To Richard Tell,
Enjoy reading about 208
exceptional women of Newark,
including Colonnade resident
Fanatie A. Washington,
and her mother, Altha B.
Alston.
Barbara Kukla
March 18, 2006

Defying the Odds:
Triumphant Black Women of Newark

Defying the Odds:
Triumphant Black Women of Newark

BARBARA J. KUKLA

Swing City Press
West Orange, New Jersey

Swing City Press
336 Northfield Avenue
West Orange, New Jersey 07052

Text type: Berkeley Book
Display type: Baker Signet
Composed by P. M. Gordon Associates
Designed by Janine White

ISBN 0-9768130-0-9
Library of Congress Control Number: 2005903317

for my soul sister

Connie Williams Woodruff | 1921–1996

CONTENTS

CONTENTS

Photo gallery appears on pages 126 through 134

INTRODUCTION

Whether the threat is a burning cross in a sleepy southern town or a female doctor bucking the whites-only hiring policies of a city hospital, *Defying the Odds: Triumphant Black Women of Newark* speaks to the remarkable fortitude of women everywhere who struggle against the everyday realities of racial bigotry and sexual discrimination. Like Maya Angelou, who had the distinction of being our nation's poet laureate, these high achievers know why the caged bird sings.

My purpose in writing this book is tied to my belief that too little attention has been paid to the contributions made to our society by the men and women brought here in shackles to fuel our nation's early economy. Absent from our general knowledge and history books are the names of hundreds of African-American writers, artists, scientists, inventors, educators, community activists, war heroes, explorers, and countless others whose labor and ingenuity helped build our country. Yet they existed and continue to exist everywhere in America, making Newark, New Jersey, no anomaly. Nevertheless, their achievements remain an enigma to the general population for many reasons, racism and resistance to change not the least of them.

In New Jersey, attempts to rectify such failings have fallen to the Amistad Commission, created by a law that requires African-American history to be taught in New Jersey public schools. Unfortunately, this effort has been slowed by a massive budget deficit. And so, with each day, the accomplishments of the state's black leaders, now and then, continue to fade into oblivion.

This book, my second about the people of Newark, focuses on the contributions of eight African-American women connected by birth, upbringing, or professional affiliation to the state's largest city. The appendix includes profiles of more than two hundred additional black women of Newark who reached the top of their fields.

The fact that all of these women have risen far above their supposed stations in life is a testament to their personal strength and to their shared belief that it is everyone's right to aspire to and share in the American dream. With grace and dignity, they have refused to succumb to the daily demands heaped on their race and sex. Instead, they have forged forward, pursuing the noblest goals of their professions. Each one, in her way, is a true visionary. Each one has a powerful tale to tell, deserving of a niche in the annals of U.S. history. Each one has remained solid as a rock—unbossed, unbowed, and unbeaten.

Considered as a whole, the accomplishments of these trail blazers paint a powerful picture of what African-American women can achieve, against the odds, in their quest for excellence. Their stories can help new generations of young black women gain strength and inspiration from a broader perspective on the challenges of being black and female. Just as important, people everywhere should know that Newark has produced many of our country's great leaders, an inordinate number of whom are African-American women.

The genesis of this book dates to 1998, when I was selected by the Friends of the Newark Public Library to deliver the annual John Cotton Dana Distinguished Lecture. Named for the founder of the Newark Public Library and Newark Museum, the lecture is given each year by a person committee members believe has provided outstanding service to New Jersey, especially to Newark and its people.

My selection placed me in the company of five famous men chosen previously for this distinction: author Philip Roth; former New Jersey congressman Peter W. Rodino, Jr., of Watergate fame; playwright and screenwriter Richard Wesley; former Newark Museum director Samuel C. Miller, Jr.; and poet and playwright Amiri Baraka.

Surprised and thrilled to be the first woman accorded this honor, I began thinking about the many other women whose gifts to our city and to the Newark community far surpass mine. I was also eager to see that the city of Newark was depicted in a befittingly positive manner. Out of those thoughts came the framework for this book.

Although I have never lived in Newark, it is my hometown. For nearly four decades it has been the focus of my friendships, interests, and longtime associations, as well as my work. To those who insist on domicile as a requisite for being a "real Newarker," I say what I always have said: "What have *you* done for Newark lately?"

In my case, it is not so much what I have done for Newark as what Newark has done for me. My ties to Newark have allowed me to meet thousands of people whose paths I would never have crossed elsewhere. As a journalist, I have been fortunate to make the acquaintance of Newarkers from every niche of the city, from ordinary folks who take an active part in neighborhood life to those like Roth and Baraka whose works attract international attention.

My involvement in Newark also has afforded me the privilege of participating in hundreds of social, cultural, and civic events that remain a mystery to those who confine themselves to the suburbs and refuse even to visit the city. What a wonderful education that has been! These are the same reasons that my first book—*Swing City: Newark Nightlife, 1925–50*—focused on Newark. Critics have called *Swing City* an important addition to the body of New Jersey literature. For me, it speaks also to my personal growth as a writer and to my respect for the indomitable spirit of so many Newarkers who struggle each day to survive yet manage to rise above their conditions.

Defying the Odds shares this theme. It, too, is about Newarkers—women who have dedicated their energies and talents to improving the lives of others. Two of these women are familiar to readers of *Swing City:* journalist/educator Connie Williams Woodruff and singer Viola Wells Evans, whose stage name was Miss Rhapsody. Their stories are accompanied by those of Gladys St. John Churchman, who was at the forefront of the U.S. preschool movement; Dr. E. Alma Flagg, the first black principal of an integrated Newark school; Dr. E. Mae McCarroll, who integrated Newark's City Hospital; Wynona M. Lipman, New Jersey's first black female senator; Mary Beasley Burch, founder of The Leaguers, an educational advocacy group for black teenagers; and Marion A. Bolden, the only black woman from Newark to serve as superintendent of public schools.

As in *Swing City,* I write once again about people I know. Nearly all these women were and are my friends. Their ranks include three who have provided me with personal support and encouragement at critical junctures in my life. Connie Woodruff and Miss Rhapsody were two of my best friends. Mary Beasley Burch, one of the most brilliant women I have encountered, was my longtime adviser.

I have many people to thank for helping me with this project. Those who were interviewed are listed in the bibliography. Special thanks go to Charles F. Cummings, Valerie Austin, James Osbourn, Robert Blackwell, and April Kane of the Newark Public Library; Lois Densky-Wolf of the George Smith Library at the University of Medicine and Dentistry of New Jersey; and Mary Capouya, Linda Blyth, Saundra DeGeneste, Dr. Karen Moore, Franotie A. Washington, Eleta Caldwell, Glenn Frieson, Jerry McCrea, Lynne Canaley Fernicola, Geri Surgent, Alice Campisi O'Keefe, and Dashanta Faucette. My aunt, Helen Kukla, who grew up in Newark's Ironbound section and is a proud product of the city's schools, was an invaluable resource. I also thank Peggy Gordon, Doug Gordon, Joan Vidal, and Janine White, production editors at P. M. Gordon Associates, for embracing this project.

If and when you have a chance, take a trip to Newark, look around and judge our city for yourself. You will see great people and witness great things.

CONNIE WOODRUFF

Advocate for All | 1921–1996

In early 1939, the Daughters of the American Revolution (DAR), a patriotic women's society whose members trace their roots to the founding fathers of our nation, denied Marian Anderson, the legendary African-American contralto, access to Constitution Hall in Washington, D.C. Within days, Eleanor Roosevelt, the nation's First Lady, declared the controversy an atrocity, driving home her disgust by resigning her membership in the DAR. With Mrs. Roosevelt's support, a new site for Miss Anderson's concert was found. That concert proved to be a historic event, attracting a crowd of seventy-five thousand to the lawn of the Lincoln Memorial on April 9, 1939.

Four years before Anderson's newsmaking concert, there was no fallout whatsoever when Connie Williams, a black youngster from Newark, was slighted by the same white women's group. In Anderson's case, the bold action of the President's wife put an embarrassing stain on the DAR, attracting worldwide attention. The incident involving the young Connie Williams, however, generated no public attention whatsoever. The only reaction was the personal injustice that she and her family felt. What was supposed to be one of the proudest moments in her young life instead became her personal Introduction to Racism 101, American style.

In 1935 Connie Williams was in the eighth grade at Monmouth Street School in Newark, a student of Grace Baxter Fenderson, one of the city's earliest black educators. An aspiring young writer, the thirteen-year-old promptly took up the challenge when Fenderson encouraged her to enter a citywide essay contest on patriotism sponsored by the DAR. Carefully choosing each word, she wrote about how proud she was to be an American in a land of such great opportunity. Because she lived in a part of Newark that was home to many first-generation immigrants, among them Germans, Poles, and Greeks, she was proud, too, to be a product of a place where people of many races and nationalities got along. Most of all, she was proud to be a Newarker.

As the girls' first-place contest winner citywide, Connie was invited to read her essay and claim her medal during a Sunday afternoon ceremony in downtown Newark. Her father could not go that day because he had to work, waiting tables at a nearby restaurant. Nevertheless, he carried the two-paragraph newspaper article about his only child's accomplishment in his wallet until it crumbled years later.

For this special occasion, Connie's mother bought her a new dress and patent leather shoes, curled her hair in tight ringlets, and gave her strict instructions about how to conduct herself. But the joy of the occasion quickly dissipated. Upon setting eyes on the chocolate-skinned adolescent from Monmouth Street School and her mother, much lighter-skinned but nevertheless a Negro, the woman in charge of the program promptly announced to Connie's mother, "There's been a mistake. We will have to send your daughter her medal."

"There's been no mistake," Connie's mother shot back. "My daughter is here to read her essay and receive her medal. She will read her essay, if it's only to me." With that, Carrie Williams flew past the woman, practically dragging her daughter to the front of the hall, where one of Connie's classmates, a boy named Louis, and his father, a Newark doctor, were waiting for the start of the program. Louis also was there to receive a prize.

Apprised of the obviously discriminatory nature of the situation, Louis's father asked to speak to the member in charge of the program, only to be told there was nothing he could do about "the problem" with Connie's mother. But the DAR was wrong. "If Mrs. Williams's daughter cannot read her essay, then my son Louis will not read his," the physician asserted. That sent the organization's leaders into a spin. After weighing the options, they decided there had been a mistake. Both children were winners. Both children would read their essays.

By this time, Connie was just as exacerbated with her mother as her mother was with the DAR. "Ma," she objected, as the situation intensified. "Don't ever question me," her mother responded. "You will read your essay!" This Connie did, enunciating every word to her mother's satisfaction.

Connie Williams's academic prowess came as no surprise to her family. Born October 24, 1921, Constance Oneida Williams was a success at everything she did from an early age. Practically from birth, her parents, Caroline Pines Williams and Frederick Isaac Williams, encouraged her to aspire to greatness. They doted on her because she was their only child, the baby they had taken as their own after Connie's mother gave birth. At the time, both Rosalee Tennessee, Connie's birth mother, and her father, a young man who became well-known in later life but never acknowledged Connie as his daughter, were students at Virginia State University. As a teenager, Connie discovered her true identity and also learned that she had two younger siblings, Gwendolyn and Leon Rochester. But she *never* let on to Carrie and Fred.

By the time she was six, Connie could play classical music with ease, entertaining family and friends, at her mother's insistence, on the beautiful baby grand given to her by her godfather, J. Leroy Baxter. Baxter, a member of one of Newark's most prominent families and a dentist by trade, was New Jersey's third black legislator, serving in the state assembly from 1927 to 1929. Connie's godmother, Rosamond Stewart Marrow, another well-known community leader, was president of the board of Kenney Hospital, which served Newark's black residents.

At home, Carrie Williams was the dominant force in the family. Freddie Williams was a hard-working, mild-mannered man who often worked two jobs. For many years he was employed as a waiter at Simon & Davis, a restaurant in downtown Newark opposite City Hall. In the 1930s, during the Great Depression, he also worked part time at a posh speakeasy on Park Street. When he was not at work, he enjoyed reading books about the law or U.S. history. Playing the guitar was another hobby.

"I don't think Freddie was outgoing enough for Carrie, particularly by comparison to the Reverend Morris Hutchins, her second husband," said Bea Boone, a relative on the Pines side of the family. "Morris was a great orator, a dynamo. Freddie was very quiet, a Mr. Milquetoast."

Freddie Williams was nineteen when he arrived in Newark in 1904, about the same time that southern blacks were heading north in a great wave to find work in the hundreds of factories that had made the city a great manufacturing center. The first influx of blacks into urban manufacturing centers like Chicago, Detroit, and Newark had occurred just before the turn of the twentieth century. In Newark, a second batch of newcomers arrived just before World War I. The third surge in Newark's black population came in the early 1930s, when Meyer Ellenstein, in his bid to become mayor, encouraged southern blacks to seek employment in the city's many factories.

Freddie Williams was not a southerner. His family came from Woodstock, Vermont, where his grandparents had been one of two black families in the late 1800s. His great-grandfather on his father's side, an Indian named Ol' Ike Williams, had drowned in a pond. His grandfather had been Woodstock's town crier.

Like southern blacks, the Williams family also was on the move. By the time Frederick Isaac Williams came along, on February 19, 1885, his father had settled in Springfield, Massachusetts. His parents and siblings— his sister, Estelle; brother Albert; and the twins, Harry and Danny—later made their home in New Haven, Connecticut, where all of them except Freddie spent the rest of their lives.

As a teenager, Freddie worked in the dormitories at Yale University. That gave him a chance to meet the sons of the captains of U.S. finance and industry. He would shine their shoes, take their clothes to the cleaners, and make sure they got to class on time. In return, these wealthy young men took a liking to "young Williams," as they called him, allowing him to read their books and occasionally accompany them to class.

At nineteen Freddie moved to Newark to look for work. No one in the family is quite sure how he and Carrie Pines met or why they were attracted to each other, given their differences in personality and considerably different outlooks on life. Freddie, a short, wiry man, wanted very little out of life other than a peaceful existence. Carrie, who was tall and lanky and carried herself with great élan, like the Third Ward socialite that she was, wanted it all.

Their love for Connie, who was their only child, may have kept them together for the nearly twenty years they remained married. After they divorced in the early 1930s, Carrie and Connie remained on Waverly Avenue. Freddie moved around the corner to a new apartment complex called the Douglass-Harrison apartments, where he lived at 107 Somerset Street until he was ninety-seven. He spent his final days in West Orange, where he lived with Connie and her husband, until shortly before his death.

Freddie Williams was 105 years old when he died on May 18, 1990. On his 103rd birthday, he described the sadness he felt in outliving all his friends. But he had few other regrets. His major disappointment was that he had never become a lawyer. "In my day, the ordinary black man couldn't even drive a garbage truck," he said. "Any thought of a man of my station practicing law was out of the question."

Years after her divorce from Freddie, Carrie married again and moved to Springfield, Massachusetts, where Hutchins, her new husband, became pastor of the city's largest Baptist church. Because of his standing in the community, she was in her glory as the church's First Lady. She was in her mid-eighties when she died years later in a nearby hospital.

As a teenager at South Side High School on Johnson Avenue in Newark, Connie Williams was a stellar student. Charming and pretty enough to woo the world with her bright smile, she was one of South Side's most popular students.

"We were neighbors on Waverly Avenue," said Mary Edmond Singletary. "Connie was a teenager when I was a little girl, but she was always very friendly and protective of me. Our mothers were great friends. Her upbringing was very middle class. Her buddies were the Lacey girls. Their father was a postman, which was a big deal at the time. She also was friendly with the Lee girls, whose father was a dentist. In our day, that was a very big deal."

Retired New Jersey Superior Court Judge Harry Hazelwood knew Connie Williams from Old First Mount Zion Baptist Church, where their mothers were among the movers and shakers. They also were friends from South Side High School, where they were classmates. "Connie was always very vivacious. She loved life and had lots of energy, but she could be tough," Hazelwood said. "She had guts, was straightforward, and got results. More importantly, she never forgot the people she knew way back."

As an adult, Connie told friends she strove for excellence because she wanted to make her parents proud. "They put everything they had into me," she said. "Until the day he died, I was always Daddy's baby, his 'little girl.' "

While she was growing up, her mother, who ran a catering business from their home on Waverly Avenue, was at the center of Republican life in Newark's old Third Ward. "My mother wanted me to be a leader too," Connie said. "She stressed the importance of a good education and vibrant personality. She believed that being smart and popular could take you anywhere in life you wanted to go. She drummed that into me practically every day of my life."

Connie's mother came from the Pines family, whose members spread out from Newark to East Orange and Montclair. For many years her cousin, Bobby Pines, ran a popular gas station in Montclair. Her maternal grandmother was Sarah Stewart, who owned a house on Washington Street in Newark next to what is now a homeless shelter called the Lighthouse Community Center. Connie's grandmother's house was her second home every day after school.

On Sundays, she went to Old First Mount Zion Baptist Church on Thomas Street with her mother and grandmother. There she sang in the choir with Sarah Vaughan, who was several years younger. Sarah, who became a jazz legend, also played the piano and organ for the choir. "When we were growing up, Sarah never sang a solo at church," Connie said. "If she did, none of us remember it. That's why we were so surprised when she won the Apollo Amateur Night contest." Vaughan, who was a teenager at the time, went on to worldwide fame.

As a young woman, Connie went to Washington, D.C., one summer to take part in a six-week institute sponsored by the national Republican Party. Its purpose was to give young leaders a better understanding of U.S. democracy by seeing government in action and meeting many of the nation's top elected officials.

Although Connie learned a lot about government that summer, being the only person of color taking part in the institute was certainly a challenge for someone who had never been south of the Mason-Dixon Line by herself. At every turn, starting with her arrival by train at Union Station in the nation's capital, she faced discriminatory behavior. Ignored by several cabdrivers, she was rescued by a white man who hailed a cab and got her a ride to the Republican headquarters.

With some time to spare, she stopped for lunch at a Chinese restaurant. "I was perfectly visible to all the waiters," she later recalled, "but no one came to take my order. I called out. Nothing happened. Everyone was walking around like I didn't exist." That really was the case. As she soon found out, she was, indeed, nonexistent to the restaurant workers. "No niggy! No niggy! No niggy!" one of them screamed as she approached him for service.

Outraged, she told the director of the institute, a friend of her mother's, every detail of her experience. But that did not help much. "This is just the beginning," he told her. "I have more bad news for you. Because you're a Negro, you cannot stay at the hotel with the other delegates. I've found a boarding home where you can stay."

Even though she was quite young, Connie was having none of it. She was determined to participate, but she was not going to stay at any boarding house. "May I please call my father's cousin?" she asked. "She works here in Washington. I may be able to stay with her." Cousin Ada, whose lifelong love was one of the leaders of the Navy's famous Golden Thirteen, an elite corps of black servicemen, was delighted to take in her young cousin for the summer.

"Ada's love interest made the whole experience very exciting for me," Connie said. "I was very intrigued by her paramour because he was a married man." To the day she died, Ada kept her lover's picture on her bedroom window sill. She was in her eighties, but he remained forever young and dashing in his naval uniform.

Because she had never been south on her own before, and because of the racial injustice she suffered during her Washington internship, Connie was homesick. "When I get back up north, I am going to kiss the ground," she wrote to her mother. But what tales she had to tell, including another discriminatory experience that turned triumphal.

As the institute wound to an end, each participant received an invitation to attend a reception at the Embassy Row home of a western congressman. Each delegate, that is, except Connie. Knowing of her spunk, the director offered a challenge: "The party is for all delegates," he said. "You are a delegate, so go if you want to go."

Wearing the party dress she had been asked to bring along, she called a cab that night and was off to Embassy Row. "The cabdriver was colored, as we used to say," she related afterward. "Girl, are you crazy?" he asked, when she told him where they were going. "We probably won't even get in the gates."

But the gates were open, and in they went. "I think I should wait," the driver said, as she exited the car, to be greeted by the maid and butler, the only other black folks in sight. The maid was just as dumbfounded as the cabdriver. Seeing this young colored girl all dressed up in a gown was simply too much. "What are you doing here?" she asked Connie.

"I'm the delegate from New Jersey," Connie answered. "Would you please tell me where to find the congressman?" The congressman, who was engaged in conversation with a small group of friends, clearly was astounded to see Connie. But he feigned composure. "He was jerking his head, nodding to his wife to join us," Connie said. "Yet he was very gracious. After I introduced myself to him and his friends, he introduced me to his wife."

"This is Constance Williams, the delegate from New Jersey," he told her, as—in Connie's words—"we engaged in what white people call chit-chat."

"You have a lovely home," Connie told Mrs. F. "And what a beautiful piano [a baby grand]."

"Do you play, my dear?" asked the wife.

"Yes, I do," Connie said demurely.

Asked if she would care to entertain the other guests, Connie said she would, which prompted the hostess to clap her hands to call everyone to attention. "Ladies and gentlemen," said the hostess, "Constance Williams, the delegate from New Jersey, has offered to play a piano selection."

"The situation reminded me of all the times my mother made me play for the white folks she worked for during our summers at Bradley Beach at the Jersey Shore," Connie recalled. "Everyone smiled and applauded and thought I was some kind of little genius, but I always felt like their little pickaninny." But she was older now, on her own and quite willing to show off her thirteen years of lessons under Newark's piano virtuoso, Dr. Eugene Alexander Burkes.

"They probably thought I was going to play some little ditty, but I went for the dramatic," Connie said. "I decided on the *Polonaise*. Dum de dum! Dum de dum de dum de dum!" Right hand extended high into the air; she ended each chord with a flourish. In a matter of minutes, Connie Williams, the delegate from Newark, New Jersey, had won over Washington's highest echelons.

In 1939, after graduating from Newark's South Side High School, Connie went to work part time at the *Herald News*, a black weekly that went out of business in the 1960s. Its rival paper, which came to town in 1941, was the *New Jersey Afro-American*, which published until it folded in 1987. Nearly a decade later, after working for the Office of Dependency Benefits, the support base for the families of military personnel during World War II, Connie went to work full time for the *Herald News*.

In her first official role as a newspaperwoman, she was off to Philadelphia to cover a Sugar Ray Robinson fight. A middleweight, Robinson was considered one of the best boxers the world had ever known. Charmed by the handsome young athlete, Connie accepted his invitation to attend a postfight party and forgot to file her story.

"I should have been fired," she said afterward. "But [Oliver] Butts Brown [the editor] gave me a break." Brown was an important voice in

Newark's black community. At a time when black reporters and editors were not welcome at white newspapers, the *Herald News* addressed many issues of importance to Newark's black community.

A short, stubby man with a penchant for fine cigars, Brown was a graduate of Lincoln University, a college for black men in Pennsylvania founded by whites after the Civil War. At Lincoln, Brown roomed with the famous poet Langston Hughes. After they graduated, they remained friends. As Brown's prodigy, Connie would often join them at Hughes's favorite haunt in Harlem, the Red Roost. "Langston was a big name in Harlem," Connie said. "He had his own booth at the Red Roost, where we would sit and drink all day."

By this time, Brown had promoted Connie. She was now the city editor of the *Herald News*, which made her one of the few black women nationwide to be accorded such an important voice in U.S. history. As the paper's editor, she followed the careers of important figures in black life, such as Gordon Parks and Thurgood Marshall, and some of the top names in show business, including Josephine Baker and Sammy Davis, Jr.

One of her most interesting assignments required her to spend a week covering Daddy Grace, a religious guru whose following among the black population numbered in the thousands. She spent the week at his Washington, D.C., mansion, watching as he ordered his closest disciples to perform such tasks as licking crumbs from the floor to demonstrate their faithfulness to him. When Connie showed her disgust, he attempted to convert her to his "faith." She responded by exposing him in the *Herald News* as a slick con artist.

Daddy Grace was not the only con man Connie met along the way. "One day when I got to the office I saw this guy putting dirt and twigs in little plastic bags," she said. "He called himself Doc Wilson. To my surprise, he had been hired as our advice columnist. People wrote letters to him and came to the office to buy these little packets for a dollar each. Supposedly, the contents would chase away their bad luck."

Connie wrote mostly about Newark, detailing the lives of prominent blacks who were involved in civic affairs and moved in the same social circle. She wrote, too, about Newark's black masses, ordinary people who made the news for a variety of other reasons.

At social events, Connie was the center of attention. Everyone knew and loved her, and everyone wanted to be featured in the newspaper. "We were very social," said Ruth Crumpton Dargan, one of the first black women employed by the Newark Police Department. "We'd go to at least three or four dances every year and see the same people. Connie was always there, writing for the paper or serving as mistress of ceremonies."

Long before they went on to the majors, black ballplayers like Don Newcombe, Larry Doby, Joe Black, and Monte Irvin, who played for the Newark Eagles, were familiar figures at many of the black community's dinners and parties. Newcombe, who later pitched for the Brooklyn Dodgers, also was active in community affairs, working closely with educator Mary Beasley Burch and her physician husband, Dr. Reynold E. Burch, founders of The Leaguers. Established in 1949 as an organization for neighborhood teenagers, The Leaguers offered young black people social and academic opportunities they would not have otherwise had.

"As The Leaguers expanded, we needed a larger headquarters than the Burch home on South Fourteenth Street," said Connie, who gave the fledgling organization a considerable amount of ink in the *Herald News*. "Don gave us the space we needed at his place on Orange Street."

Struck by the Burches' desire to help the less fortunate, Connie went far beyond her ties as a newspaperwoman in her efforts to help The Leaguers. For five decades she assisted Mary Burch as a friend and volunteer, providing helpful advice and using her personal connections to benefit the organization. "When I received the H. Alexander Smith scholarship from The Leaguers to attend Seton Hall University, Connie made the presentation," said Donald Payne, who eventually became New Jersey's first black congressman. (Smith was, at the time, a U.S. senator from New Jersey.) "When someone was in need, she was always there, just like Mrs. Burch."

Getting out the news and sharing her opinions on important issues, especially those of a political nature, were Connie's passions. Exceptionally candid and outspoken, she was a biting political pundit, frequent guest on news and talk shows, and host of several radio and TV programs. Asked once during a local TV show why she would not support a certain political candidate, she blurted out, "Because he's a crook." A comment like that was cause for taking a show off the air. Fortunately, no one complained.

On another occasion she wrote about a well-known elected official who had been arrested by state police for cocaine possession. "Coke-head!" blared the headline. Days later, at a Democratic dinner, the official confronted Connie.

"What is this cokehead stuff?" he demanded.

"I just write the stories, not the headlines," Connie responded, calling him by name. "Don't worry. This will pass."

Any other reporter probably would have faced a further lacing by the angry politician, a known hothead, or might even have been sued. Not Connie. The politician walked away and never mentioned the matter again.

However, there were times during her lengthy service to the community when things got a bit out of hand. One occurred when Connie was questioned by state officials about her involvement as a board member for a local nonprofit organization. Someone was stealing money, and they wanted to know if she was the culprit. In the end, the officials were convinced that Connie knew nothing about the organization's finances and handled none of the money. She was off the hook.

Another time, while Connie was chairperson of the Board of Concerned Citizens at the University of Medicine and Dentistry of New Jersey, she was summoned to testify when an employee brought suit against University Hospital, and she faced possible liability. Connie wound up testifying on behalf of the employee.

Through the years, Connie wrote for many newspapers, including the *Amsterdam News* and the *New York Age*, two of the nation's oldest black weeklies. Black Newarkers considered her columns—"As I See It," in Janice Edgerton Johnson and Henry Johnson's *City News,* and "Connie's Corner," an earlier version of the column that appeared in Ralph Johnson's *The Connection*—must-reads.

Twenty years after the Newark riots, in a column in *The Connection*, Connie recounted her first-hand encounter with death at the hands of inexperienced, trigger-happy young National Guardsmen. "The human explosion in Newark that July was heard around the world. For several sweltering weeks, the city was in turmoil, flames, and fear. We were afraid of snipers, cops, looters, muggers, and finally the state National Guard that Governor Richard J. Hughes sent to put down rioters and victims alike," she wrote.

"I had the unfortunate experience of running into one of those Guardsmen boy wonders on a peaceful Sunday morning en route to a meeting Governor Hughes had scheduled at The Leaguers' building on Clinton Avenue," she continued. "The Guardsman stopped me at Elizabeth and Hawthorne Avenues, ordered me out of my car, and called his partner to keep his riot gun trained on me while my car was searched from stem to stern. It dawned on me (as one opened the trunk) that I was driving my husband's car, in which he always carried his fishing and hunting gear, including a long-barreled shotgun. Sure enough, when the trunk was opened, there was the evil-looking gun. A half-hour of interrogation followed. In that short time, I found out how impossible it is to sound coherent while looking down the nose of a gun in a nervous hand. To this day, I don't know what I said or how I sounded. All that stands out in my memory is that horrible moment when good sense outweighed my normally quick temper and sharp tongue."

In the late 1950s, Connie left the *Herald News* to become an organizer for the International Ladies' Garment Workers' Union (ILGWU). Traveling from shop to shop, she organized workers and fought for the rights of ILGWU workers toiling in the area's sweatshops. At almost every shop in northern New Jersey and rural parts of New York, her primary territory, conditions were intolerable and the people were paid a pittance. Most people did not work for dollars; they worked for cents.

One of Connie's most satisfying victories came when she won the right for women who worked in the squalid shops to become cutters, a job reserved until then for men. Women had not been allowed to cut the patterns for sweaters, coats, or other items of clothing. All they could do was sew. When Connie insisted that women, too, be eligible for positions as cutters, for which the pay was significantly higher, the men she was dealing with—the owners and managers of the shops—tried to kill her with kindness. "I had so many offers of free clothing, I could have opened my own store," she later wrote.

When she refused all the offers, many of the owners caved in to the demands of this audacious black woman, allowing a few women here and there to become cutters. "I didn't get everything I wanted, but it was a start," Connie said. "More importantly, the workers knew they had someone they could count on if they had a problem. They were a bit less fearful of losing their jobs." At the time, many of the factory workers were minority women, mostly blacks and Hispanics. Connie's willingness to fight for their rights made her a revered figure in the heavily black and Latino Newark community.

Long after she left the union and retired, ILGWU women continued to go to her when they had problems. Years later, while she lay dying, a call came to her home from the granddaughter of a union worker. Her grandmother's retirement benefits were in a mess, she told Connie, and she was getting nowhere trying to resolve the situation. "My grandmother said to call you because you would be able to help her," the woman said. Connie did help. She picked up the phone and made a call to the union headquarters in New York, talked to the woman in charge of retirement benefits, and quickly straightened out the mix-up. At Connie's wake at Messiah Baptist Church in East Orange on October 23, 1996, the woman's granddaughter was one of the first people in the door. She had no idea, she said, how sick Connie was when she called, and she would remain ever grateful to her.

Connie stayed with the union for twenty years. In all that time, she enjoyed just one major promotion—from organizer to education director—a change that prompted her to establish all kinds of new programs and benefits for her members, who also benefited greatly from her personal ties to the Newark community and the connections she could promote.

Yet after so many years with the union, she felt she was stagnating. There was just one woman in the highest echelon of the ILGWU ranks, an international vice president, and it seemed almost certain that the union brass intended to keep things that way. In her fifties, at a time in life when most people would not contemplate switching careers, Connie decided to change jobs. By then, her roots in both the state labor union movement and New Jersey politics had solidified.

As the daughter of the politically active Carrie Williams, Connie was raised on local politics. "As a child, I stuffed envelopes, distributed flyers, and attended hundreds of county committee meetings with my mother," she said. "My godmother, Rosamond Stewart Marrow, also was a very influential Republican in Newark's old Third Ward."

For a while, Connie was content with Republican life, winning favor with the party by conducting civics lessons and voter registration drives for Essex County women. But the party of Lincoln was not for her. To her mother's and godmother's dismay, she eventually became a Democrat. "My days as a Republican came to an abrupt end after I trotted the wife of the GOP candidate for governor all over Newark, in and out of churches and private homes," Connie said. "At the end of the day, this hoity-toity woman had the nerve to tell me I was very nice for a colored girl but should not expect too much from the party. There was nowhere in it for a Negro to go."

As a Democrat, Connie rose swiftly through the ranks, serving first as a committeewoman at the county level and then as secretary of the party at the county and state levels. Soon influential party members urged her to run for public office. But she always demurred, remaining behind the scenes as an adviser to just about every Democrat who sought election, be it at the local, state, or national level.

In 1974, when Brendan T. Byrne became governor, Connie was offered a position as an aide to the new state labor commissioner. Because her experience and qualifications far surpassed those required for the job, she turned it down. "I've never sought a position in government," she wrote to the commissioner. "The only one I would consider is assistant commissioner. There is a vast difference between executive aide and assistant commissioner. Given my experience and many years as a labor leader, I would be overqualified to become an aide, and it would be a disservice to the people that I represent."

White candidates for public office often courted Connie's favor, looking to her for ways to win the black vote in Newark and beyond. Party affiliation did not matter. She was close to both Republicans and Democrats. Through the years, six New Jersey governors from both parties—or, as she liked to say, "from both sides of the aisle"—appointed her to state commissions. Governor Richard J. Hughes, her friend from those hot summer nights when Newark was in rebellion, was the first, naming her a member of the state judicial review committee. Needless to say, the judges who were in trouble and went before the commission, almost always white men, were not overjoyed to see a black woman among those who would decide their fate on the bench.

When Byrne became New Jersey's governor, he reorganized the state commission on women and appointed her chairperson, a position she held for the next sixteen years. During that time she also served two terms as president of the National Association of Commissions for Women (NACW), a group that lobbied for the rights of women nationwide. "She was a firecracker," Byrne said. "Anytime anyone mentioned appointing a woman to a position, Connie's name came up. She was clearly able to do any job." At the time, the NACW was almost all white. The only black woman at the highest level was one from a southern state who rarely spoke out on behalf of blacks or other minority women.

In her take-charge manner, Connie soon worked her way into the group's upper echelons, serving first on the board of directors and then as vice president. When it came time to run for president, however, she declined. Her father, then 103 years old, had suffered a stroke. She would have neither the time nor the freedom to travel as extensively as the presidency required.

Ironically, the NACW vice president was another black woman, Mary Burke Nicholas of New York, one of Connie's dear friends. For the next two years, Nicholas headed the organization. When her term was up, she very graciously chose not to seek office again. Instead, she passed the baton to Connie, who took over as president at the next convention in Washington, D.C. During the two terms that she served as NACW president, from 1983 to 1987, Connie focused on diversifying the organization by encouraging African-American and Hispanic women to join local commissions and seek leadership roles at the national level. The NACW also opened it first headquarters in Washington, D.C., and secured the services of its first executive director, Ethel James Williams.

When Connie won her second term as NACW president, at the Pasadena, California, convention in 1985, the convention speaker was

Maureen Reagan, the daughter of President Ronald Reagan. When Reagan arrived, both Connie and another officer, a white woman, were outside the Pasadena Hilton waiting to greet her. As Reagan stepped out of her car, she greeted the other woman warmly, ignoring Connie's welcome. Intentional or not, Connie felt slighted. Because she was black, she assumed that Reagan had automatically dismissed her as no one of importance, which prompted her to move into her "don't get mad; just get even" mode.

At the welcoming luncheon for Reagan, Connie was friendly and relaxed, making small talk with the guest of honor, who now realized that Connie was the NACW president. During her introduction of Reagan, Connie dazzled the delegates, pulling out all the stops, flattering the President's daughter with each new word. Obviously pleased, Reagan gave Connie a hug.

Although Reagan's speech was interesting and informative, it paled by comparison with Connie's animated introduction. When Reagan finished, Connie stepped to the microphone to request another round of applause for the speaker. But she was not done with Maureen Reagan yet. A question-and-answer period followed. The first question from the audience set the tone.

Why was Reagan heading the U.S. delegation to Kenya for an international conference on women? What did she really know about women's issues? How could she speak on behalf of minority women? Did she have any credentials other than being First Daughter?

Reagan appeared flustered but did her best to explain why she believed she was a legitimate delegate. She was not going to Kenya in a leadership role simply because her father was the President, she said. She was interested in women's issues and saw herself in a position to ignite change, a role she believed she had earned through her involvement in the women's movement.

Through it all, Connie sat quietly on the dais, letting Reagan squirm. Afterward, she walked the relieved speaker to her waiting car, gave her a hug, and cheerfully waved goodbye.

During her many years in politics, Connie supported some of the biggest names in New Jersey politics, including Byrne and Tom Kean for governor and Bill Bradley, who became New Jersey's longtime senator. Under Earl Harris, the Newark Municipal Council president, she was, for good reason, one of many key Democrats who supported Kean rather than Jim Florio, his Democratic opponent for governor.

As a young woman she had done secretarial work for Kean's father, then a U.S. senator, working at their family homestead in Livingston. Just a boy at the time, Kean remained friendly with her over the years. She liked him, and she respected him as a sincere young man who, like his father, could do great things for New Jersey.

Florio, as it turned out, was not a man to hold grudges. When Connie's term was up as chairperson of the New Jersey Commission on the Status of Women during his term as governor, he reappointed her. Again, when her term ended on the New Jersey Martin Luther King Commemorative Commission, which she chaired with her friend former Governor Hughes, he reappointed her. Years later, at Connie's wake, both Florio and Byrne were among the mourners.

Although Connie often supported male candidates, her focus was on providing New Jersey women with a stronger say in politics and government by increasing their numbers as elected officials. In East Orange, she supported Corinna Kay for the city council and Mildred Barry Garvin for a seat in the state assembly. In Newark, she supported Mildred Crump during Crump's successful run to become Newark's first black councilwoman. When Reita Greenstone decided to run for a position on the Essex County Freeholder Board in 1974, Connie became her unofficial campaign manager, crafting Greenstone's platform and engineering her decisive win at the polls.

Reita and Connie became friends because of a rift in the Democratic Party at the national level. "My husband, Herbie, and I had gone to Washington because of a split in the party over how the delegates would be selected for the 1968 national convention. Northern Democrats from Chicago, led by Mayor Richard Daley, and southern Democrats from Mississippi were at odds over the selection process," Greenstone recounted.

"Herbie was a New Jersey delegate. I wasn't, but I spoke out on the issue. In the end, they decided to split some of the votes. After that, they asked me to be a delegate. I wound up having a split vote with Connie, who was one of four women on the National Democratic Committee representing New Jersey. We both were for Hubert Humphrey, and we had a lot of common interests. By the time the convention was over, we'd truly bonded," Greenstone continued.

"Connie really had her fingers on the political pulse. She loved people, had a sense of how things should be done, and crossed all party and racial lines. She also had an innate ability to put her tremendous abilities into words and then act on them. She could have sought political office, even been governor, but she preferred to stay in the background," Greenstone said.

When Greenstone ran for county freeholder the first time, it was "almost a joke," she said. Although she was on a ticket with three other popular Democrats—Harry Callaghan and Joe Iannuzzi for two of the other freeholder spots and Larrie West Stalks for register of county mortgages and deeds—as a white Jewish woman, she was fighting an uphill battle to win a seat on the board.

On a rotating basis, three freeholder seats were up for election each year. In a county where Democrats dominated, they traditionally went to an Irishman, an Italian, and a black man. Greenstone hardly fit the bill. "I was supposed to lose," she said. "No one said I could win. But, with Connie's help and support from other sources, I did. Nick Amato, the Essex County surrogate, was my campaign manager, but Connie was my right hand. When I won, everyone was shocked."

Greenstone won a second term in 1977. By this time, she had established an enviable record. To her critics' dismay, she had taken on unpopular causes like mental health and the rights of women and won a large following. After the election, her board colleagues elected her freeholder director, the board's top spot.

During Greenstone's two-term tenure on the freeholder board, she and her late husband, Herb, a prominent New Jersey trial lawyer, often threw huge political parties at their home in Livingston, events that attracted governors and other important elected officials. Connie generally was at the center of these gatherings.

"Trial lawyers are like actors," Reita Greenstone said. "They like being on stage. Politicians are much the same because they crave power. Connie and Herbie hit it off because they both were outgoing and loved people. If Herbie hadn't been a lawyer, I think he would have liked to become a politician."

By the early 1970s, Connie was back in school. She had earned her bachelor's degree in 1958, traveling back and forth to classes at Empire State College in New York City while working for the union. In 1977, when she was almost fifty-six, she received her master's degree in labor studies from Rutgers University in New Brunswick.

With her graduate degree in hand, she decided to leave the union and enter academe. She worked briefly for the state Energy Department under her friend and trade union colleague Joel Jacobson and then decided to apply for a teaching position at Essex County College in Newark. She had all the right stuff, but the king of Essex County politics, Democratic County Chairman Harry Lerner, stood in her way.

Their feud had started a few years earlier, when Lerner tried to replace Connie on the National Democratic Committee. She had served one four-year term and was considered a shoo-in for a second term, but Lerner blocked it. As county chairman, he wanted one of his buddies, Essex County Clerk Nicholas Caputo, to take over the position. Lerner was livid when Connie bucked his authority. By that time she had more clout and more friends in high places in Washington than he did. With their support, she took her case to the Judiciary Committee of the Democratic National Committee and won.

When the time came for her to be interviewed for the job at Essex County College, Lerner was still seething. The college was a Democratic bastion of political cronyism, and Lerner was fully in control of it. On the day of her job interview, a secretary at the college whose family Connie had done a favor for called her to let her know that the interviewer was not going to show up. Lerner was playing games with her.

Connie kept the appointment anyway, waited two hours, and then left. The second time around, the same thing happened. And the third. By then, Connie had enough evidence to call Lerner and tell him in no uncertain terms to back off or she would beat him again at his own game. This time, she threatened to go public.

Days later, Reita Greenstone, Connie, and I had lunch at the 744 Club, a businessmen's private club where Herb Greenstone was a member. We were celebrating my thirty-seventh birthday. From the club, we headed across the street to Brothers restaurant for a drink. No sooner had we gotten through the door than Connie spotted Lerner. He had his own table where he held court every day. On that particular day, he was pretty far gone.

"Connie," he said, greeting her warmly with a kiss. After we told him that it was my birthday, he graciously asked us to join him. Then came the big surprise. "Ya know what?" Lerner declared to Connie. "I really respect you. I always said no one could beat Harry Lerner at his own game. But you did. So what the hell. If you want that job at the college, you can have it. I'm practically out of here, anyway. I'm retiring to Florida."

Within a week, Connie was ensconced in a ground-floor office at the college, preparing to teach labor studies courses. Two days later, George Harris, who had just become the college president, called her to his sixth-floor office. Newly arrived from Connecticut, Harris needed someone close to him who knew the community well and could interact on his behalf with the local politicians.

Harris never said whether he knew about Lerner's involvement in Connie's appointment. He simply asked her to become his director of public information and community relations. Until her retirement from the college in 1989, she remained in that position under Harris and later under Dr. A. Zachary Yamba, the current president. Her role, however, was far more than that of the average public relations person.

When college officials sought state funding for a women's center, a program Connie helped to create, and returned from Trenton empty-handed, Connie simply picked up the phone and called the chairman of the Senate Education Committee. "That's your bill?" the senator asked, promising to revive the measure. His instructions were simple: Be in Trenton for a senate session the following week. She was, accompanied by Patricia Palmeri, the center's director. Eventually, the bill came up again and was approved. Jubilantly, Connie and Pat returned to Newark with a legislative guarantee of $250,000 for the center.

As a national committeewoman Connie also was in the forefront at Democratic conventions. When the Democrats met in New York in 1976 to select Jimmy Carter as their presidential candidate, she and Senator Harrison Williams headed the New Jersey delegation. There she was on TV with Williams, casting the votes for "The Great State of New Jersey, The Garden State."

During her many years of community service, Connie served on more than thirty boards and foundations. She was a life member of the Newark Branch of the National Association for the Advancement of Colored People (NAACP), the National Council of Negro Women, and The Leaguers, and she was a founder of Newark's Attucks-King Black Heritage Parade.

For the last forty-two years of her life, Connie was married to William Woodruff, a stationary engineer and supervisor for the Essex County Sewerage Commission in Newark. Billy Woodruff was Connie's third husband. While still a teenager, she had married Horace Sims, a musician who was her mother's boarder on Waverly Avenue. "It was a mistake," she said, "so it didn't last long." A few years later she married Elmer (Rocky) Morris, a Newark bartender. That union, too, was headed for divorce when he became ill and died of tuberculosis.

She met Billy Woodruff through her friendship with his sister, Theresa Ross, a model who often appeared in fashion shows for which Connie was the mistress of ceremonies. Where Connie was vivacious and outgoing, Billy was quiet and reserved. He was a towering figure—6 foot 3 inches tall, broad-shouldered, and, at one time, 260 pounds.

Connie and Billy were married on April 9, 1955, at her mother's home in Springfield, Massachusetts. Her stepfather, the Reverend Morris Hutchins, officiated. Early in their relationship the couple lived in an apartment on Barclay Street in Newark, just around the corner from the house on Waverly Avenue where Connie grew up. Eventually they purchased their first house, on Ludlow Street, where they frequently entertained friends and family. In 1970 they moved to West Orange, New Jersey, where they spent the rest of their lives.

While Connie was at work, her father, who went to live with them in the early 1980s, was Billy's companion in retirement. Moving to West Orange at age ninety-seven was a difficult change for Freddie. He missed Newark, where he had spent fifty years as a tenant of Douglass-Harrison Homes in the old Third Ward. Built in the early 1930s as segregated housing by the Prudential Insurance Company, the 754 apartments were taken over in the 1980s by the New Community Corporation of Newark.

Soon after Freddie's death, in 1990, Billy Woodruff's health began to fail. Following his retirement from the sewerage commission, he suffered one heart attack after another. Once an avid golfer and fisherman, he was suddenly restricted to watching ballgames on TV and sitting in the backyard.

On January, 19, 1996, Billy was admitted to Overlook Hospital in Summit, New Jersey. He had had another heart attack and was showing signs of dementia. Billy never went home from Overlook. He spent two months in nursing homes before being felled by another heart attack. He died April 24, 1996, in Clara Maass Medical Center in Belleville, New Jersey.

At Billy's wake, Connie looked frail. She had spent the winter, one of the harshest in years, running around to hospitals and nursing homes. She was tired. And she was gravely ill. At first, friends thought she was finally showing her age at seventy-four, a nonfactor until that point thanks to her tremendous energy and positive outlook on life. Within days of Billy's death, however, Connie's own illness became apparent.

On May 2, 1996, she was one of one hundred men and women recognized by *City News*, the black weekly, for having the most influence on black life in New Jersey. Connie was late for the ceremony, barely arriving in time to receive her award. The sequined jacket she wore was hanging on her thin frame. Obviously, something was wrong, and this became even clearer when she suddenly announced that she was giving up smoking. Always a heavy smoker, there was hardly a time when a cigarette was not dangling from her lips or waving around in her hand as she animatedly made some point.

The diagnosis was not good. She had breast cancer, which had spread and could no longer be treated. At most, her doctor said, she had six months to live. From June until October 1996, Connie was in and out of St. Michael's Medical Center in Newark. She ran constant fevers. Little by little, she was going downhill. Most days she slept a lot. When she felt up to it, she would read and entertain friends. Her caregivers included two nurse's aides and members of her sorority, Alpha Kappa Alpha, who took turns staying with her for two hours each day.

But her days of giving to her community were not over yet. When one of the nurses caring for her told her of the trouble she was having enrolling her nephew at a local high school, Connie picked up the phone and called someone she knew to help ameliorate the situation.

Another day, one of her aides was hardly in the door before she began telling Connie her problems. "Mrs. Woodruff, I don't have enough hours," she said. "Part time is no good. I need full-time work. They told me you have clout. They said you could help me." This was one of those days when Connie was feeling miserable.

"Can't I even die in peace?" she shrieked after the woman left. "Can't they leave me alone?"

"I don't know," I told her. "Most people focus on themselves and their own needs. When you give as much to others as you have given, they expect you to help, no matter what."

Connie Williams Woodruff died on October 19, 1996, in St. Michael's Medical Center in Newark, six months after her husband's death. Their ashes are interred in Trinity & St. Philip's Cathedral in Newark, where they were longtime members. Connie's, Billy's, and Connie's father's funerals were held at Messiah Baptist Church in East Orange, where her friend, the Reverend Harry Batts, was pastor. Both Batts and Connie's friend Leonard Coleman, then president of baseball's National League, eulogized her.

Coleman, who came from Atlanta during the World Series for the service, had this to say: "If you needed advice, Connie was the one everyone went to. If you wanted to run for office, you had to go through her whether you were a Republican or Democrat. If you had a problem or needed a favor, Connie was right there. When you said 'Connie' in Essex County, New Jersey, everyone knew who you meant."

Nearly a decade has passed, yet Connie's friends still talk fondly of her. Many of them also have paid tribute to her good works. A year after her death, she was inducted posthumously by her alma mater into the South Side/Shabazz High School Hall of Fame in Newark. For several years, Project 2000, a mentoring program for black male medical students run by her friend Al Bundy at Seton Hall University, bestowed the Woodruff Award for outstanding community service. The Cornerstone Award, given by the United Way of Essex and West Hudson, also is presented in her memory annually by Maria Vizcarrondo-DeSoto, the president and chief executive officer (CEO).

In addition, the Connie Woodruff Nursing Scholarship at Essex County College, which Connie established in memory of her father, lives on through the work of her friend Bernice Sanders. Proceeds from the annual Ebony Fashion Fair, which Sanders runs, perpetuate the fund. In honor of Connie's love of Newark's young people and her interest in music, a student jazz competition sponsored by the Connie Woodruff Foundation, a nonprofit organization created by friends, also has kept her name before the public.

In West Orange, where Connie and Billy lived for thirty years, a red maple is planted in her memory between the municipal building and the police headquarters complex. It pays tribute to Connie's service to the township as chairperson of the West Orange Human Relations Commission, no easy task in a town called home by people from sixty different countries and cultures.

Former Mayor Samuel Spina said he had appointed Connie to head the commission because of her innate ability to unite people, no matter how diverse the groups. "Connie was intensely loyal, which was important to me," Spina said. "I always was impressed by the way she always got her point across. She could tell you to go to hell and have you looking forward to the trip."

Spina said he had no trouble gaining the township council's approval to plant the tree in Connie's memory. "We'd planted trees in a park to honor the contributions of others to West Orange," the former mayor said. "But you had to be a special person to have a tree planted on the municipal grounds. Connie was that special person." The plaque on the stone mounted at the base of the tree bears Connie's epitaph: *"Friend of Many, Advocate for All."*

GLADYS ST. JOHN
CHURCHMAN

Central Ward Savior | 1902–1974

From the start of the Great Depression until her retirement
in 1967, Gladys Churchman was the genius behind the
comprehensive community service agency that kept
Newark's African-American children safe while their parents
were at work. To hundreds of parents of color, she was the
savior of the Central Ward. As the executive director of the
Friendly Neighborhood House, Mrs. Churchman, who devoted her time to uplifting the lives of her young charges
and their families, was at the forefront of the U.S. preschool
movement. The agency she ran was unique in many ways.
Catering to children of all ages, the Friendly operated a
nursery for infants, served daily hot lunches to schoolchildren, and enlisted scores of volunteers from the neighborhood to provide extra instruction and homework help.

Few children who lived in Newark's old Third Ward, now
the Central Ward, did not have some connection to the
neighborhood house, whether it was through the Girl Scout
troops that Churchman ran or through afterschool study
sessions for neighborhood boys and girls. Many, if not most,
of the children served by the Friendly came from poor black
families. More often than not, their parents worked far into
the night at jobs that paid a pittance to ensure their offspring

greater success in life. Many were "latchkey kids," youngsters who wore their house keys around their necks and had no place to go until their parents got home at night. For them, Churchman and the Friendly were a saving grace and daily refuge.

In his youth, Grachan Moncur, the noted jazz trombonist, was one of hundreds of children who went to the neighborhood house every day after classes let out at Morton Street School. "That's where everyone went," said Moncur, who lived down the street from the Friendly at High and Court Streets. "Both my parents were working, but that was O.K. with me. I loved it, especially the hot lunches. I also loved the fact that I was Mrs. Churchman's boy. You could feel how much she loved children. I would never have done anything to upset her because I respected her so much."

After he was widowed as a young man, Donald Payne, New Jersey's first black congressman, turned to Churchman and the neighborhood house for help. "My son Donald was four, and my daughter Wanda was just two," said Payne. "Without Mrs. Churchman and the personal interest she took in them, I don't know what I would have done. At the neighborhood house, I knew my children were in safe hands."

Elegant and highly cultured, Churchman stood just five feet tall. Yet she was an imposing figure. She loved children, but she also ran a tight ship. Children in those days were expected to be seen and not heard unless spoken to. They also were expected to obey their elders. If the children who went to the Friendly Neighborhood House did not show respect for others, out came Churchman's paddle. "Gladys was no-nonsense," said Dorothy Gould, the principal at Morton Street during the latter part of Churchman's tenure. "Everyone from the neighborhood watched over each other's kids, so everyone was free to spank them."

"I used to call my grandmother 'the universal disciplinarian' because she spanked everyone's children," said funeral director James Churchman III, the fourth generation of his family to run the James E. Churchman, Jr., Funeral Home. Established by their great-grandfather in 1899 and presently run by his sister, Edith, the business is now headquartered at Thirteenth Avenue and South Seventh Street in Newark.

Young Churchman can still remember the first spanking he got from his grandmother after he defied her order not to play on the jungle bars at the playground. "She caught me and she whupped me," he recalled, laughing at the thought. Her hand may have hurt, her grandson said, but the larger lesson learned was the embarrassment he felt because of her disappointment in him.

One of the first spankings Edith Churchman suffered also occurred at the neighborhood house. "Because I was the boss's granddaughter, I thought I could do whatever I wanted," she said. "When my grandmother overheard me telling that to some kids, she got out her paddle. I had seen her turn other kids over her knee. This day it was my turn."

Gladys Churchman's association with the Friendly dates to 1930, when Stella B. Wright, one of the organizers, encouraged her to help underprivileged children as a volunteer. "I don't think she ever intended to stay," said Edith Churchman. But she did, for nearly forty years. By the time she retired, just about everyone in Newark knew her name. To hundreds of children who became doctors, lawyers, teachers, and other professionals and their parents, she symbolized everything that was good about growing up in Newark.

The Friendly Neighborhood House dates to 1926, three years before the Wall Street stock market crash that fueled the nation's Great Depression. Ostensibly, it was an outgrowth of the Fuld Neighborhood House, founded in 1905 by Rabbi Solomon Foster of Temple B'Nai Jeshurun to serve the area's immigrant Jewish families. The Fuld center, at Livingston Street and Seventeenth Avenue, was named for Carrie Bamberger Fuld, sister of department store magnate Louis Bamberger, one of Newark's greatest philanthropists.

Because of the burgeoning Negro population in the old Third Ward, there was a great need by the mid-1920s to provide more services for black families, especially the children. To meet that need, a group of prominent Newarkers, both black and white, met to discuss the matter. William Ashby, the executive director of the Urban League, was a key member of the group. So were Judge John C. Howe, Stella Wright, who was a recreation volunteer at Belmont Avenue School, and Louise Shuggard, who was active in civic affairs. A board of trustees was formed with Howe as president and Shuggard as vice president.

As head of the Urban League and founder of the United Way, Ashby was involved in every aspect of Negro life in Newark. Ashby's chief objective was getting safe housing and jobs for poor men and women of color at a period in time when the nation was mired in an economic depression. To help their children, he began a toy project, engaging craftsmen to make and repair toys, which were rotated among the families, much as books are circulated by lending libraries. In short order, children who lived in Newark's old Third Ward could choose from 127 toys, including scooters, skates, repainted cars and trucks, and wooden soldiers.

In those days, many black women worked long hours as domestics. This kind of work was commonly referred to as "being in service." Others worked in the hundreds of factories strewn across the city that made Newark a manufacturing hub. A few, like Moncur's mother, Ella, a beautician, operated their own businesses.

Job opportunities for black men were just as limited. Many were factory workers, porters, or garbage collectors, holding down low-paying jobs that barely fed their families. Although it was all right for a black garbage man to walk alongside his truck, driving it was out of the question because of the unwritten rules of discrimination. These restrictions were not, as many people thought, limited to the South. Such "choice" occupations as driving a garbage truck were for whites only nearly everywhere in the United States.

"Even if you had a good education, it was hard to find a job for which you were qualified," explained Ashby. "I was a graduate of Lincoln University and held a master's degree in social work from the Yale University School of Divinity. Yet I was a member of the Negro race, so I had to take a job as a waiter when I came to Newark. I can't tell you how discouraging and humiliating that was. I thought I was a failure."

The Friendly's first headquarters was a one-room storefront at Barclay and West Kinney Streets, a one-time saloon called the Tub of Blood. Stella Wright became the director. A janitor was hired, and a corps of volunteers was engaged. On Sundays, movies were shown. A small fee was charged, and the profits helped finance the activities.

Keeping the little neighborhood house running was a constant struggle. When the profits dropped off, Old First Presbyterian Church on Broad Street in downtown Newark came to the rescue. The situation stabilized when the agency became a member of the Newark Community Chest, an amalgam of community service agencies that benefited from a common fund-raising campaign.

In 1928, the neighborhood house moved to a larger storefront at Morton and Broome Streets. Concerned about overcrowded conditions at the center, Louis Bamberger offered to help. With his brother-in-law and sister, Felix Fuld and Carrie Bamberger Fuld, he bought a vacant lot at 199 Howard Street and the buildings around it for $26,000 and then deeded them over to the Friendly.

The Friendly's new quarters opened in late 1929. After that, clubs and classes steadily grew, and the noon lunch program for schoolchildren quickly expanded. Gladys Churchman came on board as a volunteer soon afterward. In 1931, at the urging of Stella Wright, Churchman joined the Friendly as a paid member of the staff, serving first as a group worker and then as associate director until her appointment as director in 1945.

From the outset of her involvement with the Friendly, she set about improving and expanding the programs offered by the agency, adding after-school and evening activities. The nursery, which serves children ages nine months to four years, dates to the move to Howard Street in 1931, the same year Churchman went on the payroll. It was financed and equipped by the Junior League of Newark.

Cheryl Wright Newby, who spent thirty-two years as a Newark teacher, was just nine months old when her mother brought her to the nursery in 1948 and enrolled her brother Eugene, a kindergarten pupil, at the neighborhood house. Until then the Wright children had been in private care, a financial drain on their parents.

Mary Wright, the children's mother, learned about the program at the Friendly from Churchman, her upstairs neighbor on Barclay Street. "Gladys thought it would be easier on me to have the children go to the neighborhood house," Wright said. "My husband agreed. The program was better socially for the children. It gave them the chance to closely interact with other children. I can't remember what we paid, but it was hardly anything by comparison to what we paid before."

The Wright children went to the neighborhood house every day after school until they were teenagers. "We loved it," Newby said. "There was so much to do, and we loved being with Aunt Gladys. It was a very important part of our young lives." Gene Wright recalls having just as much fun as his sister. "There were all kinds of things to do. We put on plays and took part in athletics. I loved all of it because it brought me into contact with other people my age," he said. "Through Aunt Gladys, I also became involved in the Cub Scouts and Boys Scouts." Later, while working his way through college, Wright became a Boy Scout leader.

In 1936 The Junior League withdrew its support for the nursery. But the Community Chest came through, providing an infusion of new funds. With the onset of World War II, the program expanded again to serve a growing number of children whose parents worked in factories to aid the war effort.

"When I graduated from West Side High School in 1940, my first job was at the neighborhood house," said Dr. Evelyn Boyden Darrell, a clinical psychologist. At that time, Garnett Henderson was the director and Gladys Churchman was the assistant director in charge of the afterschool program. "They both were very strict and business-like. There were about ten people on the staff, including a social worker, teachers, the cook, and aides who walked the children to and from school. Everyone had to be on time. They also had to do whatever was expected of them without complaint."

Darrell's job was to bring the children inside at lunchtime and monitor their behavior in the playground. She also had a special job—taking Henderson's two nieces, Harriet and Elizabeth, to her apartment at 32 Barclay Street after school, changing their clothes, and bringing them back to the neighborhood house.

After the Howard Street building was razed in 1963 to make way for the William P. Hayes Homes, a public housing complex, the Friendly moved to 165 Court Street. The new building was a handsome red-brick-and-glass structure, part of the Edward W. Scudder Homes, a public housing project that was just going up.

Just as in the past, the Friendly was the hub of neighborhood life, offering everything from youth activities and afterschool homework assistance to trips and activities for senior citizens in a new government-sponsored senior center. Amelia Garrison, who led a jazz combo at area clubs in the 1930s and 1940s, was the first director.

Prompted by the decline in the area's Jewish population after the 1967 Newark riots, the Friendly merged with the Fuld Neighborhood House, headquartered at 71 Boyd Street in the Hayes Homes, on January 1, 1971. At the time of the merger, the combined agencies had five Central Ward locations under the direction of Ida Bell Stevens. The new entity was called the Friendly Fuld Neighborhood House. Today it has two sites, one at 165 Court Street and a Head Start program several blocks away in the basement of the St. Nicholas Greek Orthodox Church.

In 1999, with the help of $200,000 in state and federal funds, the Gladys E. Churchman Infant/Toddler Program was dedicated at the Court Street facility. At the same time, ten neighborhood women were trained to care for the children, who ranged in age from three months to four years. "We are returning to our original mission—serving infants as well as older children," said Katherine Maupins, who was executive director at the time. Today, the Friendly Fuld Neighborhood House serves 360 children from infancy to age thirteen at Court Street, offering before-school and afterschool programs, recreation, and mentoring services. Jobs services and mentoring opportunities also are available to adults. Another 125 children are served by the Head Start program.

When the Court Street building opened in 1964, two rooms on the first floor, where the Newark Housing Authority offices were based, were set aside for the Friendly. One was a utility room that doubled as a kitchen. The other was a large auditorium where lunches were served and recreational activities took place. The nursery was on the top floor. Seven staff members were assigned to the nursery. Two other staff members and a corps of twenty volunteers were assigned to programs for older children. On average, 250 children and adults came through the doors each week.

With the new building up and running, there came new goals and responsibilities. The challenge now was to provide services for the 1,640 families living in the six high-rise apartment buildings that made up the Scudder Homes. The day-care program that Churchman ran, or the Day Department, as it was called, was like none other. From the time that parents dropped off their children each day before school until 9:30 at night, when the doors closed, more than one hundred children took part in activities, including dramatics, handcrafts, games, and tap and ballet lessons. After the Scudder Homes filled up, that number increased significantly.

Girl Scout and Boy Scout troops and parents' clubs also met at the center. There were plenty of programs for families, too, as well as activities for adults, including voter education classes and registration drives. "I think my grandmother recognized a very early need to help working women care for their children." Edith Churchman said. "When the school bell rang, these children didn't leave. They waited for the volunteers from the neighborhood house to come to pick them up for lunch, bring them back to school, and march them back to the neighborhood house after school, where they stayed until their parents came to get them. The volunteers were like surrogate parents.

"My grandmother was always doing things for people," she noted, a concern that did not stop when the Friendly's director locked the building at the end of the day. "At Thanksgiving, she would make up baskets for neighborhood families. At Christmas, I can remember her compiling a list of things that her staff members wanted. I'd go upstairs to her apartment and help her wrap all of the presents."

Many of the children's Christmas presents came from the otherwise feared Longie Zwillman, the mobster who ruled the Central Ward. "We saw him as a very kind man who loved helping the poor," said Dorothy Gould. "Once the gifts were ready, Gladys and I would circle the neighborhood, going up Broome, Howard, and Charlton Streets to distribute them."

Gladys Elizabeth Antoinette St. John was born on October 28, 1902, and lived in Ansonia, Connecticut. She and a younger brother, Joseph St. John, who became a jazz musician, were the children of Clara Jackson St. John and Joseph St. John. No one in the family is sure how Ansonia became home to the St. Johns. "We tried to trace our history, but the records were not readily available," said Edith Churchman. "We're not sure if my great-grandmother was born there. But I do remember going to Ansonia with her when I was about six to see first and second cousins."

After moving to Newark in 1910, the St. Johns lived at 16 Frelinghuysen Avenue. As a child, Gladys attended Washington Street School near West Kinney Street. After graduating from Central High School, she enrolled at Newark State Normal School (Kean University), where she received a general course certificate that entitled her to teach.

She met her husband, J. Enoch Churchman, who had followed his father into the funeral business in the early 1920s, while she was working for a printer on Center Street in Orange. After their marriage on November 4, 1923, the couple lived briefly on Oakwood Avenue in Orange, where one of Enoch Churchman's two funeral homes was located. Soon after, they moved to Newark.

In the late 1920s, when their only son, James E. Churchman, Jr., was five years old and about to enter Monmouth Street School, the couple divorced. Although his father remained a strong influence in his life, Jim, Jr., called Junior or Junie by friends and family, was especially close to his mother. After his maternal grandfather's death, his grandmother, Clara St. John, lived with them on Barclay Street and on Bergen Street, where he opened his first funeral home.

"My grandmother came from a family of nine children," Jim Churchman said. "She was a very nice person, so I loved to spend the weekends at my grandparents' house on Frelinghuysen Avenue. She taught piano lessons to the children of the neighborhood. I would go with her, in and out of many Italian homes, when I was very young. As a child, I was very contented just being with her." His maternal grandfather, Joseph St. John, worked for Feist and Feist, a real estate development company located on Park Place in downtown Newark. "He was part Indian. He also was a very funny man, very jovial," Churchman said.

As a boy, Jim Churchman worked for Bamberger's, the downtown department store. "When they had a promotion, I would put up all the ads in my neighborhood," he said. "At twelve, I got another job as a representative for the Scott Young Circulating Library. My territory was the top floors of the Douglass-Harrison apartment buildings, where we lived." By that time, he and his mother had moved from 17 Somerset Street around the corner to 28 Barclay Street. "In those days, the buildings were very beautiful and well maintained," said Dorothy Foster Latta, who still lives in the neighborhood. "Almost everyone who is prominent in the black community lived at Douglass-Harrison Homes at one time or another."

Through the years, the cluster of six-story red brick buildings, built as segregated housing for blacks by the Prudential Insurance Company in the heart of Newark's Central Ward in the early 1930s, were home to Connie Woodruff, city editor of the *Herald News*, a black weekly; Dr. J. Thomas Flagg, a Montclair State College professor, and his wife, Dr. E. Alma Williams Flagg, Newark's first black principal of an integrated school; and pianist Jay Cole, a brother of jazz legend Cozy Cole. Dr. C. O. Hilton, a prominent Newark physician, and Eugene Thompson, a state legislator for several terms, also lived there at one time.

When Mary Wright and her husband, Ferdinand, a barber, moved to 28 Barclay Street in the early 1940s, Gladys Churchman lived above them. "At first, I just would see her coming and going," said Wright, who was working in downtown Newark for the Office of Dependency Benefits, a federally run bureau that processed benefits for families of World War II military men who were killed or missing in action. "Over time, we became very good friends.

"Gladys was very friendly if she liked you," Mary Wright said. "There was nothing in the world she wouldn't do for me, or anything I wouldn't do for her. Every morning she would stop by my house to see if my children were all right and check to see if they'd had their breakfast. But if she didn't like you, she would snub you in a minute." Wright was one of Churchman's closest friends, an inner circle that also included Harriet Pierce, a member of St. Philip's Episcopal Church; Isabell Sauls, a travel companion; and Gould, who had been a member of a girls' club at the Friendly.

Churchman became involved in scouting in 1930, when she replaced a leader who was leaving the neighborhood house. She organized and led Troop 45 until 1956. As troop committee chairperson, she was appointed to the board of directors of the Girl Scout Council of Greater Essex

County, which presented her with the Girl Scouts' highest honor, the Thanks Award, in May 1945. It was given for "outstanding contributions to the work of the Council beyond that which is required in the normal performance of duty."

Over the years, thousands of Newark girls passed through the Girl Scouts program at the neighborhood house. "Although I was never a Girl Scout, my grandmother thought it was a wonderful training program for young girls," Edith Churchman said. Because camping was such a strong part of Girl Scouting, troop members from the neighborhood house often spent summers outside the sweltering city in the great outdoors. With Churchman, in full regalia in her leader's uniform, they also traveled to jamborees and other scouting events.

"For many years, Newark Girl Scouts never got a chance to go camping at the Oval in South Mountain Reservation on the outskirts of the city," said Gould. "After Miss Shuggard, who was on the board at the neighborhood house, built a cabin at the Oval, we had first pick. Right after school was out, I would take the girls up there to spend ten days in the woods away from the heat." At the invitation of Shuggard and Elsie Illingworth, who served on the board as well, troop members also participated each year in the Lincoln-Douglass celebration at Newark's Old First Presbyterian Church.

Children from the Friendly also went to summer camp, courtesy of community organizations like the Civ-Eds, a group of black educators who taught in the Newark schools. "During my term as president we turned over a check for $62 to the neighborhood house that was enough to send two boys and two girls to camp that summer," said E. Alma Flagg, a retired assistant superintendent of Newark schools. "That was a lot of money in those days."

The neighborhood house also was home to Boy Scout Troop 67. Its proudest product was Jim Churchman, Jr., who became Newark's first black Eagle Scout, scouting's highest achievement, as a student at South Side High School. "Scouting was a lot of fun," he said. "It also was a wonderful learning experience because we went into people's homes all over Newark to learn what we needed to know to earn the various merit badges."

The Robert Treat Boy Scout Council of America, where his mother served as a director, enlisted many knowledgeable people who were experts in their fields to assist the boys. "To earn my bird-watching badge," Churchman recounted, "I had to learn all about birds. Getting my merit badge for swimming was another matter because Newark swimming pools were for whites only in those days. There weren't that many pools, so I was sent to the one at the Y on Halsey Street. The man in charge took one look at me and said, 'You know you can swim.' That was it. I never even saw a pool, but I got my badge."

In his youth, Churchman also served as an acolyte at St. Philip's Episcopal Church, where his family has been a fixture for several generations. The church, which started off in a small building at 336 High Street (Martin Luther King Boulevard), merged in 1954 with St. Paul's at High Street near West Market. After the church was destroyed by a fire, the congregation merged with Trinity Cathedral on Military Park, one of Newark's earliest houses of worship. Today, it is known as Trinity & St. Philip's Cathedral, the hub of black Episcopalian life in Essex County.

On Sundays when Churchman was a boy, his entire family attended Mass at St. Philip's, a tradition each generation has honored over the years. As the family matriarch, Gladys Churchman was involved in every major activity. She was on the cathedral's executive committee, served as secretary of the sponsors for the Girls' Friendly Society, and was a member of the Lay Committee and several guilds.

Her closest friend at St. Philip's was the rector, the Reverend Louis H. Berry, who arrived in Newark in 1924. Under his dynamic leadership, St. Philip's flourished. At the same time, St. Paul's was on the decline. The merger of St. Paul's and St. Philip's occurred almost by accident. At a dinner one night in the mid-1940s, Reverend Berry happened to be seated next to Arthur E. Barlow, senior warden at St. Paul's.

"How's everything at St. Philip's?" Barlow asked.

The rector's answer was strategically measured: "Fairly well, but we are so cramped at St. Philip's."

Barlow responded, "Why don't you take over St. Paul's property? You and the good people of St. Philip's will take care of St. Paul's estate, and I know that you will treasure our stained glass windows and other memorials."

Almost overnight, St. Philip's took possession of St. Paul's buildings and grounds. Estimated value: $500,000. On June 24, 1954, the last Mass was held at St. Philip's. On the next Sunday, July 1, the congregation of St. Philip's worshiped in its new home. By then the congregation was the second largest of twelve Episcopal churches in Essex County.

"When I was a girl, we were at church all day Sunday because my grandmother was involved in so many activities and my father was superintendent of the church school," Edith Churchman said. In later years, her brother has assumed a key leadership role in the church, serving on the vestry.

In her spare time, Churchman loved nothing more than relaxing and socializing with her friends. "Sometimes, Gladys and I would go out to the Owl Club on Elizabeth Avenue, a hangout for everyone in Newark's black community, or stop by Little Johnny's on Montgomery Street, a neighborhood bar where everyone knew each other," Mary Wright said. "Gladys also loved going to dances sponsored by community groups at the Terrace Room on Broad Street, especially when Duke Ellington was in town.

"We also had a little pinochle group," said Mary Wright. "We met once a month at each other's homes and served dinner. There was no money involved. We played for fun, although it could get pretty competitive at times." Also in the group were Mildred Helms, who later spearheaded the construction of low- and moderate-income homes in the Clinton Hill section of Newark's South Ward; Gladys Curtis, who assisted with the children at the Friendly; and Christine Hart, another friend. Harriet Pierce also was a part of the group.

Because they looked so much alike—both were short, rotund, and had long hair, often worn in an upswept style—people often confused Mary Wright and Gladys Churchman. "One night I was out at Twin Oaks, a place near Somerville where everyone used to go, when a man came up to me and thought I was Gladys," Wright recounted. "He wanted to know what was going on at the neighborhood house. When I saw Gladys the next day, she already had heard all about it. He'd been to the neighborhood house and told her what a nice conversation they'd had the night before. 'You'd better be careful when you're out there,' " she joked. " 'They are going to accuse me of what you're doing.' " Another time, Wright met a man on Somerset Street who sold insurance. After making his pitch, he told her he would come around to see her. He did, but when he arrived at 28 Barclay Street, he went to see Churchman instead. "Gladys told me how he came by to tell her more about the insurance he sold, just as he'd promised me," said Wright.

To Mary Wright's children, Cheryl and Eugene, their aunt Gladys was like another mother. "Because of her, I started kindergarten at Morton Street School when I was four," Cheryl said. "She was always around to help me and share special occasions with my family. But she didn't take any nonsense. One day after school, I was supposed to go to music lessons. But I didn't feel like it, so I went to the playground. She spotted me as she was driving by with Miss Harriet, got out of her car, caught me by the ear, put me in the car, and took me home."

In 1966, shortly before her retirement from the neighborhood house, Churchman, a teacher by training, was appointed to the Newark Board of Education by Mayor Hugh J. Addonizio. Citing her as "a leader of high caliber," Addonizio said he appointed her because she was "someone who would make a real contribution to the improvement of education in Newark at a time of great change at the board."

One of those changes had to do with the racial imbalance that occurred when teachers were promoted. Until the early 1960s, when black teachers, led by E. Alma Flagg, fought for the appointment of black administrators, African-American teachers had no chance whatsoever of being promoted to supervisory positions.

Flagg, who held a doctorate in education and had nearly twenty years of experience, was still teaching third grade when she and some colleagues filed discrimination complaints against the board with state education officials. After a five-year battle, Carrie Epps Powell, a black teacher who was nearing retirement, was appointed vice principal at

Hawthorne Avenue School. Months later, Flagg became principal at Hawkins Street School.

But the racial turmoil at the board did not subside. By the time Churchman was appointed to the board, Newark's African-American community was clamoring for a black business administrator. When a white candidate who was less qualified than their candidate, Wilbur Parker, was chosen for the position, many blacks became enraged, picketing the board office and City Hall.

A year later, the Newark riots exploded, triggered by the arrest of a black cabdriver and rumors that police had beaten him. The source of discontent, however, went far deeper. Infuriated by more than just one incident, black Newarkers simply were tired of being treated as inferior. Parker's failure to win the administrator's position was a thorny issue. So was the construction of the University of Medicine and Dentistry in the heart of the Central Ward, which endangered the homes of many blacks.

During her tenure on the board of education, Churchman's focus was academics. She served two terms, both as chairman of the Instruction Committee. She also became chairman of the board of directors of the Newark City Hospital School of Nursing and belonged to the Mental Health Board of Essex County.

Among her other civic activities were her memberships in the Central Ward Juvenile Conference Committee and the Hill (Central Ward) Social Agencies' Council. She also was the first African-American member of Zonta International of Greater Newark. Simone Churchman, her teenage great-granddaughter, followed suit, making her the third generation of the family involved in Zonta, an international businesswomen's organization.

When school let out for summer, Churchman saw to it that Cheryl Wright and other qualified youngsters got jobs at the neighborhood house or at the board of education offices. As a teenager, Cheryl worked at both. "My summer job at the neighborhood house started when I was a teenager attending West Kinney Junior High School," Cheryl said. "As an assistant to the teachers, I did anything Aunt Gladys wanted me to do."

By the time Cheryl entered junior high school, the Churchmans were living at 397 Bergen Street, opposite Cleveland School, where Jim Churchman opened his first funeral home. His family, which by then included his wife, Corinne, and children, Edith and James III, lived on the second floor. His mother and his grandmother, who died at age eighty-nine, lived on the third floor.

"One night, when Aunt Gladys had to go out with Junior and his wife, she called to have me come to the funeral home to close up," Cheryl recalled. "I think she knew I might be afraid because she told me there was nothing to fear from dead people, only people who are alive. 'Trust me,' she told me. 'You can handle it.' That night there was nothing on TV but very scary movies, so I was very glad when Aunt Gladys called to check on me. I was gladder yet when they all got home."

For Edith Churchman and her brother, James III, who took over the family business after their father's semi-retirement, living above the funeral home was all they knew. "It was nothing unusual for us," said Edith. "That's where we always lived, and that's where I live now, above the funeral home—just like my parents and grandmother did on Bergen Street."

For some of their friends, going to the funeral home to visit always had an eerie feeling about it. Della Moses Walker, whose brother James was a friend of James Churchman III, said that was especially true at Halloween. "When I was very young, Forty [James III] always had a Halloween party," she said. "When we got to the house on Bergen Street, I was afraid to go into the basement. I thought it was where all the bodies were, so I would always go upstairs to the third floor to have ginger beer with Grandma." Walker's fear was unfounded. "We didn't keep the bodies there," said James Churchman III. "My father turned the basement into a smoking room. We also had a Ping-Pong table and lots of room for parties like the ones I had at Halloween."

Like many of the girls in the neighborhood, Cheryl Wright was a member of the Girl Scout troop run by Dorothy Gould, her principal at Morton Street School. "Miss Gould was very strict, just like Aunt Gladys," Cheryl said. "Looking back, it was almost like being in the military. Aunt Gladys would look you in the eye and bawl you out in a minute if you weren't doing the right thing. So would Miss Gould. We never could do anything that was the least bit mischievous and get away with it."

"Mrs. Churchman was very proud of her Girl Scouts," said Gould, who spent her early days at the Friendly Neighborhood House as a member of a club for teenage girls. "We learned about behavior and deportment, and we had a lot of parties," she recalled. "To fulfill our community service component, we worked with the younger children. That's why Church never had to hire part-time workers. She had a million kids she was grooming for better things."

Cheryl Wright was one of them. "When I became a teacher, I began subbing at Peshine Avenue School and applied to the board for a permanent position there," she recounted. "When my papers came back, I was assigned to Maple Avenue Annex. I didn't know anyone there and didn't want to be assigned there, so I asked again if I could be assigned to Peshine. They told me Aunt Gladys said that Maple Avenue Annex, not Peshine, was where I was supposed to be. That was where Aunt Gladys wanted me, and that was it. She was very much in control."

Churchman's influence over Cheryl's development did not stop there. "When I began dating, Aunt Gladys wanted to meet all of my boyfriends," she said. "If she didn't like one, she'd tell me he wasn't for me. To my regret, she passed away two months before I married. Jim Churchman, Jr., gave me the gift Aunt Gladys wanted me to have—limousine service for our wedding."

In retrospect, Cheryl Wright Newby sees her childhood involvement at the Friendly as life-enhancing. "Going there for so many years helped me become a more responsible adult," she said. "All of us had to work hard because there was so much of an academic focus. If we did our homework, there was a little time for play. Yet the entire experience made our lives more balanced. Aunt Gladys taught me about the many needs children have, which made me want to follow in her footsteps, both as a teacher and in the outside world. She had a profound effect on all of our lives."

"Aunt Gladys was my mentor too," said Cheryl's brother, Gene, a former Newark teacher, now a human resources executive in Owensboro, Kentucky. "If there's such a thing as a woman role model for a man, she was mine. She was the example I followed. Because she loved helping people, she encouraged me to do things that helped people. That's why I became a scout. That's why I became a teacher, and that's why I chose human relations as my field."

As a boy, James E. Churchman, Jr., often asked his mother why she spent so many hours at the Friendly. Her answer was always the same: "If I can save one child, it's well worth it."

Years later, Churchman concluded that he had "a great appreciation of women" because he came from a family of women. Both his grandmother and his mother greatly influenced the way he conducted himself. He had considerable support, too, from the women who worked for his mother at the neighborhood house. "I used to call Mrs. Ethel Jones, the chief cook, my aunt," he recalled. "She had no kids, but she loved children. She was like a godmother to me. She always had a nice word for everyone." He also was very fond of a woman named Mrs. Cobb, who died of cancer when he was a boy.

"My mother was extremely dedicated to her work and devoted to the children," Churchman said. "The neighborhood house was a very special place for women who went out to work and needed child care. She could really get things done. When people came in upset and crying that they had no money, she would make waves."

In addition to his job at Douglass-Harrison Homes, his dedicated service to the Boy Scouts, and his duties as a church acolyte, Churchman was active in sports as a student at South Side High School. During his travels with the school track team, he got his first taste of racial discrimination when the team bus stopped at a dinner in Hightstown, New Jersey. "No Coloreds," read the sign. That included him and his teammate Charlie Malone, who became a Tuskegee Airman, the only two black boys on the team.

After graduating from South Side, Churchman attended Howard University in Washington, D.C., and then joined the army. "People say that my wife, Corinne, and I met at Howard University, but that's not true," he said. "We both were at Howard, but I left for the army after my first year. Corinne and I met later on a double date arranged by a mutual friend," he explained. "My godfather was the one who arranged the double date," said Edith Churchman. "My father was with my mother's sister. My mother was my godfather's date, but my father spent the whole night peeking through the rearview mirror at my mother."

After basic training and a brief stay in Berkeley, California, Churchman shipped to Hawaii, where he served as an operating room technician at the Pearl Harbor Naval Hospital, the largest medical facility of its kind in the Pacific. From there he was assigned to Saipan on the island of Guam.

As a young man, James E. Churchman, Jr., never envisioned himself following his father into the funeral home business. As a college student and army operating room technician, his interests were medicine and applied psychology. He wanted to become a surgeon. "When I began thinking about what I was going to do after the army, I realized that the chances of becoming a black surgeon were not all that good," he said. "My father had an established business, and I'd been an apprentice with him before entering the army, so I decided to join him in it. I never had any regrets about it."

Churchman started working for his father when he was twelve or thirteen, taking care of the door at the funeral home and doing chores. At that time, the funeral home was at 32 Waverly Avenue in Newark, around the corner from where Jim and his mother lived. Although he worshiped his mother, he also was very close to his father. "When I was seventeen, I went to take the road test for my driver's license in a hearse," he recalled. "It was quite the talk of the neighborhood."

Even though his father married twice more, his parents remained friendly after they divorced. It was his father, Churchman explained, who came to the rescue when he and his mother were on a bicycling expedition through Newark's Weequahic Park and she fell and broke her ankle. "Immediately, my father came to the park and took my mother to the hospital."

After his discharge from the army, Churchman enrolled at the McAllister School of Embalming. He graduated in 1947 and became licensed to practice in 1949, the same year he married Corinne Johnstone and went to work for his father. Churchman dissolved his partnership with his father in 1952, when he decided to go into business for himself. "Shortly before I left, we had a disagreement," he said. "My father wanted to remodel the funeral home, but I had no say. But there was no bitterness when I left. My father helped me. He wanted only the best for me."

As a child, Edith Churchman loved nothing more than going downtown on Saturdays on shopping expeditions with her grandmother. "My biggest thrill was jumping in a Green cab with her to go Bamberger's. She had a favorite driver, a lady who always carried bananas and would give me one. Going to Bamberger's was a very big expedition. At that time, the store had a doorman and elevator operator. They all knew my grandmother. It was a big thing when they knew she was coming to shop."

After shopping, they would go to the store's basement to have lunch. "They had all these great desserts," Edith said. "They would put a cone on top of a scoop of vanilla ice cream to make it look like a clown, using cherries for eyes. I was hardly more than five years old, so it was a big thrill." Years later, Gladys Churchman's portrait was included in a collection of photographs of New Jersey's Outstanding Citizens put on display in Bamberger's Distinguished Citizens Gallery.

At home, Edith Churchman loved parading around in her grandmother's slingback shoes with the toes out. "They were size six," she said. "When I got older, she used to let me stretch them out for her, which made me feel very grown. I can remember how heartbroken she was when my foot grew larger and I couldn't wear them any more. In my mind, it was a real tragedy."

As if it were yesterday, she also remembers her grandmother's piano playing at the neighborhood house. "She played a little stride piano and was very heavy on the pedal, with her left hand hitting the bass chords. She had a favorite song the kids all loved:

> Johnny goes right and Johnny goes wrong;
> Two little Johnnys walking along.
> Johnny goes right.
> He always stays right;
> He always keeps out of trouble.
> But Johnny goes left.
> He stays to the left,
> And always gets into trouble.
> So when you are walking along,
> Remember the two little Johnnys.
> Always stay right.
> Like Johnny go right,
> And you will never go wrong.

"Nana also was a big Eastern Star [a Christian civic organization]," Edith Churchman said. "I can remember her getting all dressed up in her Eastern Star regalia—a white dress with a crinoline and shoes and stockings to match. They met at the Prince Hall lodge at 188 Belmont Avenue [now Irvine Turner Boulevard]. For a time, she was Worthy Matron," the equivalent of chapter president.

Gladys Churchman supported her grandchildren in their endeavors. As a member of the Newark Board of Education, she was the one who handed Edith her diploma when she graduated from Arts High School.

Both Edith and her brother, James III, graduated from Maple Avenue School in Newark's South Ward, where there were few other black students. "Going to a South Ward school in the 1960s, when the area was still predominantly white and Jewish, made us like freedom riders, except for the fact that my father drove us to school every day," she said.

"As I recall, there were just two or three black kids in my class. We were made to feel very unwelcome. Until then, I had been a very favored child in the classroom. I was always made to think I was very smart. Until then, I was a straight A student. At Maple Avenue, they had been diagramming sentences. I had not, so I was made to feel very stupid." Things got no better when Edith had trouble pronouncing the word "Schenectady" in a reading class. "It became a big issue," she said. "Much was made of the fact that I could not sound out the word. I was in a pretty hostile environment. The only good thing was that the longer my brother and I stayed there, the more integrated the school got."

After graduating from Maple Avenue, Edith went on to Arts High School and Heidelberg College in Tiffin, Ohio. A graduate of the New England School of Mortuary Science, she also holds a master's degree in rhetoric and public address from Emerson College in Boston and a doctorate in communications from Bowling Green University in Ohio.

James Churchman III is a graduate of the New York Military Academy at Cornwall-on-Hudson, New York, and Bradley University in Peoria, Illinois, where he was a business major.

At Cornwall, football was his passion. When he made the varsity team, he was elated, even though his family could not attend every game because of business commitments. To this day, however, there is one game that stands out in his memory. "The field was slick and the ball was everywhere because it was raining so hard," he recounted. "Luckily, I recovered a fumble. When I looked up, there was my grandmother, standing in the mud."

One of Gladys Churchman's perks as a school board member was a chauffeur-driven car. Despite the rain, she had gotten her driver to take her all the way to Cornwall. One of her drivers was Curtis Grimsley, later the president of a union that represented noninstructional Newark school employees.

"Having access to a driver was a big deal," said Edith Churchman. "I can still see my grandmother descending the steps on Bergen Street and hopping into the car to go downtown to a school board meeting. That's when I realized that there was a difference between people who were politically correct and people who were not. My grandmother knew a lot of people—just about anyone you could think of who was important in Newark. For the first time, too, I realized that my life was privileged, largely because my grandmother was so respected and knew so many people. In some circles, she was 'Queen Churchman.'"

Although her grandchildren were growing older and venturing out on their own, Gladys Churchman still kept in daily contact with them. "When I went away to college and my brother was in high school, she had a second phone put in, a private number, so that we could always reach her and there would never be a busy signal," Edith Churchman said. "When we were home, our friends were always welcome at my grandmother's house. Her love was unconditional."

For Edith Churchman, who is the spitting image of her grandmother, there is no higher honor than having someone remind her of the resemblance. "She's Gladys," said Evelyn Boyden Darrell. "Not only in looks, but in her commitment to the Newark community." As Edith Churchman once told a magazine reporter, "I stayed on to work here because of my pride of involvement in a family-owned business. I want people to see me as a caring person and Churchman's as a resource for the community at all times, not just when there is a funeral."

Gladys Churchman died of a stroke in Orange Memorial Hospital on January 14, 1974, at age seventy-one, after spending months in a coma. She is buried in Glendale Cemetery in Bloomfield, New Jersey.

Because of her many years of service to the Newark community, she was revered throughout the city. In October 1956, she received a plaque from the *New Jersey Afro-American* newspaper for twenty-five years of service to the Friendly Neighborhood House. In March 1959, the F&M Schaefer Brewing Company commended her devotion to the improvement of family life in the Central Ward. In April 1961, she received the annual Fellowship Award given by the Wesleyan Service Guild of the Philadelphia District, Delaware Conference of the Methodist Church.

Gladys Churchman's work has never been forgotten. Shortly after her death, her portrait was hung in the library at Weequahic High School. At Morton Street School, where her friend Dorothy Gould was principal, a plaque on the lawn pays tribute to her accomplishments.

"When you think about a day-care situation like that which existed in the 1930s, when the nation was in the depths of a depression, everything my grandmother did was pretty amazing," Edith Churchman reflected. "She really cared about kids. She really cared about people. I never heard anyone say a mean word about her."

"Hardly a week goes by at the funeral home without someone mentioning my mother's name, even though she's been dead [more than] thirty years," said James E. Churchman, Jr. "Either they were in her Girl Scout troop, went to the neighborhood house for lunch and after school, or sent their children there. My mother said that she would be happy if she could save one child from a life of poverty and despair. She saved hundreds."

DR. E. ALMA FLAGG
Pioneering Educator | 1918–

No matter how sterile the windowless E. Alma Flagg School on Third Street in Newark may seem, this drab concrete building remains a shining tribute to its namesake. For those who know Newark history, Dr. Flagg was the tireless educator who spent years pressing for the promotion of African-American administrators. Eventually, in fulfillment of that mission, she became the first black principal of an integrated public school in New Jersey's largest city.

Yet those who know her best say the greater contribution of Eloise Alma Williams Flagg to the Newark community is the modest way she has gone about helping others for more than eighty-six years. Flagg's friend Joan Henderson considers her mentor's generous spirit and importance as a role model for young people all the more amazing because Flagg has triumphed over so many adversities, including the poverty of her childhood. "Alma has worked extremely hard to accomplish what she has," said Henderson. "As a true educator, she focused solely on her students, helping them to achieve their personal goals."

Counted among those "young people" is Henderson's husband, Carroll (Timmie) Henderson, who became the Newark Fire Department's first black battalion chief. "When I was a boy, I was the editor of a little school newspaper at Eighteenth Avenue School, and she was the adviser," he recalled. "We had no other black teachers, so she was very important to me and other children like me. Then, as always, Flagg's devotion to the welfare of others was clear," Timmie Henderson said. "If you're in a pinch, you don't even have to ask. Alma will be there for you."

Flagg's innate sense of concern for others is rooted in her unswerving devotion to family and friends, her unflagging energy, and her determination to keep going no matter how rough the road ahead. "My mother's always been reluctant about asking other people for help," said Thomas L. Flagg, a Michigan college professor. "She likes to do things herself. When my grandmother and father were both sick and died within a year of each other, my mother knocked herself out caring for them. Even when there was nothing more that she could do, she felt there was."

His sister, Luisa Foley, a high school Spanish teacher, feels the same way. "This is the way my mother has been all her life," Foley said. "Her sense of drive and determination comes from her mother, who had little education yet raised five children on her own. If you understand that, you understand the source of my mother's dedication to her family and to her community."

Joan Henderson met Flagg just after graduating from South Side High School in 1957 and joining the Newark Choral Society, conducted by Dorothy Schneider, South Side's music teacher. "We stood next to each other and immediately became friends," said Henderson, describing a bond that has lasted nearly fifty years.

Without Flagg's help, Henderson probably would not have been able to make it through college. But she did, earning two master's degrees to follow in Flagg's path as a beloved teacher and guidance counselor. "Alma wasn't earning all that much herself, but she would put a blank check in my mailbox from time to time for me to use for whatever I needed," Henderson said. "She would never tell anyone this. What she does, she does quietly and without any expectation of recognition or reward."

"Useful" is the word Flagg often uses to describe herself. Her life's view, that she would "rather be useful than popular," is one she has embraced all her life. Friends call Flagg "determined," "tenacious," and "very modest." She considers the first two on point. As to the third, she demurs, attesting to its probable veracity.

Asked what led her to assume so many leadership roles—both in the Newark schools, where she served as teacher, principal, and assistant superintendent, and in Newark's community at large, where she has been president of a half-dozen major organizations—Flagg points to her desire to serve her community. "I'm not going anywhere," she is convinced. "Newark is my home. I've spent almost all my life here. This is where I'm going to stay. So I might as well be useful."

Despite her years of service to Newark and its people, Flagg often feels that she has not done enough with her life, hence her all-encompassing sense of internal restlessness, a trait that finds her forever looking for new ways to be of assistance to others. The fact is that she has led an exemplary life. "Alma is our standard bearer," Joan Henderson said, speaking for scores of students and educators who have come under Flagg's influence.

As a young teacher, Henderson was Flagg's colleague as well as her friend. After graduating from college, Henderson's second teaching job was at Hawkins Street School in Newark, where Flagg, after breaking the district's color barrier, was assigned as the first black principal of an integrated public school. "Alma was my friend, but she was tough as nails on me," Henderson recalled. "She always is fair, but she is a no-nonsense person, precise and professional in everything she does."

Alma Flagg's appointment as the first black principal of a modern-day school in Newark capped a course that had been set in motion by African-American educators nearly two centuries earlier. Newark's earliest black teachers were ministers. One of the first schools for black children was the African School. Founded in 1828 to serve fifty Negro children, it was supported by a $100 annual budget provided by the town fathers.

By 1837 the city had several schools for Negro children, separated by gender as well as by race. At the Colored Female School, a Miss Sawyer was in charge of instruction. She taught reading, writing, grammar, arithmetic, and geography.

In 1849 a school for Negro children of both sexes opened in the upper rooms of a church founded by former slaves on Plane Street, now University Avenue. In the late 1880s, church members built the Wickliffe Presbyterian Church, a beautiful brownstone edifice on Thirteenth Avenue. Abandoned after Newark's 1967 civil strife, the church was demolished to make way for Society Hill, the Central Ward complex where Flagg now lives.

As the principal at Hawkins Street, Alma Flagg followed a trail blazed by James Baxter, who went to Newark from Philadelphia in 1864 at age eighteen to teach at the Newark Colored School. Baxter eventually became the school's principal, staying on until his retirement in 1909.

Within the Newark community, Baxter was revered by blacks and respected by whites. Although his school was segregated from schools that white children attended, their principals welcomed him into the Newark Principals Association. Early on, he became the association's vice president. Because of his standing in the community, James S. Baxter Terrace, a low-rise apartment complex run by the Newark Housing Authority, bears his name.

After Baxter became principal of the Colored School, he moved its operations to Fair Street and established an evening school. Eventually the school moved to State Street, near Broad, to a building that is now home to the Newark Public Schools' Office of Visual and Performing Arts. By 1871, largely through Baxter's efforts, Negroes were admitted to Newark high schools. Within a year, all city schools, including the grammar school facilities, opened to Negro children.

Baxter's daughter, Grace Baxter Fenderson, a founder of the Newark Branch of the NAACP in 1914, also held a special place in the hearts of black Newarkers. When the public schools became integrated, she was one of the city's first black teachers. For forty-two years she taught at Monmouth Street School in Newark's old Third Ward, where her students included James E. Churchman, Jr., Connie Woodruff, and Dr. C. Theodore Pinckney, Jr. James Churchman became one of Newark's most respected funeral home directors. Connie Woodruff was a revered community leader. Theodore Pinckney became chairman of the Mathematics Department at Newark's East Side High School.

Until pioneering teachers like Fenderson and Mae Mulford, another highly regarded educator, came along, Newark's Negro children were taught by whites only. Change did not come easily. It took another forty years for Alma Flagg to break the barrier that excluded these and others of their race from attaining supervisory positions.

Finally, in 1964, the Newark Board of Education relented and named Carrie Epps Powell, who was nearing retirement, vice principal at Hawthorne Avenue School. Soon after, Flagg, the leader of the ground-breaking effort to integrate the top levels of school administration, was named vice principal at Garfield School and then principal at Hawkins Street, where most of the students and teachers were white. Ironically, Flagg's history-making appointment at Hawkins Street came exactly one hundred years after James Baxter arrived in Newark to head the Colored School. To her benefit, Flagg was in familiar territory at Hawkins Street. She had grown up in the Ironbound section of the East Ward, where the school was located, and she was a product of its elementary schools and East Side High School.

Shy and quiet as a child, Flagg was also tremendously focused and achievement oriented. "I don't know why I wanted to become a teacher," she said, for there was no particular teacher that she considered her inspiration. Perhaps it was because she was studious by nature, winning awards at Chestnut Street School for academics, deportment, and attendance. She also demonstrated a natural flair for writing, interviewing her classmates and writing poems that appeared each week in the *Newark News*. "They called it the Junior Sunbeam Club, so I guess you could say I was a junior reporter," she said.

Flagg was one of five children of Hannibal Greene Williams, a sign and house painter, and Caroline Ethel (Moody) Williams. Her older sister, Thelma Williams Gillis, called Mickey by her friends, became chief clerk of the Newark Municipal Court. Her brother, the Reverend Dr. Hannibal Allen Williams, was the founder and pastor of New Liberation Presbyterian Church in San Francisco and a former moderator of the Synod of the Pacific. Two younger siblings, Samuel Donald Williams and Harold Moody Williams, died young.

Born in City Point, Virginia, on September 16, 1918, Alma Williams was three years old when her family moved to Pennsylvania. After brief stays in Coatesville and Allentown, the family moved to Newark when she was eight.

In those days, Newark was a great manufacturing center. "It was an age of production, fueled by a tremendous work ethic," she said. "But most of the factories I knew in my early years—Hollander fur-dying, Ideal Foods, Waterman's fountain pens, Ballantine beer, and numerous leather and metal industries—are long since gone." So are the many department stores of her childhood, places like Bamberger's, Kresge's, and Orhbach's.

Upon their arrival in Newark, Alma's family lived first at 71 Kinney Street, where her father conducted his business. Although they moved frequently, the Williamses never ventured from the Ironbound section of Newark's East Ward, where Alma and her siblings attended school.

Because she was bright and eager to learn, Alma was promoted frequently, having skipped two grades by the time she completed elementary school. One of her proudest moments occurred in seventh grade at Chestnut Street School, when her teacher, Anna Gerber, presented her with a book at the end of the year for earning good grades. "Miss Gerber encouraged me," she said. The book, *Nellie's Silver Mine,* remains one of her treasures.

As a girl, she and her sister began attending Holy Trinity Baptist Church, a tiny congregation on Chestnut Street, where the pastor was the Reverend S. H. Littles. "Later, we joined Mama's Church," First Mount Zion on Thomas Street, one of the many churches that remain a staple of black life in Newark. Many others have either merged with other houses of worship or disappeared from the Newark landscape over the years.

Within the black community, one of the key mergers involved St. Philip's Episcopal Church, which took over the all-white congregation of St. Paul's. Founded in a small building on High Street, St. Philip's burned down after moving to High and West Market and then merged with Trinity Cathedral on Military Park. St. John's United Methodist Church, situated in a former Jewish temple at High Street and Thirteenth Avenue, eventually joined with Franklin Methodist; then after the merger, the church moved to Broad Street. Today Franklin–St. John is located on Keer Avenue in Newark's South Ward.

Although life was hard for the Williams family, it became even more difficult when Alma's father died of complications from asthma and heart trouble. He was forty-seven. She was just twelve and about to graduate from eighth grade at Oliver Street School. Suddenly, her whole world was in pieces.

With five children to feed and support, Caroline Williams struggled to keep her family together. "Some people wanted to split us up, but Mother never gave that a second thought," Flagg said. "She worked as hard as she could as a domestic to keep all five of us together. Somehow, we got by, but it wasn't easy," added Flagg. "Family was and always will be all-important to Alma," said Joan Henderson. "She had very little as a child, very few material things, but the family was very close."

Flagg revered her mother, who lived to be ninety-four. "In later life, Mother Williams lived with Alma and her husband, Tom, on Stengel Avenue in Newark," Henderson said. "Everywhere Alma went, Mother Williams went, even after Tom got sick. It was very difficult because Mother Williams sometimes was confined to a wheelchair in her final years."

By the time Alma entered East Side High School, her family was living on Brunswick Street, where Sarah Vaughan, the famous jazz singer, and her family were their neighbors. "We lived at 61, and they were at 74," Flagg said. "I didn't know much about Sarah, but our mothers were nodding acquaintances."

At East Side, Alma ran track—"nothing to speak of," she said, "just interclass relays and the hop-skip-jump." She also wrote verses for the school newspaper and was a regular visitor to the main branch of the Newark Public Library, downtown at 5 Washington Street. "We never went to the branches," she said. "We either went to the school library or to Washington Street."

Her high energy level and penchant for constant activity were evident early in life. For two years, she was a member of the National Honor Society. She also belonged to the Latin Club, Drama Club, and chorus. She was on the staff of *The Torch*, the school yearbook, and appeared in a class show.

After graduating from East Side High School in January 1935, she enrolled at Essex County Junior College, an institution created by President

Franklin D. Roosevelt during the Great Depression to provide students with the opportunity to learn while keeping teachers employed. The college was based at Newark State College at 185 Broadway in Newark.

Although she received a scholarship from the Howard University Alumni Association to attend Howard University, she could not afford to go. Instead, she studied for two and a half years at the junior college level and then applied to Newark State. After passing an entrance exam, she was accepted.

At Newark State, Alma Williams was one of just a few black students in the class of 1940. The class of 1939 had only two black women, Edwina Tucker Davis and Evelyn Watson Ford. Only one, Margaret Longus Jenkins, was in the class of 1938, the first graduates to receive a bachelor's degree.

"When I did my first practice teaching as a junior, there were just three of us," Flagg said. "In my senior year, a mature lady joined us, so there were four. There were few outright [discriminatory] acts, but there was always something there. One that stands out is the time my social studies instructor used the N-word in class just as if it were perfectly understood and accepted. I also can remember the dean asking me how I accounted for my intelligence. When our grades were posted in the hallway, we were all listed as 'Colored.' "

Because there was no acceptable response to such insults, Alma and her friends ignored them. "You couldn't go around fighting all the time, so whatever was said was said and done with," she explained. Nevertheless, these untoward incidents remained fresh in Flagg's memory after nearly seventy years. One of her first recollections of blatant bigotry dates to her high school days. "It was well-known," she explained, "that parts of Barringer High School were off-limits to Negro children. Those who went there sometimes were called names and taunted by white students."

Alma graduated from Newark State, following the lead of Gladys Berry Francis, another noted Newark educator. Francis, who was certified to teach in 1936, became director of elementary education for the district. Long after her retirement, she was appointed to the Newark Board of Education.

Because there were so few black students at Newark State, they all knew each other. Yet because of their low status on campus, they had few places to socialize. None of the white fraternities or sororities accepted young black men or women, so Francis joined Phi Delta Kappa, an off-campus group of black women from Jersey City and Newark. Members included Gladys Cannon Nunnery, for whom a school was later named in Jersey City; Elizabeth Houston, who later taught in Brooklyn and whose granddaughter was singer Whitney Houston; and Mae Mulford, who became one of Newark's earliest black teachers. After graduating from college in 1941, Alma joined the Beta Alpha Omega chapter of Alpha Kappa Alpha, the nation's oldest sorority for black women.

Geraldine Sims, a retired Newark school principal who entered Newark State as Alma Williams was finishing, remembers Flagg well from their college days "Even as a young woman, Alma had a strong fiber. She was not to be dismissed," Sims said. "Whatever her background, she was a crusader."

Flagg's leadership abilities may have come naturally or they may have surfaced in response to the many causes affecting the U.S. Negro of her day that required the efforts of determined and tenacious people. "There had been discrimination all along at Newark State," Sims said. "Most of the girls were encouraged to do their practice teaching at Charlton Street School in Newark because most of the students there were black. Schools in white neighborhoods, like Ivy Street and First Avenue, were not considered. Even the Ironbound, which had a sizable black population in those days, was off-limits to us. If the girls didn't go to Charlton Street, they were assigned to Oakwood Avenue in Orange. Most of them took it for granted they would go to one of those schools."

The belief at the time was that if you stood at Spruce Street and Belmont Avenue in Newark and threw stones in various directions, they would land where all the black teachers were. "Basically, that meant Charlton Street, Eighteenth Avenue, Monmouth Street, and Morton Street," Flagg said. "That told the story."

Discrimination against black students at Newark State was symptomatic of U.S. society itself, a microcosm of what life was like for people of color at every turn. Although some teachers and administrators at the college were accepting of Negroes and some Negro students seemed content with their condition, Alma Williams and Geraldine Sims saw their situation for what it was. They accepted what they had to accept but felt no apprehension about speaking out when the need arose.

"We were there to get an education," Flagg said, and there was no stopping them. They were determined to further their goals, get their degrees, and, like their white contemporaries, become teachers. Yet when Flagg graduated in 1940, there were no teaching jobs available in the Newark schools. Sims, who graduated three years later, was more fortunate. "As luck would have it, I was assigned to Fifteenth Avenue School," she said. During forty-one years in the Newark school system, she also taught at Roseville Avenue School and was principal at Maple Avenue School and Maple Avenue Annex.

By the time Sims graduated, Flagg, who had already spent two years teaching in Washington, D.C., had returned to Newark and was starting her second year of teaching at Eighteenth Avenue School. "When I told the dean at Newark State that I was going to teach in Washington, he commended me for going south to help my people," Flagg recalled, still amused by the thought. "All I wanted to do was stay in Newark and help my people here."

Flagg, however, has earned her place in the college's history. In 1966 she was named Outstanding Alumnus at the college, which became Newark State and relocated to Union, New Jersey. In 1968 she received an honorary degree. In response, she urged the instructors to see the people of Newark "with open minds as well as open eyes, to see them as real human beings who think and feel, to believe them able to learn and participate and create." By doing so, she said, everyone would benefit.

At the beginning of her career, Flagg experienced worse discrimination in the nation's capital than in Newark. "I found that it was all right for me to be a teacher in Washington, but I could not have a soda at a lunch counter," she said. "The schools were segregated by divisions. Nine of the divisions were for whites; the other four were for blacks."

After teaching fourth grade for one semester at the Douglass-Simmons School in Washington, she was transferred at midyear to the Crummell School, where she was assigned to the third grade. During her two years in Washington, D.C., she first lived in a private home and then became part of a household of young professional people from New Jersey, mostly government workers.

In the fall of 1943, she passed the Newark Teachers Examination and became an official employee of the Newark school system. During her first year of teaching in Newark, the other black teachers who joined the ranks were Dorcia Smith Berry, Gwendolyn Hall East, Mary Womble Spruel, Dorothy Turpin Smith, and Ruby G. Brown. They joined a small contingent of black women already teaching in Newark: Grace Baxter Fenderson, Mildred Morris Williams, Rose Y. Wood, Carrie Epps Powell, Gladys Berry Francis, Olivia L. Bryant, and Helen Miller. Pansy Borders was a staff social worker.

By the time she returned home, Alma Williams and J. Thomas Flagg, a top student and track star at Barringer High School and Montclair State Teachers' College, were preparing for marriage. Although she knew her husband-to-be from the days when they both attended St. James African Methodist Episcopal Church on Union Street in the Ironbound, she did not get to know him well until they met again at a college dance. They soon discovered many common interests, including their work with children. On Saturdays and during the summer after Alma graduated from Newark State, they ran a program for children at the First Congregational Jube Memorial Church at Hayes Circle in Newark. Today the building is home to Greater Mount Moriah Baptist Church.

Alma Williams and Thomas Flagg married on June 24, 1942, in First Mount Zion Baptist Church of Newark. The Reverend James H. Burks, the pastor, officiated. Thelma Williams Stephens, Alma's sister, and Robert E. Stephens, Thelma's husband at the time, were their witnesses.

J. Thomas Flagg was born in Hawkinsville, Georgia, one of two children of Joseph Thomas Flagg, Sr., a trackman on the Pennsylvania Railroad, and Hannah Polhill Flagg. At an early age, his family moved to Seabury Street in Newark, where he grew up.

After graduating from Wilson Avenue School in the Ironbound, Tom spent two years at East Side High School and then enrolled at Barringer High School, where he made headlines as a track star. To prepare for his science major, he completed three years of postgraduate high school work before entering Montclair State College. After graduating in 1940, he stayed on to study for a master's degree in chemistry, while Alma went to Washington to teach.

Soon after their marriage, Tom Flagg was summoned to serve in the army. After completing basic training at Fort Dix, he was sent to New Orleans and then overseas to Liverpool, England, where he served until D-Day, June 6, 1944. After his unit crossed the English Channel on D-Day, he was assigned to the Medical Corps in France until he returned home in January 1946.

By that time, Alma was a tenured Newark teacher. After she passed the teacher exam in April 1943, she was assigned to the third grade at Eighteenth Avenue School. One of Flagg's students at Eighteenth Avenue was Eleanor Crutchfield, who later became a Newark teacher. "To this day, I marvel at Dr. Flagg's ability to remember every detail from the time I was in the third grade," said Crutchfield. "Not only can she remember the names of students in my class, including some I've long forgotten; she can remember exactly where they sat in her classroom. These are things that happened in 1944!"

Flagg remained at Eighteenth Avenue School until 1952, when she asked for a transfer. "I was studying for my master's degree in guidance at Columbia and wanted an opportunity to get into guidance," she said. "To do that, you had to teach an upper grade. At Eighteenth Avenue, all teachers in the upper grades were men."

Eventually she was reassigned to teach the seventh grade at McKinley School, in the heart of a mixed European neighborhood. "After my arrival, I had several unpleasant experiences," she said. "I can remember one man telling me, 'They don't like your people.' " Blatant bigotry also affected the black students who attended McKinley. "They had a difficult time," she said. "Most of them lived across the railroad bridge. Sometimes the white students would block the bridge so they couldn't get across to come to school."

When homes around McKinley School were torn down to make way for the Columbus Homes public housing project, the student population at McKinley began to shrink. "They didn't need as many teachers," Flagg recalled. "Since I had been the last to arrive, I was one of three who had to go."

Following the birth of her daughter, Luisa, in 1952, she took a year off and then was transferred to Peshine Avenue School, where the students were mostly white and Jewish. "I was the first black teacher at both McKinley and Peshine," she said. "I tried, but I never got into guidance because of all these changes."

From February 1954 until June 1957, she taught the third grade at Peshine. "I was demoted," she laughed. "But I did get to teach fifth-grade arithmetic while my third-grade students took gym." At Peshine she taught writing and shared with her students her love of poetry, the vehicle she had used since childhood to capture her thoughts about life and her view of the world.

At that time, WBGO, a Newark-based station that is now an affiliate of National Public Radio, was operated by the Newark Board of Education. The studio was located on the top floor at Central High School. "Every once in a while, I'd take my students there," Flagg said. "Margaret Manley, who was in charge of the radio station, would take them on a tour and then have them recite their poems on the air. A few weeks later they got to hear themselves on the radio."

While teaching at Peshine, Flagg completed her doctorate at Columbia. "It took me forever, nine years in all," she said, "I just kept at it. Not many people imagined I would be a principal or school administrator because I was so quiet."

Flagg's life was now a balancing act on all levels. She was the mother of two children, Thomas L. Flagg, who was born in 1949, and Luisa, who came along three years later. After spending seven years in a two-family house she and her husband had bought on Tillinghast Street in Newark, the family was settling into a new home, a pretty little four-bedroom house, white with green trim, at 44 Stengel Avenue.

Despite the fact that she and Tom were both highly educated and were assets to the Newark school system, no warm welcome awaited the Flaggs in their upwardly mobile middle-class South Ward neighborhood. "The neighbors were mostly Jewish, and we were not," Flagg said. "Some neighbors were cordial, but no one embraced us with open arms."

By the time their son Tommy was ready for preschool at Maple Avenue School, the situation was no better. "I became active in the PTA [Parent-Teacher Association], but the prejudice was obvious," Flagg said. "It was clear the other women did not take to me for [no] other reason than my race." Her son, who went on to earn his bachelor's, master's, and doctoral degrees at the University of Michigan, felt none of this. "I can't recall any bad incidents," said Flagg, a psychology professor at Adrian College in Michigan. "We did all the same things other families did in those days. We didn't feel any different than anyone else. What I do remember is that both my parents were very busy, yet we always had dinner together."

Both he and his sister Luisa, who graduated from Bryn Mawr, a prestigious women's college in Pennsylvania, recounted the good times their family had on vacation each summer. "We went all over," he said. "To California, to Virginia one summer, when both my parents were taking classes at Virginia State, and to Fundy National Park in New Brunswick, Canada. We also went to the beach and to Yankee ball games."

"Going to Fundy National Park was a ritual for several summers," said Luisa Foley, who teaches Spanish at Cherry Hill High School in South Jersey. "My parents took courses while we were there, but we got to do lots of sightseeing. We always stayed in the same hotel and ate in the same restaurants."

At home, Luisa Flagg was the storyteller of Stengel Avenue. "As a child, Lu was very inventive, always making up stories," her mother said. "All the young girls in the neighborhood would gather around her to listen to them."

Although the racism that permeated U.S. society was clearly evident in the Flaggs' Newark neighborhood, not all of the neighbors shied away from the family. The major exceptions were Bill and June Seligman, whose two children were close in age to the Flaggs' children. Not only did the Seligmans, who were Jewish, and the Flaggs become friends; they interacted socially despite what others in the neighborhood may have said about them behind closed doors.

"My friendship with Alma extended far beyond mere courtesies at PTA meetings or interactions on the street," said June Seligman. "We were constantly in and out of each other's houses, and we socialized a lot. When Bill and I had a party, Alma and Tom were there, and vice versa.

From the start of their friendship, their children were friends too. "Our son Scott and their daughter Luisa were best friends," Seligman said. "Even when they went off to college, Scott to Princeton and Luisa to Bryn Mawr, they stayed in touch and visited each other. Tommy Flagg and Danny were friends at Weequahic High School."

At the time, Flagg, who was completing her graduate studies at Columbia, saw something in Seligman that went beyond their friendship. "June was bright and articulate," said Flagg. "She had the makings of a good teacher, and so I encouraged her." Seligman, who was a stay-at-home mother, still remembers the night she decided to go back to school. "Alma and I were talking on the telephone. She kept telling me I should go to college. Until then, I hadn't given it much thought. I thought my husband would think I'd gone crazy, but Bill was very supportive. He agreed with Alma."

Seligman was forty-four when she graduated from college. After applying for a job in the Newark schools, she was assigned to Chancellor Avenue School, where she taught for twenty years until her retirement. Until the end, when she had some classes that were "simply unmanageable," she "loved every minute of it."

With her doctorate in hand, Flagg was now one of Newark's most educated educators. Again, she felt it was time for advancement and expressed a desire to go into remedial reading. "There I was with a doctorate, teaching third grade," she said, shaking her head in disbelief. This time, she got what she wanted. She was assigned to teach remedial reading at two schools, South Tenth Street and South Seventeenth Street, a position she held from 1957 to 1963.

Still, no chance of promotion was in sight. Weary of the double standards they faced as black educators, Flagg and her friends decided to take action. She and Philip Hoggard, another black teacher, filed complaints against the Newark Board of Education, charging discrimination in the promotional system for vice principal. Others followed suit.

To become an administrator, a candidate for vice principal or principal had to take both an oral and a written test. Black candidates generally did exceptionally well on the cut-and-dried written part of the test. The oral test was another matter. Black candidates, no matter how bright or gifted, *never* scored high enough to win an appointment.

"Most of the manipulations that affected the outcome of the test were on the oral section," Flagg said. "That could kill you. But there were manipulations as well attached to the written section. It was not a standardized test like the National Teachers Examination." Because the test was so slanted, many white administrators remained smugly confident that no black educator would ever become an administrator in the Newark schools. "I can recall an assistant superintendent telling me that he was sure there would be no such appointment anytime in the life of the list, which generally was good for four years," Flagg said.

Instead of bucking the system from within, Flagg and her colleagues decided to appeal the board's arbitrary behavior to the state division of discrimination. Her complaint, filed in June 1959, eventually was consolidated with others. "Everything dragged on and on for several years," Flagg said. "When one complaint was thrown out, I'd file another. Some of the teachers were in and out." Discouraged, Phil Hoggard left the district to teach elsewhere. Another teacher, Ralston Gaiter, stayed on for a while but eventually left.

Flagg just dug in deeper, ever persistent in her quest to become an administrator. Frederick Raubinger, the state education commissioner, persistently sided with the Newark Board of Education. There was no discrimination against Newark's Negro teachers, he ruled, dismissing each case.

Raubinger's rulings came as no great surprise to Flagg and the three other teachers who were part of the suit at the time. Although they hoped justice would be served, they were used to the ways of the world. Then, to their surprise, Carrie Epps Powell, a 1923 graduate of Newark State, was appointed vice principal at Hawthorne Avenue School in September 1962.

But that was only the beginning. In March 1963, Flagg became vice principal at Garfield School, and in September 1963 Gladys Berry Francis was appointed vice principal at South Eighth Street School. "For years, we had no black vice principals," Flagg said. "Now, within a year, we had three."

According to a newspaper account, Flagg's appointment at Garfield School occurred because the school population had topped one thousand, creating the need for a new vice principal. Yet other dynamics were at play. In addition to the pressure applied by the teachers, changing times found Newark Negroes clamoring for better conditions. "That probably influenced their thinking too," she said. "We didn't win our case with the commissioner, but we did win."

Not that discriminatory behavior and racial insults simply vanished. "Edward Kennelly, then the superintendent, thought nothing of telling me how surprised he was that I was so efficient and skilled at every thing I did, whatever the position," Flagg said. "Yet everyone knew I was."

The 1964 announcement of Flagg's appointment as principal at Hawkins Street reverberated throughout Newark's black community. An editorial in the *New Jersey Herald News*, a Newark black weekly, concluded:

> Down through the years, Newarkers have been clamoring for a Negro principal, the same as they did for a number of years to secure a Negro judge in this community. We recall the terrific struggle that Newark teachers had trying to become vice principals. They were most successful and impressive on the written examination, but for some strange reason, their minds went blank when taking the oral examination. It is shocking to think that qualified Negroes would be held back in our Newark school system. We are happy to at last see our school officials come of age and carry out the functions of their office without fear or prejudice. Our heartfelt congratulations go to Alma Flagg for achieving this goal.

Through it all, Flagg never thought of giving up her mission to see fair practices implemented for all Newark educators. "I guess I was single-sighted, entirely focused on moving forward with the issue at hand," she recollected. "I was totally absorbed in what I was doing." Flagg's only misgiving about the outcome was its timing. Unfortunately, she said, Grace Baxter Fenderson, whose greatest wish was to see the appointment of a black principal of an integrated school in Newark, did not live to learn of her appointment. Fenderson, one of Newark's most revered educators and civil rights leaders, died in March 1962, nearly two years before Flagg's appointment at Hawkins Street. Gradually, however, scores of other black educators followed Flagg into top positions in the Newark schools.

"Dr. Flagg was a mentor to many of us," said Nathaniel Potts, a former principal of West Side High School. "A group of us who wanted to become administrators used to stop by her house to talk about the principles of administration. The group included Bert Berry, who became principal at Thirteenth Avenue School; Howard Caesar, principal at Hawkins Street, who became an assistant superintendent; the late William Brown, principal at Bergen Street School (William H. Brown Academy), who also became an assistant superintendent; and Ernie Thompson, principal at Martin Luther King and Burnet Street schools."

Even though she was the one who opened the floodgates of fairness for scores of black educators who came after her, few of Flagg's contemporaries supported her campaign to become an administrator. "A lot of them thought I wouldn't get anything, but they didn't mind benefiting from what we did," she said matter-of-factly. "Some thought they'd get a ride. But that didn't stop me. I've been single-minded all my life."

Although Flagg lacked help from some in confronting the rampant discrimination preventing the advancement of Newark's black teachers, she was admired by more people than she thought. "Alma gave everything she had to broaden opportunities for the rest of us," said Geraldine Sims. "The woman was powerful, even though she was quiet. She was like a quiet storm. Frankly, many of us were awed by her. She had ideas. She had vision. And she was determined to keep going, no matter what." That feisty resolve probably led Flagg to get her doctorate. "You had to be twice as good as anyone else to get anywhere, and Alma knew that," Sims said.

During Flagg's three-year tenure (1964–1967) at Hawkins Street, she supervised a mostly white faculty. But that did not faze her. "I just did the job," she said. "I was at Hawkins Street when the riots erupted. The first thing I was instructed to do was to tell all the white teachers to go home."

Doing so, however, meant endangering herself. "We were all worried about my mother that day," her daughter, Luisa, said. "My father didn't want my mother to go to school, but she did. On her way home, she was stopped by a group of National Guardsmen who had cordoned off our street. Somehow, she got home."

During Alma's days at Hawkins Street, Tom Flagg was in and out of the Newark school system. After teaching science at Oliver Street School from 1952 to 1955 and at Webster Junior High School in the mid-1950s, he helped develop the South Side Project, a special program for gifted students at South Side High School called SWAS (School within a School).

Subsequently he became education director for the United Community Corporation, Newark's antipoverty agency. In that capacity he was in charge of the Newark Youth Corps, the first program of its kind for inner-city youth nationwide. During his tenure the program was cited as one of the best in the country, winning the students an invitation to travel to Washington to meet President Lyndon B. Johnson.

In the early 1960s, Tom Flagg became acting vice principal at West Kinney Junior High School and then principal of the Clinton Place Junior High School Summer School. "The district had never had a black summer school principal before," said Alma Flagg. "It was quite a big thing at the time, especially in the black community."

By the time Stanley Taylor, a highly regarded educator from Brooklyn, became Newark's first black superintendent of schools in 1973, most of the children attending district schools also were black. So were Taylor's three assistant superintendents—Alma Flagg, Robert Brown, and William H. Brown.

About the same time that she became assistant superintendent in charge of curriculum, her husband was named director of secondary education. Soon after, he developed the Newark Teacher Corps program for Montclair State College. When the program ended in 1971, he accepted a full professorship in education at the college, where he taught until his retirement in 1984.

After Taylor left Newark, Alma Flagg had to make another adjustment. As part of an across-the-board restructuring, Alonzo Kittrels, the new superintendent, changed her position. "I got kicked into a director's position to do the same work I was doing," said Flagg, who also served several years as an adjunct professor at Rutgers University. "I was at the same level as many of the people I made directors."

Some people thought Flagg would leave. Instead, she decided to stay and make the best of it until her retirement in 1983. By then, she had given forty years of her life to the children of Newark and to the Newark Public Schools.

Although she stays busy in retirement, Alma Flagg, now in her mideighties, still does not feel busy enough. "I like to stir it up upstairs," she said. "I always need something new to do."

Finding time for new endeavors remains problematic because of the scope of her interests, including four decades of dedicated service to the Elizabeth Avenue–Weequahic United Presbyterian Church. "Tom and I became Presbyterians after our children were born," she said. "He was raised as a Methodist, and I was Baptist." Over the years, she has been a Sunday school teacher, choir singer, and member of the session, the church's ruling body. As the clerk of the session, the person responsible for church records, she also became an ordained elder.

Flagg also remains active with Alpha Kappa Alpha, her sorority, and takes part in many educational programs, such as the United Way's Celebrity Read, a program that brings community leaders into the schools to read to the students. For three years before her retirement from the school system, she served as education chairman of Project Pride, an advocacy group for Newark children, coordinating a radio program on WNJR called "Teen Rap." "We always had a guest, generally someone from a profession or a community leader," she said. The students got to meet and interview them.

Over the years, Flagg has served in leadership roles in more than thirty professional and civic organizations, most of them Newark-based. For a time, she was on the advisory board of the Christian After-School Program at Franklin–St. John United Methodist Church of Newark. Until recently, she was a regular volunteer at the New Jersey Performing Arts Center, the hub of Newark's cultural activities.

Commitment to community service is a family trait. Tom Flagg also was a community leader, serving as vice president of the South Ward Boys' Club and president of the Alpha Alpha Lambda chapter of the Alpha Phi Alpha fraternity. He also was active with the Frontiers Club of Newark, a community service organization for black men.

Alma Flagg's only regret about her civic involvement was her inability to save the Newark League of Women Voters from extinction. As a former president of the nonpartisan organization, she tried futilely to save the chapter after being recruited for the job by Anne Evans, the league's longtime president. "Most of us were getting older," Flagg said. "We tried, but we just couldn't get sufficient support from young people to keep going."

Over the years, Flagg devoted considerable energy to the league. In her 1983 President's Message, she appealed to each member to commit herself to "making a difference in community life. If each one of us does one new thing—write a letter, give financial support, volunteer some service, or attend a legislative session," she wrote, "that can be achieved." Dorothy Knauer, executive director of the Community Agencies Corporation, an umbrella group for several Newark-based youth service organizations, credits Flagg with keeping the league going as long as it did. "Without Alma, it would have folded much sooner," she said.

Flagg also came to the rescue when, after the 1999 death of Senator Wynona Lipman, who represented Newark in state government for twenty-seven years, she was asked to take the senator's position as board president of SHARE (Self-help and Resource Exchange), a nonprofit organization that distributes surplus foods to community groups. "Alma stepped in for a short time as interim director," Knauer said. "She knew little about SHARE or how it operated, but she was willing to fill the gap. Otherwise, SHARE would have gone under."

During Alma Flagg's years of commitment to the Newark schools and to the Newark community, many honors have been bestowed on her. At her retirement dinner in 1983 at the Robert Treat Hotel, her place in Newark history was secured when Superintendent Columbus Salley announced that a new school, then under construction, would be named for her. A year later the E. Alma Flagg Elementary School opened.

Today the school is her pride and joy, a place where she often goes to read to the students, engage them in hands-on activities, and participate in assemblies. One of her favorite activities is teaching the students to make soap. For them it is a novelty; for her it is a reminder of her youth, when buying store soap was an extravagance.

The United Way's Celebrity Read program at the school offers students a chance to interact one-on-one with their school's namesake. During a recent program she read three books, including one about Martin Luther King, to an eager group of third graders, who responded with numerous questions about the books she had read to them and her ties to their school.

Through her continuing interest in the education of Newark children, Flagg has witnessed a gradual decline in educational achievement over the years. Although she acknowledges many advances in education, she also believes there has been a tendency "to throw out the baby with the bathwater." Many good programs, she said, were abandoned simply because they were considered old-fashioned.

"When I went to Washington as a young teacher, people there were quick to acknowledge the Newark schools as among the best in the nation," she said. "They thought that coming from Newark was a positive thing. From being on the inside, I can see that some of the practices that we no longer value were important contributors to a good education," she said, citing "something as simple as teaching handwriting" as critical to success in school.

Another of her concerns is "the abandonment of memorization. I see learning by rote as a time saver, a very valuable skill," she said. "Who doesn't remember the little jingles we learned in our youth. They were important learning tools." The elimination of geography from the grammar school curriculum also confounds Flagg. "Everyone needs a general idea of where places are," she said. "Yet today, many people have no idea of where north or south may be. They're lost."

Soon after Flagg's retirement from the school system, a group of her friends and family members established the E. Alma Flagg Scholarship

Fund in her name. For twenty years, until the fund folded in 2004, a half-dozen or more scholarships were awarded annually to Newark high school students in need of financial assistance who excelled academically.

Another honor was bestowed on Flagg in 1986, when she and New Jersey's former governor, Tom Kean, were cited as outstanding graduates of Columbia University. In 1999, the same year she served as deputy grand marshal of Newark's African-American Heritage Parade, she was elected to the Newark Women's Hall of Fame. She also was one of the first elders of Newark's African-American community to be honored publicly during Kwanza festivities at the New Jersey Performing Arts Center.

In October 2004, Flagg delivered the John Cotton Dana Distinguished Lecture at the Newark Public Library. Named for the founder of both the library and the Newark Museum, the event is sponsored annually in tribute to a person from the Newark community who has made a significant contribution to the city and to the state of New Jersey. In typical fashion, Flagg wondered why she had been chosen to give the lecture and receive the accompanying $1,000 gift to purchase library books. But others had no doubt of her merit.

"Alma was a natural choice," said Rebecca Doggett, a community leader who was in charge of the program. "Because of her prominence in our community, she is a member of our board. More importantly, the struggle she went through came at a time when she might have suffered many personal repercussions, and probably did. She stood up and fought against the racial structure of the school system even though she could have lost her job, been demoted, passed over for promotions, or isolated and ostracized. Her struggle is still relevant in terms of assuring that our children secure a quality education," Doggett added. "She is someone—like our current superintendent, Marion Bolden—on whose shoulders our next generation of educational warriors can proudly stand."

More recently, Flagg's stellar career and contributions to her community received national attention when she became the April "calendar girl" for All-State's 2005 calendar honoring African-American educators.

In her spare time, Flagg still writes poetry. Three paperback volumes of her poems, written since 1979, have been combined into a single hardback, *Lines, Colors and More*. One of her proudest moments as a poet came in 1976 when she read "The Freedom Train," a poem she wrote as an anthem to the civil rights movement, at a meeting of the Newark Bicentennial Commission.

After her husband's death in 1994, Flagg decided it was time to sell the family homestead on Stengel Avenue. With her children long since grown and gone, she bought a spacious townhouse in Society Hill, block after block of new housing near Newark's downtown. There she is surrounded by her memories—programs, pictures, and other remembrances.

In one scrapbook are all the poems she wrote each week in her youth for the Junior Sunbeam Club. In another are photos and news clippings detailing her husband's days as a track star at Barringer High School and Montclair State College. Other albums contain hundreds of news articles highlighting her career as an educator and community activist. Old friends like Walter Fenderson and Grace Baxter Fenderson, leaders of the Newark Branch of the NAACP, and William R. Jackson, secretary of the Court Street Young Men's Christian Association (YMCA) and a member of the Newark Board of Education, still look out at her. Everything is there.

One of her prized possessions is a 1978 album of holiday music recorded by the South Side High School Choral Alumni and the Newark Choral Society under the direction of Frederic C. Martin. It is a memorial tribute to Dorothy Schneider, the music teacher who guided the choral society in its early days. On the cover is a photograph showing each member wearing church robes. Standing in front of Flagg is her friend Joan Henderson, both of them looking as youthful as they did in the early days of the choral society when they first met.

At home in Newark, Flagg often travels to meetings and community events with her longtime friend Willa Jackson. "Education is Alma's love," Jackson said. "Her style of doing things is very quiet, without fanfare, but she gets a lot done. She's done a lot for people because she wants them to succeed. Her reward is to see them succeed."

DR. E. MAE MCCARROLL

Revered Physician | 1898–1990

Dr. E. Mae McCarroll, namesake of the Newark Department of Health and Human Services building, was the first African-American doctor appointed to the medical staff at Newark City Hospital. Until her appointment, in early 1946, black doctors in Newark and many other U.S. cities could refer their patients to white hospitals but could not treat them there. That all-important locale of patient care was reserved for white physicians only.

Known as the First Lady of the National Medical Association (NMA), the organization that represents African-American doctors, McCarroll spent nearly fifty years as a Newark physician, toppling racial barriers at a time when segregation was an ingrained way of life for most Americans.

When McCarroll arrived in Newark in 1929, many Newark neighborhoods were integrated, yet the downtown business district remained off-limits to blacks. "If you looked in the window of Child's, the restaurant where all the white folks went for lunch, someone would come out and shoo you away," old-timer Bill Roberts recalled. "Blacks, or Negroes, as we were called in those days, were not welcome on Broad Street. Our lives revolved around our neighborhoods."

Whatever their status, life remained a daily Catch-22 for Newark's black residents, a microcosm of racial ills that ran rampant across the nation. Getting quality health care, therefore, was a continual uphill battle for Newark's men and women of color. Only the Booker T. Washington Community Hospital on West Kinney Street, which accepted patients of all races, allowed black doctors to admit and treat their patients.

Community Hospital was founded by Dr. John A. Kenney, personal physician to Booker T. Washington and George Washington Carver, two of the most prominent black Americans of their era. After serving as medical director and chief surgeon at Tuskegee Institute in Alabama from 1902 to 1922, Kenney relocated to Newark to escape death threats from the Ku Klux Klan (KKK). He had become their target for demanding equal rights for Negro doctors in the institute's newly built Veterans Administration building.

In his quest to ensure black families better medical services, Kenney settled at 132 West Kinney Street, the present location of New Salem Baptist Church. There he established a small private hospital, named Kenney Memorial in memory of his parents. Residents called it Community Hospital.

In 1939 Kenney returned south to head the Tuskegee Institute Hospital, deeding his Newark hospital to the Booker T. Washington Hospital Association, a group of prominent Newark blacks. He called it his gift "to the Negro people of New Jersey." Five years later he moved north again, to Montclair, New Jersey, where he practiced medicine until his death in 1950 at age seventy-five.

From the start, Community Hospital struggled financially, lacking the funds to purchase much-needed equipment or hire dedicated staff and doctors. That effort came to an end in July 1953, when the financially strapped hospital closed it doors.

But the hospital's board of trustees did not disband. Under the leadership of board president Rosamond Marrow Stewart, a $300,000 fundraising drive for a new hospital at a new location in Newark was initiated. Just as the old hospital was about to close, Stewart told the press, "The board will stay together and will work with a committee of professionals and lay people to sell the present building and make plans for a new institution." Plans called for the installation of an elevator, substantially more space, and "suitable facilities for proper care."

Despite the board members' fund-raising efforts, the new hospital was never built, and eventually the Booker T. Washington Community Hospital shut down for good. By then, McCarroll's year-after-year campaign to obtain a position on the medical staff at City Hospital had paid off. In 1946 she was invited to join the staff, surmounting the persistent racial divide that had separated the services of the city's black and white physicians.

According to written accounts, the struggle to integrate the medical staff at Newark City Hospital was initiated in 1934 by the Newark Interracial Council. Eventually, the hard-fought effort gained the widespread support of many civic, religious, political, and social groups. Further momentum came in March 1939, when the New Jersey State Temporary Commission on the Urban Colored Population issued a report that blamed state government for its "complete failure" to protect its "colored citizens" from racial prejudices. Addressing the situation at Newark City Hospital, the survey observed, "Despite the fact that City Hospital is supported by public funds and because of unhealthy living and working conditions, Negroes are forced into ill health. The School of Nursing has no Negroes among its ninety students, nor has it ever had one. Neither has it a Negro physician on the staff, nor does it provide facilities for Negro interns."

When McCarroll applied for a staff position, she was told she was ineligible because she was not a member of the American Medical Association. "But the AMA didn't permit Negro members," she explained. Undaunted, she continued to apply each year, accompanied by her friends from the Phyllis Wheatley Society, a cultural organization for black women. "We'd all pile into an open-air car that one of my friends owned and go down to City Hospital so that I could make my plea to join the staff," she said. "It became an annual ritual because there was never any response."

All that changed in late 1945, when a *Newark Evening News* reporter wrote about her determined effort. Why, he wanted to know, did she keep coming back each year, since it was apparent she would not be appointed? "I do so because I know that someday someone like me, some person of color, will be appointed if we persevere," she answered. "If you are determined to do something, you cannot give up. We are tired of leaving our patients at the hospital's front door."

By then, the hospital's Jim Crow policy was a smoldering issue in the November 1945 municipal elections, prompting a heated commission hearing at City Hall that resulted in a resolution calling for an investigation into the matter.

After the *Newark Evening News* article appeared, McCarroll received a telephone call from the chief of the medical staff at the hospital. He wanted her to become his assistant. "He was a proctologist," McCarroll said. "A lot of people said I should not accept his offer because proctology was not a field for women. They thought the offer was a ploy—that the doctor and his colleagues were being patronizing because they were convinced I would never take a position in proctology. My feeling about the matter was entirely different. The chief of staff was a man I respected. I thought he was quite sincere and sensitive to the issue at hand. Breaking down racial barriers and stereotypes was not an easy thing. The news article helped. It was such an embarrassment to the hospital that it opened the doors to me as a Negro physician. It gave the good doctor an opportunity to hire me."

On January 3, 1946, McCarroll reported for work at the hospital, breaking new ground for the black physicians who came after her. Within the medical community, however, there was no universal celebration. Some of the city's black male doctors, including several still on a "waiting list," supported McCarroll. Others argued that her appointment should have gone to a man.

"Black women always fought the frontline battles," said Rosetta Lee, a nurse's aide during World War II at City Hospital and at St. Barnabas Hospital when it was at Montgomery and High Streets in Newark. "The women could calm the waters and get into spots that the men would fight over." In those days, City Hospital was segregated in every way imaginable. "When women of color had their babies, they had to stay on the first floor of the hospital, away from the white women," Lee recalled. "When their husbands came to see them, the men had to stand outside and talk to their wives through the windows. They couldn't come inside."

McCarroll, in her dignified way, sloughed off all criticism of her appointment. "What I did, I did for our patients, not necessarily just for doctors," she said. "But they benefited too. Everyone benefited." In a news article shortly after her appointment, McCarroll told why she had entered the medical profession: "I wanted to be able to stand on my own two feet, be my own boss, and be in a position to help overcome intolerance. Everyone has been very nice to me at the hospital and at the clinic, and I'm very happy with my work."

Of the many awards McCarroll received through the years, one of the most cherished came that year from the New Jersey State Federation of Colored Women. The Achievement Award, presented to her on July 17, 1946, recognized an active career in which she had enriched the community by years of constructive work. She was commended for becoming the "first Negro physician appointed to the staff of the City Hospital of Newark, N.J."

Earnest Mae McCarroll was born in 1898 in Birmingham, Alabama, the fourth of eight children of Francis Earnest McCarroll, a teacher who later worked for the post office to support his large family, and Cornelia Burrell, who lived to be one hundred years old. The children, in the order of their birth, were Curtis, Anne, Henry Francis (Frank), Earnest Mae, Alyce, Edward, Leon Harold, and Elizabeth.

Very little is known about Curtis, but his niece, Eleanor Stoller, suspects that he and his brother Frank left home at an early age because their father was so strict. "When Eddie came home one night after 11 P.M., long after he was grown, Cornelia had to let him in through a window," Stoller said. "Eddie was one of the younger ones, so you can imagine how hard my grandfather must have been on Curtis and Frank." Frank eventually settled in French Lick, Indiana, where he worked in a hotel. Curtis was rarely heard from again.

Anne McCarroll Griffin, Stoller's mother, was the oldest girl in the family. She became a teacher after graduating from Talladega, a historically black college in Alabama. She earned a second degree at Tennessee College, now the University of Tennessee at Nashville.

Alyce McCarroll Wilson, who graduated from Fisk University in Nashville, Tennessee, became a social worker in Omaha, Nebraska, where she lived with her husband, Milton, a prominent businessman. In later years, Cornelia McCarroll went to live with them. "Aunt Alyce was quite active in Omaha," said Stoller. "A women's center there was named for her. When a group of young people began causing trouble, the mayor asked her to talk with them to help quiet things down. She was quite respected. When she came to Omaha, they thought she was white. She was very light-skinned and had blonde hair. Everyone in the family was light."

After graduating from Talladega, Eddie McCarroll became a teacher in the Birmingham schools. At his sister Mae's invitation, he later moved to New Jersey. After a stint in the army, where he played in the band and attained the rank of sergeant, he became an adjudicator for the U.S. Veterans Administration.

After high school, Leon McCarroll moved north to Philadelphia to live with Mae, who had just begun her medical practice. He later moved to Newark, where he became an assistant purchasing agent at the Newark Post Office. Betty, the youngest McCarroll, also graduated from Talladega College. From there she went to New York to study nursing at Harlem Hospital.

After Mae McCarroll's graduation from Talladega, she decided to enter medical school. "I'm not sure why Aunt Mae wanted to be a doctor," Stoller said. "It probably was because she loved helping people so much, especially children. But my grandfather did not want her to attend medical school. My mother had to make a special trip from Nashville to Birmingham to convince him to let Aunt Mae go."

In her senior year at college, McCarroll was accepted to the Women's Medical College of the University of Pennsylvania with the provision that she take supplemental chemistry and physics classes to improve her grasp of science. After completing those courses at Fisk University, she entered medical school in 1922. She was one of three black women in Penn's class of 1925. One of the others died before graduation. The third, Virginia Margaret Alexander, was McCarroll's lifelong friend.

Following her graduation from medical school, McCarroll traveled to Kansas City, Missouri, to serve her internship at the Old Kansas City No. 2 Hospital. "No. 2 meant Negro," she explained.

After practicing for two years in Philadelphia, she married James Leroy Baxter, a dentist from Newark's old Third Ward, and moved to Newark in 1929. About the same time, Baxter, nearly twenty years her senior, was ending a two-year term in the New Jersey General Assembly. He was the state's third black legislator, serving from 1927 to 1929. He followed Dr. Walter G. Alexander (1921–1922) and attorney Oliver Randolph (1923–1932).

The Baxters made a dashing couple. She was lanky, beautiful, and full of energy. He was charming, politically adept, and the son of one of Newark's most highly regarded citizens. His father, James Baxter, a revered Newark educator, had been principal of Newark's Colored School from 1864 to 1909.

Both Baxter and his brother, Louis, a veterinarian, graduated from the University of Pennsylvania. Their sister, Grace Baxter Fenderson, an alumna of the Newark Normal School, later Newark State College, was one of the first African Americans to teach in Newark's integrated schools. A longtime civic leader, she was instrumental in the founding of the Newark Branch of the NAACP in 1914, three years before her marriage to Walter Fenderson.

"Mrs. Fenderson had a gorgeous townhouse at 17 Elm Street about a block from the post office, where she would hold NAACP meetings," said Harry Hazelwood, a retired state superior court judge. "That's where I met people like Roy Wilkins [the NAACP's executive director] and Thurgood Marshall [an attorney for the civil rights group who became the first black U.S. Supreme Court justice]."

Clem Moorman, the father of singer Melba Moore, and his older brother Wilson were among the young people invited to the Fendersons' home for NAACP meetings. "Wilson was eighteen, and I was fifteen," said Moorman. "Mrs. Fenderson offered us advice that I've never forgotten. She urged us not to go along with the crowd—to find something to believe in and stick to it. Mrs. Fenderson always looked so perfect," Moorman noted. "Her clothes. Just the way she spoke made her a very distinguished woman. Her house also stands out in my mind because it was so beautifully furnished."

To the family, the Fendersons' home on Elm Street, purchased by her parents years before and presently on the fringe of a path for a new sports arena, was known as "the House." The 106-acre farm that the family owned and Louis ran in rural Liberty Corner, New Jersey, between Far Hills and Bernardsville was called Baxter Farm. "Everyone in the family pitched in to buy it," said Louis Baxter's daughter, Julia, who was raised there with her half-sister, Louise Baxter Fields.

In 1934 Julia Baxter Bates made history as the first black student at Douglass College, the women's unit of Rutgers University. Although her application included the requisite photo, school officials were startled to find that the light-complexioned Baxter was an African American. Perhaps, they suggested, she would be "more comfortable" at another college. But her father would have none it. At his insistence, she was allowed to stay but was not permitted to live on campus with the white students even though the dean, Margaret Corwin, lobbied on her behalf.

Rather than commute from Bernardsville, Julia went to live with her beloved aunt Grace and uncle Walter in the House on Elm Street in Newark. "It was easier for me to take the train from Newark to New Brunswick than it was to commute from Far Hills," she said. "I also liked living with my aunt and uncle."

As a collegian, Julia Baxter also spent a considerable amount of time at her uncle Leroy and aunt Mae's house on Hillside Place, a tiny street in Newark's South Ward. This was where McCarroll had her medical offices. "The first time I met Aunt Mae I was about seven or eight years old," said Bates. "Uncle Leroy brought her out to the farm in Far Hills, where my father had his veterinary practice. She was very warm and friendly. She gave me a hug. I guess I liked her because I didn't get much affection. Our family was a bit standoffish. I can't remember my father ever kissing me. My mother died when I was three, and my stepmother and I didn't get along."

Like her aunt Mae, Julia was an extremely accomplished yet humble woman. After graduating magna cum laude from Douglass in 1938 and earning a master's degree at Columbia University, she took the only available job she could find as a young black woman yearning to become a teacher—a position at Dillard College in New Orleans. She subsequently spent twenty-five years as research director in the national office of the NAACP in New York.

"She never told us that Thurgood Marshall and Roy Wilkins were her friends," said Jeannette Robinson, a Newark college administrator, who was her closest friend. "We had to find out." Nor did she say anything about her importance as chief researcher for the historic 1953 *Brown v. the Board of Education* decision that outlawed segregation in the nation's schools. As the NAACP's chief attorney, Thurgood Marshall's compelling arguments propelled him to national fame, paving the way for his eventual appointment to the U.S. Supreme Court.

"All of this about Judy [Julia's nickname] is all news to me," a friend from the New York Smart Set, a women's social group, said at Bates's 2003 memorial service at Essex County College. "I knew her for fifty years, but she never said a word about any of her involvement in *Brown v. the Board*."

Bates's best friends in her youth were her cousins, Malcolm and Douglas, who were nine and eleven years old, respectively, when her uncle Leroy married Mae McCarroll. Their mother, Kate, who came from Providence, Rhode Island, had died of tuberculosis at a very young age. "She was a very beautiful woman, absolutely gorgeous," said Bates. "Uncle Leroy met her when he was in college and she was a student at Mercy Hospital in Philadelphia. After their marriage, they lived in Orange, where he had his dental practice."

After Baxter married McCarroll, Malcolm—"Mac" to family and friends—lived with the couple for a while on Hillside Place in Newark and then moved in with his aunt Grace and uncle Walter on Elm Street. "Malcolm and I shared the third floor," said Bates. "I had the front bedroom and a little study and he had the back bedroom."

Douglas Baxter, who sold farm-fresh eggs for a living, lived with the Fendersons for most of his life. After their deaths, he stayed on alone on Elm Street. "Years later, there came a time when we didn't hear from him for a while," Bates said. "My sister called the police. They found him in the house. He'd been dead for ten days."

Malcolm Baxter, a World War II army veteran, met his wife, Nicole, while serving in France. Until his retirement in 1980, he was a chemist for the GAF Corporation in Bound Brook, New Jersey. Afterward he turned his attention to La Champagne, a family-owned restaurant in nearby Flemington. He died in November 2001 at age eighty-six.

Julia Baxter Bates also was eighty-six when she passed away on July 10, 2003. After teaching at Dillard and working for the NAACP, she returned to Newark and spent twelve years as education director at NewArk Prep, a residential alternative school that served fifty boys and girls. Until her retirement in 1996, she worked in the Human Resources Department at Essex County College in Newark, helping to secure millions in federal grants to benefit first-generation college students.

In her youth, Bates's other great friend was Leon McCarroll, Mae's younger brother, who left Philadelphia to live with his sister in Newark. With Malcolm Baxter, they went to ball games and movies and engaged in other activities that appealed to young people of their era.

"We were all inspired by my aunt," Bates said. "Aunt Mae was a motivator. She loved encouraging people to strive for their goals, so I loved being with her. Everyone did." Eleanor Stoller also adored her aunt. "From the time I was a child, I always was enchanted by Aunt Mae," Stoller said. "As a girl, she always sent me nice presents. One was a beautiful bisque doll that I named 'Annie Mae' for my mother and for her." Stoller, who taught kindergarten at Miller Street School in Newark for thirty-five years, until her retirement in 1987, also lived with McCarroll for several years. During this period, she assisted her aunt, helping with the medical records and preparing the paperwork McCarroll needed for reports to the NMA. At the time, an office visit was two dollars.

In the early 1940s, Gwen Cooper became Dr. McCarroll's nurse. "My husband was in the army, so I came to Newark to live with my uncle at 151 Badger Avenue," Cooper said. "That very same day, Dr. McCarroll offered me a job. "When I arrived at my uncle's house, the woman who lived upstairs was hosting a meeting of the Phyllis Wheatley Society," Cooper recalled. "I went up to meet them. When I told Dr. McCarroll I was a graduate of Provident School of Nursing in Baltimore, she asked me to be her nurse. Mrs. Fenderson, who I came to call Aunt Grace, also was a member of the group.

"Mae worked long hours," said Cooper, a public health nurse in Newark for thirty-one years. "She made her hospital rounds in the morning and then went downtown to spend most of the day at the city clinic, where she was an epidemiologist. After that, she'd come to the office to see her patients. Then, she would make house calls all over the city, generally two or three a night. I lived nearby, so I would go along with her."

By that time, McCarroll had long since divorced Leroy Baxter. In the 1950s she began dating Bob Hunter, an affable young man who worked at Howard Bank. Although he was many years her junior, friends considered them quite compatible. They married on August 16, 1958. "Mae told me that she married again because she was tired of going to conventions where all the other women physicians had doting husbands," said Ruth Crumpton Dargan, Newark's first black female detective. "Bob was much younger than Mae, but he was very loving and took wonderful care of her. She'd get off an elevator and there he would be with her mink coat, waiting to escort her."

Whereas Baxter could be arrogant and showy—he owned a Mercer, one of the most expensive automobiles on the market—everyone loved Bob Hunter. Cooper, who stopped working for McCarroll in 1946 while awaiting the birth of her daughter, Carol, made the doctor her baby's godmother. Her second child, Eric, was Hunter's little buddy.

As a boy, Eric Cooper loved visiting his aunt Mae and uncle Bob at their home at 96 Milford Avenue, opposite South Side High School. She still maintained her practice on Hillside Place, but her apartment there was rented out. "Mae owned quite a bit of real estate," Gwen Cooper said. "She loved it. I often thought she'd rather be in real estate than medicine."

"The house on Milford Avenue was beautiful," said Eric Cooper, a chemical company worker. "Uncle Bob was very handy. He was always crafting pieces of furniture. When they moved to Hansberry Avenue, he was always down in the basement doing electrical work. He tried to show me, but I was at an age where I wasn't interested."

Years later, one of the pieces that Hunter made, a lovely stereo cabinet, became a fixture at Court Towers, the senior citizens apartment house where McCarroll went to live after his death and her retirement from practicing medicine. Above the cabinet was a lovely painting of McCarroll by Bertram Jones, a family friend. Eric Cooper liked spending time with his uncle Bob "because he always made me feel good. He was a very funny man, always jovial and joking. It really hurt me when he began deteriorating and was hospitalized. I went to see him, but he wasn't the same person."

Cooper also noted, "Uncle Bob and Aunt Mae also were very generous to my sister and me. On our birthdays, they would give us U.S. Savings Bonds." Carol Cooper Cross, who lives in San Diego, commented, "Because my birthday was on Christmas, Aunt Mae always gave me two gifts. They were very pretty things—lovely little dresses that were very expensive. Often, she'd give my mother money so that she could dress me nicely."

As he grew older, Eric became keenly aware of "how much Uncle Bob loved Aunt Mae. From what I could see, he not only loved her; he worshiped her. Aunt Mae was more private. She didn't open up like Uncle Bob."

Carol spent more of her time with McCarroll. "She was a very determined woman," said Cross. "She didn't demand respect, but you had to respect her. What impressed me most when I was a teenager was that she didn't have office hours. She stayed open late, and people just wandered in."

Clearly, McCarroll was a connoisseur of the finer things in life. She drove a Lincoln, including one that was pink and black to match her bedroom color scheme. On Hillside Place she also had a walk-in closet, the first in the neighborhood. At 96 Milford Place, the pièce de résistance was McCarroll's treasured white living room carpeting. "When Aunt Mae and Uncle Bob had a party, which they often did, some people were afraid to go in there for fear of spilling something," Cross said. "It was a symbol of Aunt Mae's lifestyle."

Nevertheless, McCarroll was down-to-earth. Although she had a housekeeper, a devoted friend named Lucille Way, she loved to cook and liked nothing more than making her own meals when she had time. "She was good at it," said Cross. "Everything she made tasted terrific. But there was always a certain formality to it. We always sat in the dining room."

Jeroline Lee, a neighbor who lived on Ridgewood Avenue, just down the street from McCarroll, described the area around South Side High

School as very friendly and close-knit at that time. "It was a small circle of people," she said. "Everyone knew everyone. If your kids were doing something wrong, one of the neighbors would step in. I didn't know Dr. McCarroll that well," said Lee, who worked for the Newark Health Department for many years and was on the committee that named the city's new health building for the doctor in 1984. "But from what everyone said, she was an excellent doctor who helped a lot of people, especially people who could not afford health care otherwise."

Because of her longtime involvement in community affairs, Lee also came in contact with Bob Hunter. "With a group that included Danny Williams and Rudy Kinchen, we formed the Independent Citizens Alliance, one of the first African-American groups in Newark," Lee said. "Bob wasn't affiliated with the group, but he came to a lot of our affairs."

After living on Milford Avenue in the early years of their marriage, the Hunters moved to 73 Hansberry Avenue. "They were one of the earliest black families in the neighborhood, if not the first," said Mildred Crump, who became Newark's first African-American councilwoman. "They were here when we moved here."

Crump, who still lives in the same house, and her late husband, Cecil, became friendly with the Hunters through their involvement in the Hansberry Avenue Block Association. "There was excellent camaraderie because we wanted to preserve the integrity of the neighborhood," Crump said. "Friendships grew also because the group had a very active social side. Hardly a week went by when someone on the block didn't have a party."

Crump considered McCarroll "a wonderful neighbor who kept the children on the block in line. If she saw one of our children doing something we would disapprove of, she let them know that she would tell us in a minute," Crump said. "Bob was equally wonderful. He always had a friendly greeting. Our neighborhood was a place where people cared about each other's families."

Early on in her Newark medical practice, McCarroll became gravely concerned about the increasing incidence of syphilis and gonorrhea among her patients. It was not clear, however, where she stood with regard to research conducted by Dr. Louis T. Wright, a prominent African-

American physician trained at Harvard Medical School. Wright, who wrote columns during the 1930s for *The Crisis*, the magazine of the NAACP, and published the scholarly *Harlem Hospital Bulletin,* took issue with the idea that African Americans had higher rates of syphilis and infectious disease than the general population. McCarroll made no such distinction. Her concern was Newark's African-American community, where the scourge proved rampant enough for her to initiate a citywide crusade to stamp it out. "That was because so many of my patients were suffering from blindness," she said.

In 1934 she was appointed clinical physician with the Child Hygiene and Venereal Disease bureaus of the Newark Health Department. After returning to school to earn a master's degree in public health from the College of Physicians at Columbia University, she became assistant epidemiologist for the city of Newark. Her postgraduate work was done at the Harvard School of Public Health.

Armed with a movie projector and a film about venereal disease provided by the Prudential Insurance Company, McCarroll began traveling the city, church by church, to warn women about promiscuity and the dangers of sexually transmitted diseases. On Saturdays, she taught hygiene classes for neighborhood children. Kitty Kearney Taylor, who years later became Newark's Ambassador on Aging, was one of them. "Dr. McCarroll lived at 59 Hillside Place, and I lived at 55," Taylor said. "I was about ten when she started the classes. All the girls in the neighborhood went."

"What I remember most about Dr. McCarroll is how kind she was," said Jackie King, who grew up in the neighborhood near McCarroll's Milford Avenue office. "I was fascinated by the fact that she was a woman doctor. For some reason, the one memory that stands out is how she used to give us Kool-Aid with lemons in it."

McCarroll's undivided commitment to her profession often worried her family and friends. "Sometimes, when I came to the office, I'd find her asleep at her desk," said Carol Cross. "Day after day, she kept up a frantic pace."

Soon after she integrated City Hospital, McCarroll and a group of women friends began crusading for another racial cause. Tired of being forced to sit in the balconies of downtown theaters, they decided to act on this affront to their dignity and humanity. "My sister, Janet Foster [a supervisor at the federal Office of Dependency Benefits and later a Newark schoolteacher], Dr. McCarroll, and a bunch of their friends decided to stage a protest at Proctor's Theatre," said Dorothy Foster Latta, one of the first black practical nurses at City Hospital. Other community leaders, including Marjorie Moore (who became Marjorie Moore Van Dyke) and Marjorie Tate, also were in the group. Signs in hand, the women went to the Market Street theater near Bamberger's department store and began marching around. Before long, blacks could sit anywhere they wanted in any theater in Newark. Just as McCarroll had integrated City Hospital a few years earlier; she and her friends integrated Proctor's Theatre.

McCarroll's medical practice grew steadily over the years, and she became one of the city's best-known, most beloved physicians. "My mother was a friend of Dr. McCarroll's, so she became our family physician," said pianist Clem Moorman. "As a boy, I was embarrassed about going to a woman doctor. But there was no choice. My mother said we had to go, so we did. No child would ever think of questioning a parent in those days. What your mother and father said was law. You just did it, and that was that."

Bobie Cottle, a police officer who later served as Essex County surrogate and president of the Newark Branch of the NAACP, was among McCarroll's first patients. "He was just a little boy then," McCarroll said. "Every time I tried to take his temperature, he'd run around the room and try to get away from me." Ruth Crumpton Dargan also was a patient. "She was my primary physician," Dargan said. "She was very beautiful, but very professional, a no-nonsense person."

Esther Lester, who lived on Montgomery Street in Newark, was trying to have another child when a friend recommended McCarroll to her. "I had a blockage and was having trouble conceiving again," said Lester. "Dr. McCarroll knew her job. In 1956 I gave birth to my fourth child." Lester liked the idea of having a woman doctor treat her. "I liked going to her because she knew about women's parts," she said. "A man had to study about them."

In 1953 McCarroll broke another barrier when she was named deputy health officer for the city of Newark. Through that position, she gained privileges at two other Newark hospitals, Beth Israel and St. Michael's.

As one of Newark's most prominent professionals, she was very active in community affairs, serving on the board of the Newark Branch of the NAACP and the Friendly Neighborhood House and as an adviser to the Neighborhood Guild. She also was on the Advisory Committee of the National Alliance of Postal Employees and belonged to the League of Women Voters, Daughters of Elks, and the Delta Sigma Theta sorority.

"Even though Mae was no longer married to my godfather [Baxter], we remained very close over the years," said Connie Williams Woodruff. "As a little girl, I spent a lot of time at their house. I also visited her often after she married Bob Hunter because he was my good friend."

Woodruff's friendship with McCarroll lasted through the years. "After her retirement, Maesie moved to Florida, but she would call me whenever she came to town," Woodruff said. One of those times was May 5, 1984, when McCarroll returned to Newark for the dedication of the city's new health building.

"The night before the dedication, Aunt Mae was supposed to have dinner with the family," said Eleanor Stoller. "She didn't come because she was too busy preparing her speech." Actually, McCarroll and Julia Bates, her niece through her marriage to Baxter, were writing the speech together. "I helped her with it, just as I helped her write many of her reports for the National Medical Association," said Bates. "She would gather the information and tell me what she wanted to say. Aunt Mae was chairman of the NMA's Publications Committee, so there was lots of writing to do."

The night of the dedication of the new building at 110 William Street, Connie Woodruff and I had dinner with McCarroll at her friend Susie Miles's downtown apartment at Court Towers. One of the first things I asked the doctor was why she had not made an acceptance speech that afternoon. "The program was very long and it was getting too hot in the sun," she answered. And so, when she rose, she simply said, "Thank you for the honor" and sat down. Others gave a different account of why she failed to deliver the three-page speech she had labored over the night before. "I think it was because the politicians spoke for so long there was no time on the agenda for Aunt Mae," said her niece Julia.

During the ceremony, accolades abounded for McCarroll and Arnold Haskin, who ran the city clinic for many years. "The new Haskin-McCarroll Public Health Building is another example of Newark's commitment to the health and well-being of its citizens," said Newark Mayor Kenneth A. Gibson. "Protecting our citizens from disease and illness is an honorable duty which we are proud to perform and from which we will never deviate."

Dennis Cherot, the city health director, said the new building gave the city the capacity to house most health services in one area. "It enables us to provide more effective care for our citizenry," he said. "Newark residents deserve the best possible care. Our expert staff and the health center will provide them with such care for many years to come."

The speech McCarroll never gave was full of tributes to others, along with a synopsis of how health care for Newark residents had improved over the years. "This occasion marks, in one sense, a new beginning—a re-dedication to the health goals all communities should seek—a happy childhood for all youngsters, hearty, outgoing adolescent school days, fruitful work, fulfillment during the vigorous midyears, and serene contentment for those who reach life's true prize," she wrote.

When she went to Newark in 1929, she recounted, Dr. Charles Craster was the city's chief health officer, Dr. Julius Levy headed the Child Hygiene Division, Dr. Robert Sellers was in charge of the Venereal Disease Division, and Dr. Arnold Haskin ran the clinic. "It was a privilege to serve under the direction of these dedicated and farsighted physicians," she said. "Those of us who did were the envy of our colleagues. Payment was unthinkable. The opportunity afforded us to work in their shadow, which was greater than remuneration."

Recounting her history with the department, she told how Levy made it possible for her to work at his neighborhood Keep Well stations. "Mothers would bring their tiny babies, many of whom bore the unpleasant consequences of untreated conditions—sightlessness and other physical deformities. How strongly we prayed in those days for some means of educating our neighborhood communities in the dangers to life and health that venereal infections bring with them."

Within a short time, she found, the incidence of venereal contagion posed a formidable threat to the safety of community health. After studying departmental records, she began formulating a program intended to mitigate the effects of the plague. When Craster learned what she had in mind, he called Sellers. The next day she began working in the Venereal Disease Division of the Newark Department of Health.

At that time, Newark had the highest population percentage of black residents of any city in the nation and the highest rate of venereal disease of any city its size in the United States. McCarroll and her colleagues set out to curb it, spending endless hours working out the logistics.

At the neighborhood level, a case-finding program was started and expanded. In-service training for staff was initiated. Testing for food handlers and domestic workers began. The Prudential Insurance Company pitched in by giving the department a projector and two films that health officials used to illustrate how venereal diseases were contracted, how they could be avoided, where contagion had occurred, and how it could be cured. "We lectured in established churches, storefront churches, in schools, and at rallies. We spoke to workers on lunch hour. Wherever groups would accept us, we were there. In its way, our work made Newark history," McCarroll said.

"The social health of any city is measured by the extent to which its citizenry remains protected, informed, and educated," McCarroll concluded. "The dedication of this building today is, in its silent way, a measure of the distance Newark has come, and of the distance Newark must go."

Ever the newspaperwoman, I asked Dr. McCarroll that night if it would be possible to tape an interview with her. "Your story would be so inspiring to other women, especially to young black women," I told her. She reluctantly agreed, telling me her life story as her friend Susie Miles prepared dinner. In those few hours, it was clear to me that I was in the presence of greatness, for here was a woman of great beauty and intellect whose concern for others outshone all her other admirable qualities.

Early the next morning, the phone rang. Dr. McCarroll was on the other end of the line. "Barbara, I'm calling because I really don't want an article in the newspaper," she said. "I'm not that public a person. I like my privacy. I'm calling so early [7 A.M.] because I didn't want to waste your time if you'd started writing." Of course I had not begun. I was still in bed. Anxious to tell her story, I pleaded a bit because what she had to say was so uplifting, so admirable. In the end, I felt compelled to abide by her wishes. There was no story.

Dr. McCarroll was a woman of great faith. While she was married to Leroy Baxter, she belonged to St. Philip's Church, later Trinity & St. Philip's Cathedral, where the members of his family were stalwarts. After her marriage to Hunter, she converted to Catholicism. "Somewhere in the early 1960s they appeared in the rectory, asking to take classes and join the church," said Monsignor Patrick McGrath, former pastor of Blessed Sacrament Church in Newark. "They began coming to see me once a week.

"Mae was a delightful person to know," McGrath added. "She also was the most intelligent woman to whom I ever gave instructions. I can distinctly recall her taking notes each week. No else had ever done that."

As a friend of the Hunters, the priest often was a guest at lavish parties they gave at their South Ward home. For years, they were at the center of South Ward social life in the black community.

When McCarroll retired from medicine in 1977, she was honored by many organizations, including the NMA, which she had joined in 1925. "The programs which she arranged as chairwoman of [the organization's] Public Health Committee in the 1930s and 1940s have landmark significance in the history of the association," a colleague wrote in the NMA medical journal.

A past president of the North Jersey Medical Society and the New Jersey State Medical Association, McCarroll also was chairwoman of the NMA's Committee on General Practice from its inception until 1955 and then, after its merger with another committee, until 1968. For thirty-five years she was also a ranking member of the NMA Publications Committee, helping to turn the NMA journal into a first-rate medical periodical.

In the 1970s, color portraits of prominent black physicians by Maida Willette Page appeared on the cover of the association's journal. McCarroll's portrait made the November 1973 cover, accompanied by an article written by Dr. W. Montague Cobb, the journal's editor.

Despite her leadership qualities and the urgings of her colleagues, Mc-Carroll steadfastly refused to have her name placed in nomination for the NMA presidency. Nevertheless, she was the medical society's First Lady. "There is no doubt that the respect in which she was generally held within the organization would have made her the first woman president if had she elected to run," Cobb concluded. "The NMA—past and future—is in the permanent debt of its First Lady, who has radiated so much good, so far and so long."

Another honor came McCarroll's way soon after her retirement. That November, black women doctors in New York and New Jersey, whose ranks had grown from 65 in 1920 to 1,050, honored five early female black physicians. She was one. The others were

- Dr. Lena F. Edwards, who spent forty years in medicine and was still making home visits to patients in Jersey City and Lakewood, New Jersey, at age seventy-seven, even after suffering several heart attacks.
- Dr. Agnes Griffin, who was still practicing ophthalmology in the parlor office of her Brooklyn brownstone at age eighty-one. She was the only black woman in the graduating class of 1926 of Columbia University's College of Physicians and Surgeons.
- Dr. Mae Chinn, the first black woman to graduate from the University of Bellevue Medical Center in New York, in the early 1920s, and the first to intern at Harlem Hospital. Until she turned eighty, she provided medical services for day-care centers with the New York City Department of Health.
- Dr. Myra Smith-Kearse, the only woman in the 1926 graduating class at the Howard University Medical School. It took her fifteen years to integrate the staff of Howard University Hospital. The catalyst, she said, was a shortage of white doctors during World War II.

Dr. Chinn, a founding member of the Susan Smith McKinney Steward Medical Society, the group that sponsored the Sunday afternoon tribute to the physicians, said her mother, who "scrubbed floors and hired out as a cook," was the driving force behind her educational aspirations. Her father, who had been a slave, opposed her going to college and to medical school.

Ironically, Chinn said, some of her first patients at Harlem Hospital preferred having a white doctor. They resented the fact that she was the one treating them, especially since she was an intern. Black male doctors, at the time, said Chinn, were divided into three groups—"those who acted as if I wasn't there, another group who took the attitude 'what does she think she can do that I can't,' [and] the group that called themselves supporting me by sending me to their night calls after midnight."

After her retirement, McCarroll moved to Washington, D.C., where, to the surprise of her friends and family, she married a third time. Her husband, Dr. Theodore J. Johnson, was an old friend, a dentist she had known for years. "My guess is that Mae married again after Bob's death because she wanted companionship," said her friend Gwen Cooper. "She and Ted were great friends, and they had many common interests."

In retirement, McCarroll divided her time between Washington, her husband's hometown, and Miami, Florida, where she had bought a two-bedroom, two-bathroom condominium at Parkway Towers, a luxurious building with a circular drive. She still returned north frequently, including a trip to Philadelphia for the fiftieth anniversary of her class at the Women's Medical College of Pennsylvania. For that auspicious occasion, the women doctors wore caps and gowns. A photograph of the event shows McCarroll, program in hand, smiling into the camera with three of her friends, Dr. Jual Keefer-Kendall, Dr. Mary D. Varker, and Dr. Rebecca Rhoads.

In her travels, Dr. McCarroll never forgot Newark. Of all the places she had been, it was where her heart was. "When she came back to Newark, she always stopped by and came to church," said Father Paul Schetelick, Monsignor McGrath's successor as pastor at Blessed Sacrament.

One of those times was in 1984 for the dedication of the health building. Another was in 1988, when the University of Medicine and Dentistry of New Jersey and the university libraries presented an exhibit titled *Pioneering Women Physicians of New Jersey*. The exhibit's opening reception at the George F. Smith Library of Health and Sciences at the Newark campus honored Dr. Palma Formica, the first woman president of the Medical Society of New Jersey. Dr. McCarroll and Dr. Eva Brodkin, her friend from medical school, were front and center, chatting with medical students and posing for photos in front of the exhibit case where McCarroll's career and contributions to medicine were documented. Copies of those materials are now in the permanent files of the Smith Library. The originals, many of which were provided by McCarroll, were returned to her brother Eddie in Miami, where he had a condominium in the same building where she lived.

McCarroll was approaching ninety years old when she traveled to Newark for the opening of the exhibit. Outwardly she was in very good health, still spirited and mentally quick. Soon afterward, however, she suffered two strokes. In an April 3, 1989, letter to Barbara Irwin, archivist and head of special collections at the Smith Library, Edward McCarroll reported that his sister had suffered a stroke and was a resident of the Villa Maria Nursing Home in Miami.

"She has not recovered her speech or the use of her right limbs," he wrote. "Otherwise, she is receiving excellent care from the hospital nursing center. Her loyal friend and employee of over thirty years, Miss Lucille Way, visits her every day. Lucille will read your letter to Dr. Mae. I am sure she thanks you very much."

Way, the doctor's friend for almost fifty years, is not exactly sure where they met. "I think it was when I went to see her to get a health card that I needed to get a job," she said. As McCarroll's employee, Way did whatever needed to be done. Sometimes she worked in the office, sometimes in the house. She also did most of the cooking.

In 1955 Way began traveling to NMA conventions with McCarroll. While McCarroll was busy with the work of the convention, Way went sightseeing and shopping. Following McCarroll's retirement, she and Way were part of a group that spent twelve days in Israel and Jordan on a trip sponsored by the Gideon Bible group.

When McCarroll sold her house on Hansberry Avenue and retired from practicing medicine, she and Way moved to Court Towers, the downtown senior citizens building at Court and Broad Streets in Newark. "We weren't there long," Way said, "less than a year. It was an in-between thing until we moved to Florida."

Although her Newark roots date back several generations, Florence Johnson, the manager at Court Towers, had no idea who McCarroll was when the doctor came to rent an apartment at the senior citizens building. "She simply introduced herself as Mae McCarroll," Johnson said. "She never mentioned anything about being a doctor." But it did not take Johnson long to catch on. "Right away, some of the tenants spotted her. The older ones had all kinds of stories to tell about how she had helped them and their children."

During her stay at Court Towers, McCarroll spent a good deal of her time socializing and entertaining friends in the recreation room. "She was very ambivalent about moving to Florida because the friends she loved most were here in Newark," Johnson said. "When she left, she gave me a beautiful note and a lovely strand of pearls to remember her by."

When McCarroll moved to Miami, Way went with her. When she became sick, felled by back-to-back strokes, Way went to see her every day. "I was on three weeks' vacation in Newark and Dr. McCarroll was in Washington when she had the strokes," said Way. "I called to see how she was doing and cut my vacation short after they transferred her to the nursing home in Miami. She thought she'd improve and come home, but she never did." Way, who is now in her eighties and living once again in Newark, visited her friend faithfully at the nursing home until McCarroll's death on February 20, 1990. Her daily visits were interrupted only by bad weather. "I wanted to be sure she was getting the attention she needed," Way said.

McCarroll's work—the many years and faithful service she dedicated to improving health conditions for her patients—was her legacy. In 1993, three years after her death, she was one of several African-American doctors whose work was highlighted as part of a traveling photographic exhibit on view at the Smith Library on the University of Medicine and Dentistry of New Jersey campus in Newark. It was titled *The Afro-American Presence in Medicine, 1850–1930*. The curator was Dr. Doris Wilkinson, a faculty member at the University of Kentucky who had researched and compiled the information as a visiting scholar at the W. E. B. DuBois Institute at Harvard University.

Although McCarroll's love of Newark and her contributions to its residents remained fixed in the hearts of the city's old-timers, there are some who have no knowledge of who she was or how many barriers she overcame to improve their lives. Today, thousands of people who pass through the portals of the Health Department building at 110 William Street in Newark have no inkling that the building bears her name. A small sign outside simply designates the Newark Health Department. Inside, a small metal plaque denotes the dedication of the Haskin-McCarroll building on May 5, 1984.

5

VIOLA WELLS
(MISS RHAPSODY)

Newark's No. 1 Brown Gal | 1902–1984

To the music world, Viola Wells, known professionally as Miss Rhapsody, was at the forefront of the emergence of jazz as America's vernacular music. Whether Ellington or Basie, Holiday or Fitzgerald, there was hardly a jazz artist she did not know or who did not know her. Hers was not an internationally known name, but her dazzling way with a lyric and crystal-clear diction gained her colleagues' complete respect.

To her fans in Newark, where she was born at the turn of the twentieth century, Miss Rhapsody was one of the city's most beloved entertainers. Behind the scenes, however, her positive outlook and upbeat personality belied a life tougher than most. Yet she was a strong Christian woman sustained by her faith, convinced that her fate, no matter how unsettling or unfair, was God's will.

In retrospect, her life was punctuated by a series of faith-based triumphs over an unending series of tragedies. She was just four years old when her mother died in childbirth. When she was nearly fifty, her father was murdered by their family minister. In her early seventies she lost her only child to alcoholism. And at age seventy-seven, she became an amputee after a fan accidentally stepped on her diabetic toe while she was touring Europe. Because her heart was weak, doctors said she would never walk again. But she fooled everyone. Within a year she was back singing again at a posh nightclub on New York's upper West Side for a fifty-three-week run.

Through every adversity, her Christian beliefs remained unshakable, even after the 1949 trial and sentencing of the Reverend H. Beecher Jackson, the man who murdered her father. Standing on the steps of the Essex County Courthouse in Newark that September, she was approached by a *Newark Evening News* reporter. "Do you think justice was done?" he asked, after Jackson, one of Newark's most prominent ministers, was sentenced to life in prison.

Hardly missing a beat, she responded, "Yes, I do, for I am my father's child, and he believed that no man has the right to take other man's life. As a good Christian, he believed that you should turn the other cheek, no matter what, not take an eye for an eye or a tooth for a tooth." Other members of Rhap's family were angered by her response, especially her stepmother. They wanted revenge. They wanted Jackson sent to the electric chair.

Years later, after the New Jersey courts did away with death by electrocution, Governor Richard J. Hughes downgraded the sentences of many prisoners. Jackson, a model inmate who had spent nearly two decades behind bars at Trenton State Prison working in the library and counseling other prisoners, was among those paroled.

Jackson, a flamboyant preacher and gifted elocutionist, arrived in Newark from Chicago in the early 1940s to serve as pastor of Thirteenth Avenue Presbyterian Church. Founded by a group of former slaves soon after the Civil War, the Central Ward church, built of hewn stones, was among the most prominent in Newark's African-American community. As a black preacher, Jackson gained notoriety after he gave a fiery speech on the steps of City Hall in 1947 during a visit by President Harry Truman. For African Americans, this was an uplifting occurrence at a time when Newark was strictly segregated, a sign that times were changing.

A very learned man and a gifted speaker, Jackson was very troubled too. "He also was subject to tirades," said Geraldine Sims, whose family left the Thirteenth Avenue Church two years before Wells's death because of their displeasure with the minister's conduct. "He'd open the doors of the church and invite people to leave if they didn't like a certain topic he was speaking about," said Sims, a retired Newark school principal.

When Jackson began carousing at downtown bars and was reputed to be running around with a woman from another church, the leaders sought his removal, appealing to officials of the Presbytery of Newark to oust him. "I was just a teenager, but I used to see him all the time at the Novelty Bar on Market Street," said Evelyn Boyden Darrell, whose family belonged to the church. "My friends and I would be in the front having sandwiches when we'd see him sneaking in the back to the bar. I told my mother, but she didn't believe it."

But others did. "There was a terrible stew among many of the church leaders, which led those who were disgruntled to complain to the Presbytery about Jackson," Sims recalled. "The church leaders wanted him out." Their ranks included many leaders in the black community, among them Dr. Charles Bomar, a dentist in Orange, and Dr. C. O. Hilton, a physician for Newark schools. "Unfortunately, none of the [white] officials of the Presbytery cared about the concerns of black people," Sims said. "It's terrible to say, but many church members felt vindicated after the murder of Mr. Wells. It proved that they were right about Jackson."

On the evening that seventy-year-old Earle Wells was murdered, a family party was underway at his home on Newton Street, a short distance from the church. Retired from the factory in Elizabeth where he had worked for fifty years, he spent much of his time tending to the church building and grounds. "We were celebrating my sister and brother-in-law's anniversary when my father said he was going to see Reverend Jackson for a few minutes," Miss Rhapsody said. "That was about eight o'clock. He never came back. We went and knocked on the church door, but it was locked. We waited and waited, then called the police."

Early the next morning a man walking his dog in the Vauxhall section of Union Township, several miles from Newark, found Wells's body. He had been stabbed to death with an ice pick. The family was notified and Jackson was called to police headquarters in downtown Newark for questioning. C. B. (Carlton B.) Norris, Newark's first black detective, was assigned to the case.

"They had just brought in Jackson when I got there," Miss Rhapsody said. "Norris wanted to know why I'd come downtown. 'I'm Viola Wells,' I told him, just as he realized that 'Miss Rhapsody' was my stage name. 'I'm Mr. Wells's daughter.' " Police questioned Jackson extensively but had to let him go. They suspected he was the killer, but they did not have enough evidence to make an arrest.

The next day, Sunday morning, Jackson was in the pulpit at Thirteenth Avenue, preaching on the text "Faith, hope and love: And the greatest of these is love." The church was packed. Word of Wells's death and the suspicion that Jackson might be involved had spread quickly. More than thirteen hundred people crowded the pews, including Norris and his fellow law enforcement officers.

"I was sitting with my mother and brother midway in the church, where my mother had a pew," said pianist Clem Moorman. "No one believed then that Reverend Jackson was guilty, although he'd had several confrontations with the ruling body. The older members of the church were conventional and didn't approve of many of the things he was doing. He was too radical for them. He was a shrewd character. If you weren't on to him, he would win you over. We were very upset because my mother [Louise Moorman] and Mrs. Wells [Miss Rhapsody's stepmother] were close. They both were members of the Missionary Society. Everyone thought Mr. Wells was a wonderful man. He was a father figure who advised all the young people."

Minutes after Jackson finished his sermon that Sunday, he was arrested in his study and led out of the church by police. His alibi—that at the time of Wells's murder he had gone to Proctor's Theatre in downtown Newark in a 1948 blue Packard borrowed from his friend Cleveland Pinckney, a church leader—had not held up. By that time, Norris and his team of investigators had thoroughly checked the car. Bloodstains Jackson had tried to wash away were found all over the backseat.

Pinckney's son, Ted, former chairman of the Mathematics Department at East Side High School in Newark, was on the football team at South Side High at the time. "That Saturday, we had a game in Asbury Park," he recounted. "When I got home, C. B. Norris was there questioning my parents. My father hadn't seen the car yet. He had a space in a public garage where Reverend Jackson had returned it."

The Pinckney family had joined Thirteenth Avenue Presbyterian because of Cleveland Pinckney's longtime friendship with Jackson, dating back to their days as South Carolina schoolboys. When Jackson arrived in Newark, the Pinckneys were regulars at Bethany Baptist Church. Soon after, the family switched to Thirteenth Avenue.

Jackson's trial caused a huge sensation. For days, news accounts flashed photographs of Wells and Jackson across the front pages of the local newspapers, black and white. When the trial began, a flood of spectators, anxious to get courtroom seats, prompted the Essex County sheriff's office to assign extra men to duty.

The prosecutor was a young attorney named James Giuliano. Years later he became a judge of the New Jersey Superior Court, handling all assignments in Essex County. There was no doubt in Giuliano's mind that Jackson had killed Wells. Jackson, who had a wife and two children, was living beyond his means, spending money far too freely for a man who earned a modest salary. It was rumored that he had become involved in some failed business ventures and was deeply in debt. On the night of his death, Wells had gone to the church to confront Jackson about his having fraudulently taken out a $10,000 second mortgage on the building to use for his own benefit.

In court, Jackson's attorney portrayed Wells, the elderly church sexton, as the violent one. He argued that Jackson, who was thirty-seven, acted in self-defense after Wells physically confronted him. That argument was far too thin to stand up. After Giuliano urged the jury to send Jackson to the electric chair, Jackson caved in and pleaded nolo contendere. It was not an admission of guilt, but it meant that he would be punished. His sentence: life without a pardon.

Many years later, Miss Rhapsody and I were having lunch at the Bridge Club, a popular restaurant on Washington Street in Newark. We were seated by the back door. When it opened, in came Jackson. Carl Jones, who owned the Bridge Club and was seated at the bar, kept shaking his head knowingly. Miss Rhapsody was in the house and so was Jackson. It was time to go. I paid the bill, and we left. Rhap never said much about the chance meeting, other than that she had heard Jackson was out of prison but had had no idea where he was until then.

In September 1991, seven years after Miss Rhapsody's death at age eighty-two, I hosted a book-signing party for my first book, *Swing City: Newark Nightlife, 1925–50,* at the Bridge Club. All of the singers and musicians who were Rhap's friends and mine were there that night, signing autographs and having a good time. For most of the evening I sat in a booth autographing books for people who had formed a line. "Please sign this one to 'The Reverend H. Beecher Jackson,' " a woman requested.

There in a back corner, glowering at me, was the man who had killed my good friend's father. "Tell him I will sign it to H. B. Jackson, but I will not address it to 'The Reverend Jackson,' I told her. He will know what I mean." He was, to my mind, no man of the cloth.

Viola Gertrude Wells was born on December 14, 1902, at home at 21 Scott Street in Newark, a short block between Broad and Mulberry Streets in the area where the Peter W. Rodino, Jr., Federal Courthouse now stands. Like many southerners, her parents, Roberta Simmons Wells and Earle Wells, had traveled north to Newark from Virginia at the turn of the twentieth century to make a better life for themselves.

Her mother's father, a former slave, the Reverend Morgan Simmons, was the founder of several churches in and around Surry County, Virginia, where his family lived at least from the time of his birth in 1853. One of his churches was in the tiny community of Ivor, Virginia, where family members still worship.

As a teenager, Morgan Simmons helped support his family by working on a plantation outside Smithfield in nearby Isle of Wight County. From the time he was a young man, it was clear that he was a person of great promise and ambition. Records at the Surry County Courthouse, a stately building embellished by a statue of a Confederate soldier on the front lawn, show that he bought 301 acres of farmland at $1.50 per acre in 1874. He was just twenty-one. When he died in the 1930s, his six children inherited fifty acres each.

Viola was four years old when her mother, barely into her twenties, died giving birth to her sister, Estelle. Soon thereafter their father sent Viola and the baby back to Surry to live with his wife's parents. Long after she was grown, Viola referred to herself as "a motherless child," wending her way through life without the benefit of the caring advice and love that only a mother can provide.

Life on their grandfather's spacious farm south of the James River was good for the Wells girls, especially in summer, when Viola, her sister, and their cousins got to roam the fields and play in the barn. From the time she arrived in Virginia, Viola was the leader of the pack. "I was only four when I heard Ethel Waters singing on the radio," she said. "The other kids would laugh, but from that moment on, I knew what I wanted to do. I wanted to be in show business."

Barely of school age, she began staging talent shows in her grandfather's barn with the help of her uncle Charlie, a fun-loving young man who lived in New Rochelle, New York, but frequently went south to Surry. "We'd hang a clothesline and put a blanket over it for a curtain," she recalled. "Then, each of my cousins would take turns singing and dancing. Uncle Charlie would dance too. I was the announcer, so I always went last. One of my favorite songs was 'Sugar,' an Ethel Waters tune. She was my idol."

One of the most frequent visitors to the Simmons's Big House, a rambling farmhouse eight miles from the courthouse, was Grace George Slade, the young teacher at the one-room school halfway to town. She had taught Viola's mother, Roberta, and her twin sister, Rebecca. Now she was Viola's teacher too.

Six days a week, the Reverend Morgan Simmons farmed peanuts and soybeans. Sundays were spent preaching fire and brimstone as he traveled from church to church throughout the area. When Grace George married and became a Slade, he conducted the ceremony in the Big House. "We were like family," the teacher said. "I called Viola's grandmother Aunt Annie. Reverend Simmons was Uncle Morgan."

In her later years, Slade lived across the James River from Surry in a house in Hampton next door to her son-in-law, Jasper Simmons. Jasper was Viola's cousin on her father's side of the family. In her mid-nineties when she died, Slade was one of Hampton University's oldest living graduates.

When Viola was nine, Earle Wells married again and brought his daughters back to Newark, where they attended Central Avenue School. Alice Polk, the woman he married, loved children. "We loved her too, because she was so much fun," Rhap said. "She loved to play with us and make us clothes. She also made all our favorite things to eat."

In the meantime, Wells, a supervisor at a factory, became one of the movers and shakers at Thirteenth Avenue Church, the focal point of his family's life. At twelve, Viola joined the Salika Johnson Chorus, led by Ruth Reid, the church organist. For her age, her voice was full and rich. She was a standout. Soon Reid began taking the chorus on the road, traveling to places like Philadelphia to present concerts at churches and auditoriums. The group also gained widespread popularity in Newark, singing on the radio.

"For me, this was heaven. I was doing exactly what I wanted to be doing," Rhap said. She also was a top student, skipping a semester of the seventh grade at Cleveland School. After graduation, she went to work as a domestic for a family in Rutherford to help support the family. "I wanted to go into show business, but I didn't want to offend my father while I was living in his house," she said. "He did not approve of singing outside the church. Nor did I want to be sneaking around." But every once in a while, when pressed, she would sing at a party.

When her stepmother died suddenly, Viola was devastated. Things got worse when her father remarried a year or two later. "I was eighteen, and my new stepmother and I didn't see eye to eye," she said. "I thought I was a woman and she thought I was a child." With no real income of her own, she did what she thought was best. She married Howard Nicholas, a handsome young man from Jersey City. But their union did not last long. "We were both far too young to understand what marriage was all about, so we went our separate ways," she said.

Once she was on her own, she began hanging out at Newark's Orpheum Theater at Court and Washington Streets, which catered almost exclusively to black audiences. She got her first big break when a musician who heard her sing at a party recommended her for a job as a stand-in for blues singer Mamie Smith, the star of the *7-11* show at Miner's Theater, up the street from the Orpheum. Smith was a huge star, famous for her 1920 hit "Crazy Blues" on Columbia, which made history as the nation's first official blues record.

Viola Wells was a hit too, dazzling audiences that often included her friends and neighbors. In their eyes, she was their hometown star. At Miner's, she met Eddie Durham, a trombonist from Texas who became a fixture in Count Basie's orchestra. Decades later, the two of them worked together in the Harlem Blues and Jazz Band, a group of veteran musicians who regularly toured Europe.

Early in her career, she appeared mostly at local nightspots. But she was still her father's daughter—a product of the church. "That's why I only sang one time at the Kinney Club on Arlington Street," she said. "It was too rough." The Kinney Club's reputation was unsavory because it was a hangout for pimps and prostitutes. Gambling. Drugs. You name it. You could find it on Arlington Street, three blocks west of Broad Street in an area rightly called the Barbary Coast because it was as dangerous as the high seas where pirates once roamed. "Risque" was the way most people described the place. "The girls would have to do 'ups' [pick up a bottle between their thighs for table tips]," said entertainer Little Sadie Matthews.

By the late 1920s, Viola had taken to the road, traveling with Banjo Bernie's band. "He was from Baltimore and would book spots up and down the East Coast, from there to Florida," she said. Her boyfriend, Harold Underhill, played guitar in the band. "Banjo Bernie didn't handle money very well, so they made me the treasurer," she said. "I'd collect all the money, pay the bills, and pay the boys." She also did all the cooking while the band was going from place to place and saw to it that the band members' uniforms were fresh and clean.

Although she had encountered racism in Newark, those experiences paled in comparison to what she and the band endured traveling through the South. "Often, we'd play for the white folks one night and black folks the next night," she said. "You never knew who was going to turn you away. There were that many whites-only policies. Sometimes we couldn't buy gas. Sometimes we couldn't find a place to stay or eat. Most of the time we had to go in the back door of the places we played. Mostly we stayed in colored-owned boarding houses." One night while entertaining in a small town in Georgia, she did a split at the end of her act but was unable to get up. "A white man came to front of the auditorium and gave me his hand to help me get up," she recalled. "That was tantamount to treason. It darned near caused a riot."

After three years on the road, Rhap returned home to Newark at the height of the Great Depression. Newark was a town of taverns and speakeasies, so work was plentiful. But she was looking for something better, an opportunity to become more than an ordinary singer. On her own, she began booking shows and emceeing them. "When we needed a replacement for a shake dancer at a club in Scranton, I called down to Philadelphia and they sent a girl named Pearl Bailey," she said. "Pearl could sing too, so I formed a trio with her, another girl, and me."

When they were both much older, Bailey wrote a letter telling Rhap how much she had looked up to her when she was starting out in show business. Fondly, Bailey recounted how much fun they had had in the old days at Scranton's Chinchilly Club. That, too, was where Rhap got her nickname. "A reporter for the *Pittsburgh Courier* began calling me 'Miss Rhapsody' because I always sang 'Rhapsody in Rhythm' and 'Rhapsody in Song,' " she said. For the rest of her life, she was "Miss Rhapsody," or simply "Rhap" to her audiences and friends.

In the early 1930s, Rhap married again and had a daughter named Yvonne, a child everyone called Toots. Again, she had made a poor choice in a husband. Although she was enamored of Melvin Evans, he was a hustler with a penchant for getting into scrapes with the law. Soon after they married, he was sent to prison for a string of petty thefts. Forced to support herself and her daughter, Rhap took Toots and headed for Ohio to take a job with Mighty Sheesley's Circus. It was rough work, not the kind of job she really wanted. But she had to make a living for herself and her child.

Before long, she got an offer to join a show in Oklahoma. Blues singer Ida Cox, a big name among black entertainers, was the headliner. Rhap's first show was a huge success. The audience loved her. The next day, when the show was reviewed, her name hit the headlines. Cox was furious. Calling Rhap into her dressing room, she made it clear that *she* was the star of the show. No young upstart was going to upstage her. Rhap was out.

Cox's manager, Jack Schenck, was beside himself. Trying to make up for Cox's vindictiveness, he offered to drive Rhap to Kansas City, where jazz was the new sensation, thanks to Count Basie's reception at the Reno Club. Rhap wound up at the Sunset Crystal Palace in Kansas City, where the bartender was the famous blues singer Joe Turner. Soon she began running amateur night contests, emceeing the shows and singing a tune or two. One of the winners was Walter Brown, whose signature song, "Confessin' the Blues," became a hit recording.

Across the street at the Kit Kat Club, the attraction was singer Julia Lee, who made a slew of records on the Capital label in the 1940s. She was the sister of George E. Lee, the famous Kansas City bandleader. "Julia and I became fast friends," Rhap said. "When she saw me coming in the door, she'd shout out, 'Hold all the women, 'cause we got the men.' "

Rhap stayed in Kansas City for eighteen months. In 1938 she took a bus back to Newark and began singing again at hometown clubs. Soon thereafter she was booked into the famous Apollo Theater in Harlem, where she performed with three prominent bandleaders—Claude Hopkins, Erskine Hawkins, and Bunny Berigan. Her appearances at the Apollo were prompted by the fantastic reviews she had gotten playing Kansas City's top clubs.

With the help of an agent, she began singing at some of the most important night spots on 52nd Street in New York. Because there were so many clubs and the music went on all night, it was called "the Street That Never Slept." From 1940 to 1944, Rhap was billed regularly at Kelly's Stable, one of the Street's top spots.

Benny Carter, the famous bandleader, who had just returned from an extended stay in Great Britain, was the headliner the first time she appeared at Kelly's. Billed by the owners as "the Ebony Stick of Dynamite," she was at the bottom of the bill. "The print was so small, you needed a spyglass to see my name," she told friends. Nevertheless, she wowed her audiences. By the time the Nat King Cole Trio played Kelly's for the first time in 1940, she was the co-attraction.

Although Carter was five years her junior, Rhap had a tremendous crush on him. In 1944, when she recorded for the first time on Savoy, she wrote a song for him, "I Fell for You." It was a sweet song: "I fell for you, the moment that I looked into your eyes. This time it's true, I know by every star up in the sky. I love you; yes, I do." Carter, one of the biggest names in jazz, was oblivious to her infatuation.

While appearing at Kelly's Stable, Rhap often got gigs for her friends from Newark. One of them was Joe Gregory, who is still singing and dancing in his mid-eighties. At Kelly's, Joe played drums. "I got paid $150 a week, a huge sum at the time," said Gregory. "It was far more than I ever made anywhere else. I was in the chips."

Rhap also played talent scout for the highly regarded stride piano player Donald Lambert. First she got him a New York union card. Then she got him a gig at Kelly's. But Lambert was a loner. He did not like New York, so he stayed just one night before returning to Wallace's Tavern in West Orange, New Jersey, where he played until his death twenty years later.

In the mid-1940s, Rhap formed a trio, The Three Sportsmen of Rhythm, with Jay Cole on piano, Harold Underhill on guitar, and William (Bass) Lindburgh on upright bass. They toured the East Coast, appearing on the radio and at posh clubs like the Town Club in Virginia Beach, Virginia.

By the early 1940s, the Swing Era in Newark was in full gear. There was no competition yet from television. A major manufacturing center, Newark had at least five big breweries as well as several smaller ones. Consequently, hundreds of taverns were scattered throughout the city. Music, most owners felt, was a sure way to attract customers, so many of them hired piano players or small musical combos.

At the larger clubs, full-scale revues attracted audiences that lined up for blocks on Saturday nights. There was the Kinney Club on Arlington Street, the Nest Club on Warren Street, the Picadilly on Peshine Avenue, and Dodger's Bar and Grill on Bedford Street. Rhap played them all but was a particular favorite at Dodger's, just off Springfield Avenue. Like many club owners at the time, the Campisi family had links to the mob.

Regardless of his family's reputation, Rhap considered Gus Campisi, who ran Dodger's, a great guy and good friend. In 1943, when she was in

Detroit during a race riot, Gus sent her the money that got her back to Newark. It was a favor she never forgot. She also became friendly with the Campisi women, including Gus's mother, who lived above the club and could look out onto the dance floor from a second-floor balcony. "She'd always make Italian dishes for me," Rhap recalled. "She also had a favorite song. She'd ask me to sing 'My Mother's Eyes.' "

When *After Hours*, a black weekly, took a poll of the city's favorite singers in the early 1940s, Rhap was always at or near the top of the list. Grace Smith, her friend from childhood, was her major competitor. "Grace could sing it all—ballads, blues, or jump tunes," Rhap said. "She was known for tunes like 'Exactly Like You.' She could really swing."

Rhap liked being at home in Newark because it offered a more stable environment for Toots. By the early 1950s, Melvin was out of prison and living with them in the back of a restaurant she had opened on Bergen Street, opposite what is now the Pathmark Shopping Center. Rhap told everyone she left show business to open the restaurant, but the real reason was the malaise she felt after her father's death. To the world, she seemed like the same old Rhap. Inwardly, she was hurting, so much that even singing—the activity in life that gave her the most joy—could not lift her spirits.

Her restaurant thrived because she knew everyone in town and they knew her. People who had not seen her perform most likely had seen her photo or read stories about her in Newark's two black weeklies, the *Herald News* and the *New Jersey Afro-American*. One of her most fervent fans was Bob Queen, editor of the *Afro*. As a businesswoman, Rhap was generous to a fault. Often she would cook huge batches of soup and stew, which she gave away to those who were down and out. "If a guy looked scruffy," said waitress Fannie Wright, "Rhap would give him one of her husband's shirts."

"If you needed $100 and Rhap had a dollar, she'd go out and borrow the other $99 and not think a thing if you didn't pay her back," singer Celeste Jones recalled. Rhap also spent a considerable amount of her time trying to help show business friends who were awash in drugs and alcohol. When singer Lawrence Miller fell victim to the evils of drugs, she stayed with him round the clock while he went cold turkey.

Making clear her high standards and disdain for the perception among the general public that many entertainers were lowlifes, she told a *Pittsburgh Courier* reporter in 1944, "I don't like the idea that all Negro singers are considered pistol-packin' mamas. That's not the way it is with me, and that's not the way that it is with most of my friends in the business. I have absolutely nothing in common with hard-drinking, cussin' women like [blues singer] Bessie Smith."

Eventually, Rhap returned to singing, mostly at local fund-raisers and social events. After closing her restaurant in the early 1960s, she took over the kitchen at Pitt's Place, a popular club on Hartford Street in Newark. Wearing her apron, she would often emerge from the kitchen to sing a tune or two. Milton Pittman, who started out as an entertainer before going into the insurance business, owned Pitt's Place. Like Rhap, he was a generous soul. When Millie Williams, a singer who was one of Newark's oldest entertainers, died without a dime, Pittman paid the entire funeral bill.

While she was at Pitt's, Rhap was rediscovered out of the blue by Derrick-Stewart Baxter, an English jazz critic and radio personality whose book about black American women blues singers is a classic in the field. He had run into blues historian Sheldon Harris while in New York at a formal affair called the Black and White Ball and, to his surprise, learned that Rhap was still alive and singing occasionally in Newark. For years he had been playing the twelve sides she made for Savoy in 1944 and 1945 on his Brighton, England, radio show, thinking she was dead.

The next night the two men headed for Newark to interview Rhap and Leon Eason, who had the house band at Pitt's. Immediately, Stewart-Baxter offered Rhap a chance to record her first album. Rather than waste time looking for a label, he offered to sponsor it with financial help from Harris and Bill Daynes-Wood, a British jazz fan. Before long, Rhap was in a New York City studio, recording her first LP, a mix of sacred and secular music.

Accompanied by Grace Gregory, her church pianist, she was almost late for the session. Traffic was a mess because of a downpour and some kind of protest near the New York Public Library. Huffing and puffing, they arrived late at the studio, where the precious time paid for the rental was dwindling. "Rhap barely had her raincoat off before she was into the first tune," Harris recalled. "She was on. She knew the boys. With the exception of Ivan Rolle on bass, they were all from Newark: Jay Cole on piano, Danny Gibson on drums, and Eddie Wright on guitar." The LP on the Matchbox/Saydisc label soon was part of recording history.

At nearly seventy, Rhap's voice, though deeper than it was when she recorded for Savoy in 1944, was still rich and clear. If there was one thing she was a stickler about, it was enunciation. "I don't go for 'dem and dose,' " she said. "People should be able to hear every word of a song."

For her first album, Rhap chose all the tunes she loved best. On the sacred side, she sang her favorite hymns: "His Eye Is on the Sparrow," "Face to Face," "How Great Thou Art," "Power in the Blood," and "In the Garden." The secular songs included some blues ("Downhearted Blues" and "Blues in My Heart"), a jump tune ("See, See Rider"), and the tune she had written for Benny Carter ("I Fell for You"). The pièce de résistance was "Brown Gal," her signature song.

Harris, who wrote the liner notes for the album, had this to say about it: "When she moves into Lil Armstrong's 'Brown Gal,' her personal theme song for well over thirty-five years, she becomes a vignette of pure happiness and warmth. She is stage-center again at chic Café Society, the amber lights flowing gently off her soft face, her long sequined gown sparkling, her arms arcing in deliberate, slow gestures. She is once again the Brown Gal offering help to those who have since risen about her: the Joe Turners, the Pearl Baileys, the Walter Browns. The voice is not proud. But reflective."

At Harris's urging, Rhap began singing again on a regular basis. One of her first performances was at the International House in New York, a home away from home for students from all over the world. Even though she was old enough to be their grandmother, the students loved her show, warming to her uncanny ability to command her audiences no matter what their age or background.

This was the late 1960s. Rhap had long since given up the restaurant business. She was working days as a housekeeper for a wealthy family in Clifton, New Jersey, and singing at night when she could. At the time, I was new to the *Star-Ledger.* After seeing a brief clip of Rhap on CBS-TV while she was singing at the International House, I arranged an interview at her North Ward apartment.

I could immediately see how warm and friendly Rhap was, but it was also clear that she was a no-nonsense person. It was evident, too, that she had struggled to support herself and her daughter, who was then in her thirties and a gravely ill alcoholic. Nevertheless, Rhap was proud of all she had accomplished and thankful to God for many blessings, rather than focused on the rough spots in her life. Seated beside me on her living room couch, she told me her story, one filled with names of musicians like Jimmie Lunceford, Joe Turner, and Benny Carter that were mostly unfamiliar to me.

Soon after my article appeared, I got a call from Ada Cole, the wife of Jay Cole, Rhap's friend and accompanist. She wanted me to hear Rhap sing at a Saturday night dance at Ebony Manor in Newark. I went but got there late, just as the band members were packing up their instruments.

The first time I heard Rhap sing was at a party in Larchmont, New York, at the home of Albert (Doc) Vollmer, an orthodontist who devotes himself to reviving the careers of well-known jazz artists, and his wife, Dot. Their home was a magnificent stone mansion on Long Island Sound that looked like a castle. Famous musicians were everywhere in the house and on the spacious grounds, talking about the old days, telling stories about friends who had died or with whom they had lost contact through the years.

When I arrived, Rhap was at the center of it all, talking to Eva Taylor, the 1920s blues singer and wife of Clarence Williams, the music publisher. Taylor was one of the first singers to record "race records"—those directed at black audiences—on a label created by Thomas Edison. Nearby was Edna Mae Harris, the star of a string of movies shown in southern theaters for blacks only.

Rhap began introducing me to her friends. I did not know any of them by reputation, but I was familiar with their bandleaders. Buddy Tate, Earl Warren, and Eddie Durham were from Count Basie's band. Russell Procope and Franc Williams played with Duke Ellington. George James was a saxophonist with Louis Armstrong. Al Casey, the highly regarded guitarist, was part of a combo led by Fats Waller. The oldest musician present was Fess Williams, whose orchestra ruled the Savoy Ballroom in Harlem before the Savoy Sultans took over as the club's house band in the mid-1930s.

Before long, groups of musicians gathered in the dining room, empty except for a piano and drum kit. Jay Cole was first at the piano, performing jazz standards with a group that included Clyde Bernhardt, his Newark neighbor from Barclay Street, on trombone. In the early 1930s, Bernhardt was a key member of a legendary unit led by King Oliver. At another point in the impromptu concert, Gene Rodgers, famous for his opening piano solo on Coleman Hawkins's heralded recording of "Body and Soul," was at the piano. Tommy Benford, whose brother Bill often accompanied blues singer Bessie Smith, was at the drums.

In the early 1970s, after hosting a series of similar parties, Doc Vollmer formed the Harlem Blues and Jazz Band. Bernhardt and Cole were the co-leaders. Benford was on drums, Franc Williams on trumpet, George James on sax, and Barbara Dreiwitz on tuba. Rhap was assigned to handle the vocals. With the exception of Dreiwitz, a young woman, all the musicians were in their seventies or older. Before long they were playing on college campuses, in clubs, and at jazz association concerts.

During that time, Bernhardt rediscovered Princess White. Like Rhap, she lived in Newark and was a member of New Eden Baptist Church on South Twelfth Street. "When I was a boy delivering telegraphs down South, I used to see her perform," Bernhardt recalled. "She was a good tipper and the best performer I'd ever heard."

In her heyday, Princess White was the star of a traveling show called Silas Green from New Orleans. Despite its name, the troupe had nothing to do with New Orleans. Its home base was North Carolina. From there the entertainers traveled by train, putting on tent shows in nearby southern states.

Princess White was long retired from show business when she moved to Newark. Bernhardt met her when he went to worship with Rhap at New Eden. "Princess was ninety-four, but when she sang one of those hymns, her voice was so powerful you could hear her down on Broad Street [a mile away]," he noted. Before long, Princess and Rhap were both singing with the Harlem Blues and Jazz Band. Princess made her debut in

1975 at the Holiday Inn in Meriden, Connecticut, where the band gave a concert for the Connecticut Traditional Jazz Club. The place was packed when she took to the stage in a beautiful black sequined gown.

"You know," she told the audience, "in my day you didn't have a microphone. No radio. No television. All you had was a voice, and you had to sing. You *had* to sing. So, I don't know. I'm going to try. You know I'm ninety-four." The crowd went wild, practically drowning out her intro to "Exactly Like You." From the first note, the tone and quality of her voice had "star" written all over it. When she growled, the folks were on their feet. And when she danced, raising her gown just a speck above her ankles, she tore the place down.

Princess sang four songs that night, including a blues number she had written in what old-fashioned singers called "stop time," plus a mournful love song called "Old-Fashioned Love." When she finished, the audience gave her a five-minute standing ovation. When she returned to her table, some of her newfound fans followed her, congratulating her as they lined up for autographs.

Princess was exhausted, barely able to breathe. "Barbara," she called to me across the table. "Get my nitro. It's in my pocketbook." Nitro? I had driven this woman all the way to Connecticut to learn that she had a heart condition? Nervously, I searched her pocketbook, finally turning it upside down out of desperation. There was no nitroglycerine. No medication of any kind. Fortunately, the spell passed. She was all right but in no shape to take the long trip back to Newark that night. Instead, we stayed overnight, returning home on Sunday morning.

Before her ninety-fifth birthday that January, Princess made several other appearances with the band, including one at the Roosevelt Hotel in New York for the Overseas Press Club's Jazz Club and one at an outdoor jazz concert in Mamaroneck, New York. She also made a recording with the band.

In late 1975, after suffering a heart attack, Princess was admitted to Clara Maass Hospital in Belleville, New Jersey. Soon after, she had another attack. By late January, she was at home again on South Eighteenth Street in Newark under strict orders from her doctor to stay put. Stubborn as ever, she did what she wanted. And so it was no great surprise to find her at the Emelin Theater in Mamaroneck, New York, where the band was playing and Rhap was singing on March 21, 1976.

Princess was planning to go on, and she did—for the last time in her life. Wearing an airy opalescent gown imprinted with butterflies (a symbol perhaps of her free spirit), she and Rhap sat side by side in the wings of the theater until it was time for her to perform. Once on stage, she sang two tunes. Then she told the crowd, "I'm a little tired now, so I'm going to rest. But if I can, I will be back to sing another song, one that I wrote. I'm going to deal a deck of cards."

With that, Al Vollmer went on stage, took her arm, and led her into the wings. While he went to fetch her a glass of water, she and Rhap were alone again. Minutes later a flurry of activity occurred in the lobby of the theater. The Mamaroneck police headquarters, located opposite the theater, had received an emergency call. Someone at the theater had collapsed.

Within minutes, three officers, armed with an oxygen tank, were headed backstage. Anxiously, I followed them, knowing that either Rhap or Princess was in serious trouble. It was Princess, crumpled on the floor like a bird with broken wings. Rhap was standing over her, waving her arms helplessly as the medics tried to revive her friend. As she later explained, Princess simply squeezed her hand, closed her eyes, and passed away peacefully as they sat in the wings. Although Princess was officially proclaimed dead at a nearby hospital, we knew then that there was no hope of survival. Several days later her funeral took place at New Eden Baptist Church, where she was the oldest member.

Because many of the faithful consider the blues the devil's music, gossip about what Princess was doing in Mamaroneck was flying everywhere. Why was she out there singing the blues? Why, at ninety-five, did she not stick to the music of the church? When it came time for me to speak about Princess, I decided to address the issue. "Why not?" I asked. "If you had been in Mamaroneck that day, you would have seen three hundred smiling faces. Is it wrong to make people happy? Is that a sin? Think about it."

After Princess's death, Rhap again was the sole singer with the Harlem Blues and Jazz Band. Later that year, the band was hired to play a concert in rural Maryland. What we did not know was that the area was home to the KKK. Although the sponsors expected three hundred people for each concert and a Saturday night Creole dinner, just twenty or so showed up for each of two performances.

Perhaps we should have guessed that trouble might be brewing when the manager of the scraggly motel where the band was staying refused us entry into our room earlier in the day. We would have to wait until Al Vollmer arrived with the band to get into our rooms, he said. "We've had a long drive, and we would like to rest," I told him. "How much is the room?"

"Twenty dollars," he said, still reluctant to let me pay in advance.

Later, we found out that George James, the saxophonist, and his family had been similarly rebuffed. After arriving early, they had spent an hour driving around the countryside, waiting for the rest of the band to arrive.

Just one black couple attended the band's first show. The woman said they arrived early so they could get home at a decent hour and not run the risk of encountering trouble along the way. In hushed tones, she spoke of her fear of the KKK. According to a local newspaperman, the concert was "a banned event." Whites, he said, would not come out to hear an all-black band. Blacks were "too afraid to come." By Sunday afternoon we were all glad to get out of town.

In Europe, where jazz fans abound, the band's reception was far different. Once their records gained popularity, invitations to perform at jazz festivals, clubs, and concert halls in England, Belgium, and Germany poured in. As a result, Vollmer began booking month-long European tours each year.

Before touring Europe for the first time with the band, Rhap made her first visit to the Continent with me as part of my research for *Swing City*. In May 1975, we spent one week in London and another in Paris. In London we spent time with Gilbert Gaster, a well-known jazz writer; Laurie Wright, the editor of *Storyville,* a jazz magazine; and Kitty and Jack Harvey, Rhap's good friends with whom she often stayed while on tour. We also took a train trip to Brighton to visit Rhap's friend Derrick Stewart-Baxter.

Rhap was seventy-three years old but as energetic as ever. In Paris, Jean Christophe Averty, a legendary producer of jazz programs, did six half-hour TV shows on her life and career. The rehearsal was at the country home of Claude Bolling, the highly regarded pianist. Bolling's house was amazing, replete with a professionally equipped studio. There, Rhap met Claude Luter, the clarinetist, who for many years led the band that featured Sidney Bechet, one of America's most famous jazz musicians.

Bolling arranged for Rhap to sing sixteen songs in-studio over the course of the next few days. During the rehearsal, his two adorable sons, ages five and seven, sat attentively on a bench. Each time Rhap finished a song they would clap loudly and urge her on. "Zing, Miss Rhapsody!" they implored. "Zing!"

In the television studio the next day, it was evident that Averty, who resembled the French actor Louis Jordan, was a taskmaster. He wanted perfection. Rhap, who was wearing a silver sequined gown that glittered when we watched the takes, sang each song over and over, to the point where I suggested that he move on. "She's seventy-three," I told him. "She may run out of steam." By the third day Averty had recorded all sixteen songs, including Rhap's favorite, the old Ethel Waters's tune "Am I Blue." Later that day he sat her in an oversized armchair and interviewed her from off camera. The program was a wrap.

Soon after, Rhap returned to France, touring several cities with the band. After one of those trips in 1978, she returned home in a wheelchair. A British fan, anxious to get an autograph, had stepped on her foot during a gig in London, flattening her toe. Kitty and Jack Harvey, with whom she was staying, thought she should stay in London to seek treatment while the band continued its tour, but Rhap was having none of it. If she could go on the same night her father was murdered, she could go on now.

By the time she got home to Newark, her injury was worse. She was a diabetic, and the toe was not healing. After six months of treatment, doctors amputated her right leg below the knee. By that time she was in agony. Although the idea of using of drugs sickened her, she was begging for morphine to ease her pain.

Amazingly, she was her old self again immediately after her operation. As the aides rolled her back to her room, she was almost joyous. "Bar-

barita," she called to me. "Thank God almighty! That leg carried me seventy-seven years. Enough is enough!" When her sister arrived, Rhap stayed up until seven that night, talking and laughing as if nothing had happened.

Nevertheless, for the first time in her life, Rhap looked frail. She was nearing eighty and had lost sixty pounds over the course of six months. After taking medication for diabetes for more than a decade, her heart was extremely weak. Doctors said she probably would be confined to her apartment for the rest of her life, never to perform again.

But Rhap knew better. She was a believer—and a fighter. During three months of therapy at the Theresa Grotta Rehabilitation Center in West Orange, she did a hundred daily repetitions, using weights attached to a broomstick, to strengthen her arms. Once the stump healed sufficiently, she did daily exercises faithfully for the rest of her life to make certain it did not curl. Otherwise, she would not have been able to use her prosthesis.

Soon after her arrival at Theresa Grotta, Rhap began giving shows for the patients, with her friend Clem Moorman on piano. There were three in all. After the first one, Rhap lifted herself ever so slightly from her wheelchair to take a little bow. The second time around she was able to stand on a stick with a shoe attached to it that served as her temporary prosthesis. The third time, after many hours of therapy, she was walking without the aid of a cane. She was ready to go home.

From then on, there was no stopping her. She went everywhere she wanted and did everything she desired. Days after she returned home, she began driving again, taking a trip to Brooklyn to see her oldest granddaughter. In a matter of weeks, she was back singing on Sunday nights at the Ginger Man, near Lincoln Center in New York City. Ram Ramirez, who wrote the jazz standard "Lover Man," was on piano. Al Hall, a mainstay for many years with Erroll Garner, was on bass. Their fans responded by flocking to see them. "You learn from Rhap because you feel her truth and you feel her need to express her experience," Curt Davis wrote in the *New York Post*. "Doing the blues is not a choice but a given truth for her. It's an attitude as well as a voice."

Sadly, however, Rhap's daughter, Toots, ravaged by alcohol abuse, was on a downward spiral. When Toots died of a heart attack, several of her alcoholic friends showed up for the service at Perry's Funeral Home in Newark. Through it all, Rhap remained stoic, urging her three grand-daughters to hold their heads high. "These were your mother's friends," she told them. "What they are and what they do has nothing to do with you."

After a year of singing on Sunday nights at the Ginger Man, Rhap re-tired from show business, but she still made occasional appearances. Of-ten, she accompanied her friend singer Carrie Smith on gigs, singing a tune or two on the program. Her last appearance, in December 1984, just days before her eighty-second birthday, was at Sweet Basil's in Greenwich Village, where her friend Eddie Chamblee, the saxophonist, was playing. Rhap did not feel well but insisted she would be fine if she had a cup of tea. Afterward she got up and, as always, wowed the crowd, earning an encore.

A week later, after dinner at the Ginger Man to celebrate her birthday, Rhap called me late that night. She was in a panic. She thought she was having a heart attack. By the time I got to her apartment, the paramedics were there administering oxygen. Doctors at Clara Maass Medical Center, where she was admitted, thought she had the flu. On Saturday, three days before Christmas Day, 1984, she was about to go home. That morning, without warning, she suffered a heart attack and died. She is buried in Heavenly Rest Cemetery in East Hanover, New Jersey, where the name-plate on her grave bears a fitting inscription:

Viola Gertrude Wells
(Miss Rhapsody)
December 14, 1902–December 22, 1984
Newark's No. 1 Brown Gal

PHOTO GALLERY

Above, Connie Williams Woodruff playing to her audience in her baby carriage. (Author's collection.)

Top right, Connie's father, Frederick Isaac Williams. (Author's collection.)

Bottom right, Connie's mother, Caroline Pines Williams. (Author's collection.)

Top, Connie with Sugar Ray Robinson (*left*) and Newark boxer William (Jazz) Jones in 1948 at Robinson's training camp. (Author's collection.)

Bottom, Connie at Newark's first Crispus Attucks parade in 1964, flanked by community leader Queenie James and co-announcer Rudy Kinchen. (Courtesy of David Booker.)

Above left, Gladys St. John on Confirmation Day at St. Philip's Church. (Courtesy of Dr. Edith C. Churchman.)

Above right, Gladys St. John Churchman. (Courtesy of Dr. Edith C. Churchman.)

Above left, Gladys Churchman and board members at a fund-raiser for the Friendly Fuld Neighborhood House. (Courtesy of Katherine Maupins.)

Above right, Gladys Churchman with a group from Trinity & St. Philip's Cathedral. *In the rear:* The Reverend Louis H. Berry, rector *(second from left)* and Gladys Churchman's son, James E. Churchman, Jr. *(center).* (Courtesy of Dr. Edith C. Churchman.)

Above left, E. Alma Williams, East Side High School Class of 1935. (Courtesy of Dr. E. Alma Flagg.)

Above right, E. Alma Flagg reading a poem at a 1970s community event. (Courtesy of Dr. E. Alma Flagg.)

Above left, A group of Newark educators in the 1950s. *From the left:* E. Alma Flagg, Philip Hoggard, Marjorie Tate, Mary Vickers, William R. Jackson, Grace Baxter Fenderson, and attorney Herbert Tate. (Courtesy of Dr. E. Alma Flagg.)

Above right, E. Alma Flagg receiving the Kean University Alumni Award in 1966 from the president of the alumni association. *In the background, from the left:* Eugene G. Wilkins (the college president) and Alma Flagg's mother, husband, and children. (Courtesy of Dr. E. Alma Flagg.)

Dr. E. Mae McCarroll, Newark City Hospital's first black physician, conducting a research project. (Author's collection.)

Dr. E. Mae McCarroll *(right)* and her friend Dr. Eva Brodkin at an exhibit on women doctors at the George Smith Library of the University of Medicine and Dentistry of New Jersey. (Courtesy of Gwen Cooper.)

Dr. E. Mae McCarroll on the cover of *The Crisis*, the Urban League's magazine, in 1934. (Author's collection.)

Dr. E. Mae McCarroll with her husband, Robert Hunter. (Courtesy of Gwen Cooper.)

Miss Rhapsody with trombonist Clyde Bernhardt in the early 1970s on the balcony of her Newark apartment. (Author's collection.)

Miss Rhapsody and the Harlem Blues and Jazz Band in Denmark in September 1976: Tommy Benford, George James, Clyde Bernhardt, Franc Williams, Miss Rhapsody, Barbara Dreiwitz, and Dill Jones. (Author's collection.)

Viola Wells, Miss Rhapsody. (Author's collection.)

Rhap singing the blues on a 1970s tour of Europe with the Harlem Blues and Jazz Band. (Author's collection.)

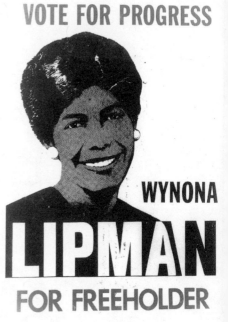

Above left, Senator Wynona Lipman (right) with her aunt, Lillian Moore Wallace; her sister, Eloise; and their father, John W. Moore, Sr., at the family homestead in LaGrange, Georgia, in the 1940s. *Seated in the foreground:* Her younger brother, Donald Moore. (Courtesy of Saundra DeGeneste.)

Above right, Election poster from Wynona Lipman's first run for Essex County office (1967). (Courtesy of Saundra DeGeneste.)

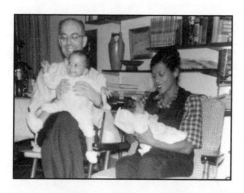

Above left, Matthew and Wynona Lipman at home in Montclair, with Karen on Matthew's lap and baby Will on Wynona's. (Courtesy of Saundra DeGeneste.)

Above right, The senator addressing a luncheon audience. (Courtesy of Saundra DeGeneste.)

Above left, Mary Beasley's high school graduation photograph. (Courtesy of Dolores Ollie.)

Above right, Mary Beasley Burch and Dr. Reynold E. Burch at a Newark social event. (Courtesy of Dr. Robert Spellman.)

Above left, Leaguer youngsters taking part in an early cotillion. (Courtesy of Dr. Robert Spellman.)

Above right, Mary Burch and her assistants planning an event at The Leaguers' office. (Courtesy of Dr. Robert Spellman.)

Top left, William Alexander and Bernice Murray on their wedding day in 1944. (Courtesy of Marion A. Bolden.)

Top right, A reluctant Marion Bolden going for a ride at age three. (Courtesy of Marion A. Bolden.)

Bottom left, First day of school, 2001: The superintendent gets a hug. (Courtesy of Marion A. Bolden.)

Bottom right, Marion Bolden all dressed up for a night out. (Courtesy of Marion A. Bolden.)

6

WYNONA M. LIPMAN

The Steel Magnolia | ?–1999

The night was sultry, filled with the scent of magnolias wafting through the hot summer night's air of LaGrange, Georgia. Ten-year-old Kathryn Penn, visiting her grandparents on school vacation, and her cousin Wynona Moore, roughly three years her junior, were asleep in an upstairs bedroom of the family homestead on the edge of town. Suddenly the sky was aglow. A huge wooden cross was burning on the front lawn.

"When the sky lit up, it looked so beautiful I called out, 'Grandma! Grandma! Come see the pretty lights,'" Kathryn said, reflecting on that night years ago when the reality of racism came calling at her family's doorstep. In a flash, Wynona's parents, John Wesley Moore and Annabelle Torian Moore, rushed to the children's bedrooms, hurrying them away from the windows to a safer part of the house.

"As a little girl from the North, I knew nothing about racial discrimination or the Ku Klux Klan," said Kathryn Penn Carr, whose father, the Reverend William Garland Penn, was an esteemed Chicago preacher. "That was the first time I was aware of being treated differently than anyone else." But it was hardly the last. Soon after, a country carnival came to town. "We were having lots of fun," said Carr. "Then

I saw a group of white women point at my cousins and me, saying, 'Those children are a good bunch of little niggers.' "

As they now knew, they were and it seemed they always would be second-class citizens. Negroes. Coloreds. Niggers. Whatever those who looked down on them wanted to call them, behind their backs or to their faces. And there was no escape, other than through their ingenuity. In those days, LaGrange, located midway between Atlanta and Tuskegee, Alabama, had a population of about twenty thousand—three-quarters white, the rest black or Native Americans.

As for many southern families, life in the Moore household revolved around hearth and home, their huge house with its welcoming wraparound porch at 508 Union Street. Set in the middle of a triangular strip on the outskirts of town, amid a grove of tall trees, theirs was one of the largest houses around, an attraction of sorts because it was owned by Negroes. "Often, poor whites stopped by to ask for tours," recalled Lipman's niece, Saundra DeGeneste. "My grandmother would just shoo them away."

From a child's perspective, growing up in LaGrange, even in the midst of the Great Depression and despite the hostility of the KKK, was almost idyllic, according to Carr, a retired Los Angeles library supervisor. Carr's mother, Marie E. Moore, was the sister of John Wesley Moore, Wynona's father. "As children, Wynona and I were very close," she said. "Every Sunday we went to Warren Temple Methodist Church, where my uncle was a trustee. We were always on the program. I would read a poem and Wynona, who loved to dance, would do the Dance of the Seven Veils." At night, the children often entertained the family, a common practice in U.S. homes in the days before the advent of television and the widespread use of automobiles led to a myriad of distractions from family unity. "We loved to put on plays with the adults as our audience," Carr noted.

At the same time, however, Kathryn and her cousins were beginning to come to grips with the reality of coming from an African-American family that was well educated and upwardly mobile in a small southern town where most of the white population consisted of poor, uneducated farmers. Until the night of the cross burning, neither Kathryn nor her cousins John, Eloise, Wynona, and Donald Moore had any idea that their very existence was cause for threats to them and their family. Nevertheless, organizations like the KKK were the order of the day in the South and beyond. No black person was truly safe.

As far as family and friends can remember, Wynona Moore Lipman never mentioned the cross burning or the incident at the fair in later life. Yet those incidents taught her to cope with discrimination, whatever its form. Years later, after she became the first black woman in New Jersey elected to the state senate, she experienced all sorts of slights, particularly in the early part of her twenty-seven-year tenure. As the only female member and the lone black woman in the senate for most of that time, whatever anger Lipman felt when challenged because of her race or sex, sometimes both, was tempered by her understanding of the situation, along with her southern graciousness and superb sense of humor.

"Ya can't teach an old dog new tricks," she told friends when the cadre of mostly white men who ruled New Jersey government refused to address her as "Senator," insisting that "Mrs. Lipman" would do. Yet she was "one of the boys" when she had to use the bathroom. Because the senate had no women's lavatory, she was forced to use the men's room with a state trooper standing guard outside the door.

All this time, "Wynona was laughing at those old coots," said Lipman's niece, Dr. Karen Moore, an Atlanta pediatrician, whose father was Wynona's youngest brother, Donald. "In our family, we were raised to believe that we were the smartest and the best. What white people had to say didn't matter." Lipman, a Fulbright scholar who taught French to Dr. Martin Luther King, Jr., before settling in New Jersey after her marriage, could more than handle the situation.

Candid yet gracious, she faced with ease every challenge that confronted her as a black woman in a white man's world. She used her intellectual superiority to deflect any and all criticisms. In the long run, she was the one who endured, winning reelection time and again over the course of nearly three decades, as her most ardent critics in the legislature gradually fell by the wayside.

"Wynona was a maverick in every sense of the word," said Mary Singletary, a former director of the New Jersey Division on Women. "She was very determined to get her issues across and her bills passed. That didn't sit well with the men. It was hard for them to respect a woman, never mind a black woman. That's why she wasn't part of the club."

Even so, Lipman rarely complained, sloughing off the constant urgings of her aide, Nia Gill, to lash out against such terrible treatment. "She'd tell me, 'Baby Doll, there's more than one way to skin a cat,' " said Gill, who encountered similar criticisms years later after her election to the senate. "Eventually, I learned that the senator was better at the game the old boys were playing than the old boys themselves. Instead of challenging the system, she transformed it." For the most part, the challenges Lipman faced in Trenton stood in sharp contrast to her upbringing.

Despite his lack of a formal education, the first John Wesley Moore, Wynona's paternal grandfather, owned his own contracting company. According to family lore, he used matchsticks to figure his finances because he could not add or subtract. Like many southern families, the Moores were racially mixed. Lipman's paternal grandmother, Mary Edmondson Moore, was a twin, the daughter of William P. Edmondson, a Scottish farmer from nearby Antioch, Georgia, and his concubine, Mary Ann Stewart. It is believed that Stewart, the family cook, was a full-blooded Creek, brought to Georgia from North Carolina. She was just twelve or so when northern soldiers rode through LaGrange, telling blacks that the Civil War was over and they were free.

Her twins, Mary and Mark, were given the surname Edmondson. Interestingly, the 2000 census shows 400 people named Edmondson and 250 others named Edmundson living in LaGrange. Despite his children's racial mix, Wynona's white great-grandfather insisted that his kin, regardless of color, get to know one another. Through the years he encouraged them to interact at weddings and funerals, even though many relatives, both black and white, disliked being associated with the other side of the family.

To their credit, some family members got along famously. "My grandmother's half-brother, who was from the Scottish side of the family, was the chief of police in LaGrange," said Carr. "When they saw each other, they would run and hug," no doubt a strange site in a segregated southern town during the 1930s.

Like her grandfather and father, Lipman's white great-grandfather was a successful businessman. Not only did he own five hundred acres of land; he also ran the only grocery store in Antioch. Nevertheless, Lipman's father, who became John Wesley Moore, Sr., at his father's death, is considered the source of the family's wealth. For thirty-three years he operated the People's Drug Store on Hines Street in LaGrange, but his ambition did not stop there. He also was a contractor for the Newman Construction Company and was affiliated with the Daniel Lumber Company, building scores of houses and stores in and around the town.

When Moore died, in December 1951, his death was noted on the front page of the local newspaper, a testament to his standing in the community. Generally, Negro death notices were confined to the "colored section" of the paper, but his obituary, which told of the death of a "prominent Negro," was up front on page ten.

Lipman's mother, Annabelle Torian Moore, was born in Hopkinsville, Kentucky, in 1894 and raised beginning at the turn of the century by her grandmother, a black woman named Clara Hatcher. Little is known about Annabelle's parents, Elizabeth Torian Hatcher and James H. Torian, except that they died before she was six years old. In the 1900 census, Annabelle Torian is listed as a "mulatto" (of mixed white and black heritage). Apparently she was a privileged young lady, for she attended the Haines Normal and Industrial Institute, a boarding school for Negro girls in Augusta, Georgia. Founded in 1886 by Lucy Craft Laney in the basement of Christ Presbyterian Church, the school was a teacher training institution. In 1912 Annabelle enrolled at Atlanta University.

Lipman's father, one of ten children, attended Atlanta University in 1905 but dropped out. Family members believe he returned to LaGrange to help with the family business. They also presume he met his wife, Annabelle, a decade later while two of his younger sisters, Alice and Hattie, were students at Atlanta University. Whereas the senator's mother was progressive and well educated, her father was from the old school. "Her job, as he saw it, was to stay home and raise their children," said DeGeneste, a supervisor in the Newark Public Schools.

John Wesley Moore, Sr., and Annabelle Torian married on July 2, 1915, as the nation was about to enter World War I. Wynona was the second of their children. Both she and her sister, Eloise, the only remaining sibling, pursued careers in teaching. Their brothers, John Wesley Moore, Jr., the oldest child, and Donald Torian Moore, the youngest, both graduated from Meharry Medical College, one of just two black American medical colleges at that time. (The other was Howard Medical School in Washington, D.C.) John Wesley Moore practiced general medicine in Detroit for many years. His brother Donald, an obstetrician-gynecologist, became the first black surgeon to perform an operation at Duke University.

When Annabelle Moore died, in July 1945, Donald Moore, her youngest child, was just twelve. By that time, her son John was a captain in the army on medical duty in San Francisco. Wynona was teaching in Atlanta, not far from LaGrange. Eloise was a teacher in Washington, D.C. In a letter to John following their mother's death, which occurred just days after her parents' thirtieth wedding anniversary, Wynona told how, after their mother became ill and the family doctor could not be located, their father had "searched this broken-down town" to find a physician.

"This is one of the most difficult letters that I have ever had to write," she informed her brother. "I don't know where to begin or what to say. If you could just be here, telling it would be so much easier." Lipman told how their mother was "stricken ill on Tuesday before last" after showing no signs that anything was wrong. "She went to the show with us Monday night and was the life of the party," she wrote. "Tuesday morning, she got up, fixed Daddy's breakfast, got up the clothes, and went out to work in the yard. She got an awful headache, came in the house, and went to lie in her bed. By noon she was very ill."

On Wednesday, at their mother's request, Wynona and Eloise packed a bag and took her to the hospital. Through Saturday she remained in the same condition, rallying a bit at times but nevertheless very sick. She had a bad heart and also was suffering from kidney trouble. The following Monday night, Wynona wrote, "Weese [Eloise] woke her for her supper and was feeding her when Daddy came and suddenly, without anyone realizing what was happening, Mama went away. We thought that Daddy would die too," she went on. "I walked the backyard with him for hours."

"The service was Thursday," Wynona related. "Mama had friends everywhere. She looked so pretty lying there. Her dress was gray and white and the bier steel gray. Son [her brother's nickname], as if it were by a miracle, all the worry lines smoothed out of her forehead and it seemed that she was about to smile. We had all the songs she loves and her grave seemed a carpet of magically growing beautiful flowers. It was so beautiful that it practically tore me apart."

The dilemma after the funeral was what to do with young Donald. Who would raise him? Wynona and Eloise both wanted to watch over him. In the end, Donald stayed in LaGrange, as his father wanted, since his father's youngest sister, Lil, soon would be coming to live with them. "Poor little fellow," said Wynona. "He did love his 'buddy' [their mother] so much."

At the time, Eloise was teaching music. Wynona, who had completed her undergraduate work at Talladega College in Alabama and received her master's degree from Atlanta University, eventually would be off to Europe to continue her studies. As fate would have it, Wynona could not have met Matthew Lipman, her husband-to-be, in a more romantic place. "We were both Fulbright scholars on our way to Paris aboard a beautiful ocean liner," Matt Lipman recalled. "The crossing took us eight days."

Right off, they clicked. In addition to their scholarly pursuits, their personalities meshed. They liked doing things together and began keeping company. At the Sorbonne, she studied French. He was studying for his doctorate in philosophy. Young and idealistic, they found it an exciting time to be in Paris. And there were lots of interesting people to meet. "Wynona was staying at the International House," Lipman said. "The singers Matawilda Dobson and Leontyne Price also were staying there, probably because that's where most foreigners stayed."

After marrying at City Hall in Paris in 1952, the Lipmans spent the next several months in Vienna. "I was stretching out my Fulbright grant," he said. The fact that it was in philosophy was odd, for Lipman came from a farm in Woodbine, a rural community in southern New Jersey near Vineland hardly known for its wealth of philosophers.

Although some members of Wynona Lipman's family believe there was some consternation over their interracial marriage—he was white and she was black—Matt Lipman said he was never aware of any such concern.

"There was no problem at all with either of our families," he said. "Matt was a great guy," said Wynona's cousin, Dr. William Edmondson, who lived in Montclair and visited the couple often during their twenty-two years of marriage. "We had a lot of great times together. We never had any problems."

After graduating from high school, Matt Lipman studied for a year at Stanford University and then transferred to Columbia University in New York. He became a philosophy professor and taught at colleges for more than four decades. Both Lipman and his wife received their doctoral degrees from Columbia in 1954. Soon after, she was offered a professorship at Spelman College in Atlanta by Dr. Benjamin Mays, the president of Morehouse College. At Spelman she taught French and tutored many students, including Martin Luther King, a Morehouse man.

"During that time, I didn't have a full-time job," Matt Lipman said. "Wynona stayed in Atlanta three years and then came up to New York, where we got an apartment in Greenwich Village. She had a job teaching at a high school. At some point, the secretary at the school told us about a house being built in Montclair. We decided to take a look at it."

The large rambling house at 121 Chestnut Street, opposite Montclair High School, was just what they wanted. By that time their income had improved significantly. He was now on the faculty at Columbia University, where he taught for eighteen years. He also held part-time teaching jobs at City College of New York and the Mannes School of Music.

After the move to Montclair, Wynona left Elizabeth Irwin High School in New York and took a part-time job at a school for neurologically impaired children. Soon she and Matt Lipman had two children, Karen, who was born in 1960, and Will, who arrived a year later. Years later, she suffered the most painful experience of her life when Will, who was just twenty-two, died of Hodgkin's disease. Karen later moved to Atlanta, where she operated her own business.

Wynona Lipman got into politics the way many people do—as a district leader representing the people of her neighborhood. "There was some kind of issue over snow piling up near the school our children attended," Matt Lipman said. "With other parents from the PTA, she went to a town meeting to protest. At that time, the Montclair Democrats were split, so they would always lose to the Republicans. They liked the way Wynona presented herself and decided she should be Democratic chairman of the town. They thought she could unite the two sides, which she successfully did."

At Wynona's urging, Nia Gill, the family babysitter, also was getting a taste of politics, assisting the senator-to-be with voter registration drives and setting strategies to bring Montclair Democrats back into power. "The senator's home was a hotbed of activity in those days," said Gill, whose pastime as a college student was discussing philosophical issues with Matt Lipman. "Wynona had a hundred things going on at the same time, and she handled them all equally well," said Gill. "Her persistence got people to work with her. They gravitated to her. If you worked, she'd open up avenues for you."

Soon after Lipman united Montclair's Democratic Party, she was tapped to run for county office. From her earliest days on the stump, friends said it was apparent that politics and public life consumed her, sometimes to the detriment of family life. Whatever the case, and however it affected their marriage, Matt Lipman had only good things to say about his former wife and her entry into big-time politics in 1967.

"Harry Lerner, the county chairman, urged Wynona to run for a seat on the Essex County Freeholder Board, which she did and won," Lipman said. "He thought she was the kind of neutral person who would make a good board president, so she became president of the board. It was a rough job," he said, looking back on his former wife's election to the board. "Budgets had to be examined, and there were all kinds of legislative issues to be considered and arguments to settle."

One of the most heated arguments Wynona had was with Essex County Assignment Judge James Giuliano. "I don't remember many of the details, except that it was eventually settled," Lipman said. "Wynona didn't back down easily. She accused the judge of being unfair politically. She thought she could successfully challenge him, and she did."

The clash between Wynona Lipman and Giuliano occurred during the freeholder board's budget hearings in January 1971, at a time when the board members were risking a contempt-of-court order for refusing to appropriate certain court-mandated items. Lipman became irate after Giuliano spent an hour before the board criticizing John Cryan, the county sheriff. That tactic, she charged, was a subterfuge meant to camouflage $2 million in excessive spending by the courts.

She subsequently sent a stinging letter to New Jersey Chief Justice Joseph Weintraub, blasting Giuliano for conduct she claimed was "disrespectful" and "disruptive." In a separate action, she urged the legislature to exert "control over the court's runaway spending practices." Giuliano refused to comment publicly on the matter, but another member of the freeholder board, C. Stewart Hausman, characterized Lipman's criticisms of the judge as "unwarranted." He argued that it was Lipman who owed an apology to Giuliano. "If the board doesn't want to apologize, then I don't want to be associated with the letter," Hausman said. He then issued his personal apology to the judge.

Although those who knew Lipman best described her as a warrior when she perceived an injustice like the Giuliano incident, some of her friends thought she bent too much to the whims of New Jersey's political bosses. "Everyone used Wynona one way or another because she was a good heart. People liked her for her candidness, but she also was a soft touch," said Lipman's friend and Montclair neighbor Jennie Brown.

"But as smart as she was, she really was a creature of the system." Brown said. "Politics consumed her. She was not a TV watcher. She was not terribly into gossip. When I'd joke with her, after her divorce, and tell her to get a boyfriend, she'd just laugh and say, 'I don't see anyone out there.'" Not that Lipman lacked an eye for handsome men. Years later, after meeting President Clinton, she told her friend Dorothea Lee in her fluid southern drawl, "Dor-o-thea! He's gor-ge-ous!"

Another friend believes Lipman's political feistiness mellowed as she grew older. He pointed particularly to Wynona's association with Newark Mayor Sharpe James, who succeeded her in the senate. "Whatever Sharpe wanted done in the legislature, Wynona did," he said. "As a loyal Democrat, she never questioned him. She was his point person in Trenton."

One thing was for sure—Lipman was a survivor. As elegant as she looked in her couturier clothes and as unruffled as she seemed, she knew exactly how to play politics. While other legislators came and went, she won election time and time again. Not that fretting was alien to her.

"Wynona was a worrier," said Brown. "To the end, she feared that someone would come along and beat her. She also worried about being dumped off the Democratic line. But there was no one out there. No worthy opposition. I'd tell her no one was going to beat her or take her off the line. But she was still worried." The reality, of course, was that Lipman had nothing to fear. Elaine Guarino, the last Republican to run against her, in 1997, found that out when Lipman captured 86 percent of the vote. When the final count was in, she always swamped her opponents.

At annual fund-raising breakfasts that Lipman gave to support her campaign drives, she often told the crowd that her legislative colleague Assemblyman Willie Brown planned to run against her. Although other politicians viewed him as a possible opponent, he denied any such intentions "She'd say that," said Willie Brown, who met Lipman when she was running for freeholder-at-large in Newark's South Ward, where she settled after moving from Montclair, "but it wasn't true. I wasn't crazy. I knew that there were more women than men in the district. Why would I run against her and lose, when I could run with her as a team and win?"

On the stump, Lipman was humble, sincere, and friendly, just as she was in everyday life. She shook every hand, listened to every problem, and acted on every issue affecting her constituents. Whereas other senators concerned themselves with the demands of big businesses and special-interest groups, her favorite issues were the rights of women, children, and families. As evidenced by the bills she introduced and worked doggedly to turn into law, she was their protector. Her bills addressed issues such as domestic violence, child abuse, child safety, welfare rights, education, and HIV/AIDS. No matter what some of her friends thought, she always stood up for what she thought was right and fair, a methodology that did not always sit well with the Democratic party bosses.

"Within the party or outside of it, Wynona knew what it took to win and how to do it," said longtime friend Dr. Julia Miller. "The first time I ran for district leader in Montclair, I lost. The next time, Wynona took me down to the courthouse and showed me the ropes. I won 10 to 1. Wynona and I knew each other from the Unitarian Church in Montclair, where we were both active," Miller said. "But we didn't become good friends until I ran for district leader."

By that time, a reform movement was underway in Essex County. Soon Lipman and Miller—Judy to her friends—were in the forefront of the Good Government Democrats, a group of black Democrats mostly from Montclair and Newark. When Harry Lerner, a longtime Democratic pol, decided to challenge Essex County Democratic Chairman Dennis Carey for control of the party, the black Democrats propelled themselves into the catbird seat.

"When they came to us, we behaved like we had many more members than we did," said Miller. "We included every black committeeman and committeewoman in Essex County in our count, although many of them did not know it. We wanted the county leaders to think we were in total control of the black vote, even though we weren't. If we were going to deliver our vote for the party, there were things that we wanted, we told Lerner and whoever else came our way," Miller said. "We had issues, and largely with Wynona's help, we set our strategy. Primarily, we wanted a black freeholder on the Democratic slate, and we wanted a black judge. Wynona, of course, was the freeholder candidate. Herb Tate, Sr. [a prominent black attorney], also from Montclair, was the one we wanted for judge." After Lerner won the chairmanship, the black coalition, known as the Black Block, failed to win a judgeship for Tate. But Lipman got the nod for freeholder, ran on the Democratic line, and won. Soon after, the Black Block disbanded.

As a member of the freeholder board, the county's legislative arm, Lipman went right to work. She was all over the place, speaking on the radio, meeting with constituents, and sponsoring workshops to better inform the public of issues that affected them and their rights. Early on, she won praise for phasing out the county sanitarium, an obsolete facility that operated more like a prison than a hospital. She also got the state to take charge of the few remaining patients.

With the county's reform Democrats firmly in charge of the board by a 6–3 margin, she was elected freeholder director in December 1970. She replaced Raymond Stabile, a Republican who was loyal to a dissident faction of his party. In her new role, one of Lipman's major concerns was wanton spending by county officials. In early 1971, just weeks after she became director, she ordered a review of the county budget, calling for massive cuts in spending, an issue that led to her flare-up with Giuliano.

"The cry for economy in government cannot be ignored," she said. "It is our responsibility to do whatever is necessary to save every penny possible. Despite our reduction of nearly $10 million in our proposed budget, I believe a professional study of every department will enable us to effect even greater savings. Major changes are needed," she concluded, "changes that can be accomplished only with the cooperation of the legislative and political leaders in both parties."

One of the freeholder board's key concerns was the overwhelming burden of public assistance and other residuals of poverty paid for by the average person. At the time, Essex taxpayers were picking up 80 percent of the $111.8 million county budget. The county court system was another burden. "While I'm no efficiency expert, the amount of work which seems to have built up on warrants which the sheriff has assigned his detectives, seems a vast amount," Lipman concluded. She then requested a meeting with New Jersey Chief Justice Joseph Weintraub to discuss the possibilities of a state takeover of the county courts.

Similarly, she wanted the state to assume a larger portion of the staggering cost of welfare benefits in Essex County. Local welfare agencies, she argued, were spending far too much for fraud investigations with little to show for it, thereby jeopardizing the chances of the county to obtain an increase in the state's share of welfare costs from 75 percent to 90 percent. "The state would hardly care to relieve the county of a financial burden only to have more funds squandered at the county level," she declared.

In her role as a county official, Lipman also campaigned fervently for the rights of prisoners and drug addicts. When five inmates were brutally beaten at the Essex County Corrections Center in Caldwell, she called for a grand jury investigation. "It is better that a grand jury act to prevent a crisis before it occurs than to be brought in afterward to perform a post-mortem exercise," she told the press. Soon after, she came up with a jail reform plan to relieve overcrowding at the center. In an effort to assist county residents being treated for drug addiction, Lipman argued that employment was key to their rehabilitation.

That concern led to her 1971 appeal to Newark Mayor Kenneth Gibson to assist methadone maintenance patients being treated at county facilities. She wanted the mayor to hire patients who were Newark residents by using $4.6 million in federal funds received under the Emergency Employment Act of 1971.

"Wynona was a scrapper," said Judy Miller. "She'd fight for what she wanted, no matter what." That brand of independence, however, did not always sit well with the party chiefs, particularly coming from a woman. Although they could tolerate Lipman's devotion to other issues, her speaking out so frankly on political matters greatly troubled them. As a result, she knocked heads with Lerner, the iron-fisted party boss, soon after she became freeholder board director.

Bucking the Old Guard, Lipman decided to support a group of Democrats seeking the reform of county government. They were pressing for a county executive at the helm, a change that would greatly diminish the freeholders' power. Not only did Lipman support the reform movement; she also supported Peter Shapiro, the movement's candidate. With her help, he became Essex County's first executive.

When Shapiro won the election, Lipman was elated. But Lerner was furious, and she had to face his wrath. Surprisingly, Lerner took an easy way out. Rather than dump Lipman, whose popularity in the community was growing, he made her Essex County's Democratic candidate for the state senate. "Harry Lerner decided to kick me upstairs," she told friends.

For both of them, but especially for her constituents, the move proved to be a stroke of political genius. For the next three decades, she was a Democratic force at the state level, rarely taking a respite from seventy-hour weeks. "What I admired most about Wynona was the strength and courage that she possessed and her willingness to help people, regardless of what walk of life they came from," said her niece Saundra DeGeneste. "To the very end of her life, she was still helping people."

By the time Lipman accepted her party's nomination and ran for the senate in November 1971, the house on Chestnut Street in Montclair was like a substation of the Democratic Party. "It was very busy," said Matt Lipman. "The kids were running around. And all kinds of people were in and out, stuffing envelopes, discussing issues, and developing strategies."

Ordinarily, Lipman would have been a shoo-in for the senate. That all changed when the area she would represent was redistricted. To run in Newark, as the party now wanted, she would have to live in Newark. Lipman said his wife's decision to move to Newark practically came out of nowhere. "I think the worst thing for me was that it came as a surprise," he said.

Before long, their marriage of more than two decades had crumbled, and they divorced. She moved to Newark. He stayed in Montclair. To this day, the mild-mannered Lipman bristles when he thinks of the news coverage of the divorce. "Reports that it was acrimonious were totally untrue," he said. "Unfortunately, Wynona thought some of the incorrect information that appeared in the newspapers came from me." Nevertheless, they stayed in touch over the years, talking on the phone and getting together occasionally. Long since remarried, Matt Lipman still lives in Montclair.

In Newark, Wynona Lipman settled into a spacious apartment at Bel Air Towers, a luxury building overlooking Weequahic Park. Unfortunately, it eventually began deteriorating and was shuttered in 2001, two years after the senator's death. "When it started going downhill, I used to beg Wynona to move," said Jennie Brown. "She'd talk about it, but she always came up with all kinds of excuses." For years, however, the simple fact that a state senator lived in what was then a luxurious building seemed to keep the owners and managers in check. "I guess they were afraid she would use her political influence if things weren't right," a neighbor said.

Lipman's senate office was downtown at the Robert Treat Hotel at 50 Park Place, cramped but adequate for her purposes, since she was in Trenton so much of the time. Although she introduced 130 bills during almost three decades of service in the senate, she was just as well known for her devotion to her constituents. "She always helped people from the community," said Abbie Stebbins, a longtime Democratic district leader in Newark. "When I worked at the Family Service Bureau of Newark, it was very difficult for people in need to get Supplemental Social Income, so I'd call her office. She never said no."

Over the years, Lipman had many aides. Two of them, Nia Gill and Christy Davis, went on to important political careers of their own. Gill served several terms in the state assembly before being elected to the senate after her mentor's death. Davis, who once ran the New Jersey office of U.S. Senator Frank Lautenberg and then became campaign manager for

U.S. Senator Jon Corzine, is now the vice president in charge of governmental affairs at the University of Medicine and Dentistry of New Jersey.

"As a teenager, I thought the senator was too hip," said Gill. "She had lived in Greenwich Village, studied in Paris, and wore one long braid down her back. At thirteen or fourteen, I wanted to emulate her. As her aide during college and law school, my appreciation of her grew day by day. She would permit me to represent her even though I had an Afro and wore African traditional clothes. Being sent by the senator provided a safety zone for me, a level of acceptance that men give other men but women rarely get from each other." Gill was also struck by Lipman's intellect. "The senator had a mind like a steel trap, which greatly impressed me," she said. "Yet she never used her superior intelligence or education to make others feel inferior. She taught me to look at a situation, determine the level of power involved, and take it from there."

Like Gill, Desiree Gordon was a teenager when Lipman hired her in 1968 to stuff campaign envelopes at a Bloomfield Avenue storefront in Montclair. "What I remember most is that she always treated us with respect and did so much to help so many people in the community," Gordon said. "We were just kids, but she made sure we got our working papers and Social Security numbers. She paid us and made us feel like we had real jobs."

Della Moses Walker, who worked for Lipman in the early 1980s, recalled how impressed she was with Lipman long before she went to work for her. "My aunt Vera [Brantley McMillon], was getting an award at a dinner," Walker said. "After Senator Lipman spoke, she went from table to table. She shook every hand, which I thought was pretty amazing because you could see how sincere she was. She just wasn't campaigning. "When I became her aide, I learned everything there was to learn about the work ethic from her. Her aides had three shifts—from 8 A.M. to 4, 4 to 8, and 8 to midnight. She started at 8 in the morning and finished at midnight." Walker's main responsibility was Lipman's telephone log. "Every time one of her constituents called, my job was to record the person's name, phone number, and problem," Walker said. "Senator Lipman would call in every thirty minutes, get the list, and personally answer every call. She was remarkable. She helped everybody."

"In the way she lived her life, Senator Lipman was the conscience of the senate," Senator Richard Codey, her Essex County colleague, told reporters after her death in 1999. Codey, who became New Jersey's acting governor in 2004, added, "She was the senate's most active voice for equality and the preeminent role model for women in New Jersey."

Although outwardly Lipman was always smiling and gracious, the epitome of the southern belle, inwardly she was a pit bull, fiercely protective of her turf. The paradox won her the nickname "the Steel Magnolia." Lipman's political savvy and resilience became apparent in 1985, when Senator John Russo, a fellow Democrat, attempted to replace her as head of the State Government Committee. Quickly, she struck back where it hurt most—in the press. "I didn't cotton to the idea," she told a reporter. "He consistently voted against minority bills." Russo vehemently denied the charge, saying each of his votes was based on the merit of the situation.

About the same time, Lipman laid into Senate Majority Leader John Lynch for attempting to create a study commission for pension bills. His bill, which required a review of each measure before it went to her State Government Committee, was merely a subterfuge for gutting it, she argued. "It seemed awfully insulting that we should have this committee digest the work of the committee before we do it."

Lipman's quirky habits, as well as her sex and race, made her an anomaly in the senate. Some senators labeled her spacey. For years, rumors abounded that she was a heavy drinker. Her family said she was not. "Other than wine, I can't ever remember her having a drink," said DeGeneste. "Wynona was very disarming," said former Governor Brendan Byrne. "She often gave the impression that she wasn't listening, but she knew everything that was going on. She'd let you know what she wanted you to know. There were times when I had to bring her into my office to discuss certain pieces of legislation, but I don't think there was ever a time that we differed philosophically. We were on the same track."

One of the most painstaking tasks Lipman took on was cleaning up the sexist language that permeated New Jersey laws. After convincing her male colleagues to establish a commission to carry out that task, she became its chairperson. "It didn't matter to Wynona that I was a Republican," said Mary Singletary, who served on the commission as director of the New Jersey Division on Women. "The important thing was that we were both interested in the same issues. This was one of them."

Over the years, Lipman sponsored scores of bills that focused primarily on the rights of families, the young, and the downtrodden. Though it seemed simple, her strategy was very clever. Systematically, she set about making change. Once a bill on one of her favorite subjects became law, she would build on it, introducing one companion measure after another. A review of the bills she sponsored on domestic violence attests to this point:

- 1978: Permitted domestic violence shelters to be located in residential areas of towns.
- 1979: Established clear legal definitions of domestic violence, toughened penalties for domestic violence, and required reporting of domestic violence incidents by municipal and state police.
- 1994–1995: Allowed domestic violence victims to register to vote without disclosing a street address.

"She knew what she wanted to achieve, but she understood that she might not get it all in one big bite," Kathleen Crotty, executive director of the senate Democrats, told the press.

Many of the times that Lipman went to Trenton to sponsor education bills, her friend Judy Miller accompanied her. "Watching Wynona in action was wonderful because she was so deceiving," said Miller, a former director of African-American Studies at Seton Hall University. "She would sit very quietly, slowly and carefully developing her ideas on what she thought should be done and how it should be done. Then, she'd zing them. She was always calm but very strong. From the time we were Good Government Democrats, it was clear that she was the most capable one among us," Miller said. "She always knew what we needed to do, which was true in the senate too. Her analysis was sharp, and she was very vocal."

Although Lipman proved exceptionally skillful at getting her bills past both legislative houses and signed into law by governor after governor, she did not win all of the battles. When Lipman introduced a 1996 senate bill that called for the creation of a needle-exchange pilot program to allow syringes to be sold over the counter without a prescription, a furor erupted. Opposed by Governor Christie Whitman and Senator Ronald Rice, the bill languished in the legislature.

"We all knew that Wynona wanted to stop the spread of AIDS, but the bill she proposed was very controversial," said former assemblyman Willie Brown, whose career in the lower house paralleled Lipman's in the senate. "Although I was from Newark too, the needle-exchange bill put me in a dilemma," he said. "Most people thought it was tantamount to legalizing drugs. That was the main argument against it."

"Wynona liked taking the train to Trenton, but I'd drive her and her aides back, dropping them off along the way,' said Ron Rice, who served also as West Ward councilman in Newark. "We used to have it out in the car, debating all the issues she thought I'd voted on the wrong way. In her southern drawl, she'd say, 'Ron, now why did you do that?' Her needle-exchange bill was a constant argument."

Nevertheless, Lipman pressed on. Despite Rice's opposition to the measure on the home front, Lipman found support in Newark for the bill from Central Ward Councilman George Branch, who introduced an ordinance to allow a needle-exchange program within the city limits. That measure, too, failed to garner enough votes. Again, Lipman was devastated, a wound that never healed "In her final days, I asked her if she felt her life was a failure in any way," Jennie Brown said. "This, and the fact that she didn't spend more time with her children, was her greatest disappointment."

By the mid-1990s it had become clear that Lipman was slowing down. Some friends thought it was because she was getting on in age, although few people knew how old she was. Whenever the question of age came up, generally for a newspaper article, she would say that there was no official record of her birth. Sometimes she claimed that the Georgia courthouse where the papers were kept burned down long ago.

With her health failing, Lipman looked haggard. Always thin and elegant, she was thinner yet. She had dropped at least ten pounds, said Saundra DeGeneste. For DeGeneste, who grew up in Detroit, Lipman's illness offered an opportunity to truly get to know the aunt she had rarely seen as a child. "I knew that my father had a sister in New Jersey who was married to a white professor, but that was it," she said. "The family was not all that close, so I'm not surprised we didn't see more of each other.

"After Wynona, married, I didn't hear much about her. I'm not sure if the fact that Matt was white entered into it at all. My guess would be that the men in our family, my father included, were chauvinists. As a result, they were not all that supportive of Wynona or interested in her accomplishments."

DeGeneste's first encounter with her aunt came in 1967 during a visit to Montclair. "Detroit was country by comparison, so I was greatly impressed by my aunt," she said. "She was so cosmopolitan. So beautiful. So worldly. She had been to Paris. Here was this woman, my father's sister, who spoke French and had a doctorate." Despite the fact that the Moores come from mixed blood—more Native American than black or white—DeGeneste said she was enchanted, too, because her aunt had entered into an interracial marriage. "It was all very sophisticated to me," she said.

Fifteen years later, after moving to the Newark area, DeGeneste renewed her ties with Lipman, who was by then a state senator. Soon she began helping out part time at Wynona's office, designing campaign flyers. "Wynona was just like my grandfather—a workaholic," DeGeneste noted. "All of the Moores—my grandfather, my father, my uncle, and me—had that work ethic. My Dad worked until the day he died. Something must have happened at 508 Union Street, LaGrange, Georgia, that turned these people into workaholics."

Another common thread ran through the family— a commitment to serve others. "Wynona's interest in politics didn't surprise me because everyone in our family loved helping people," DeGeneste noted. "Both her brothers, my father and my uncle, were doctors, and their sister, Eloise, was a teacher."

Because her aunt was divorced and on her own, they would sometimes do things together socially. "We'd talk on the phone, and, when her time permitted, go to Martha's Vineyard, to Oak Bluffs," DeGeneste said. When Wynona Lipman became sick and was dying of cancer, DeGeneste became her caregiver— a challenging role, to say the least.

The Steel Magnolia was withering and having a hard time facing the reality of her situation. "Wynona clearly needed someone to care for her, and I felt it was my responsibility," her niece said. "But she could be very difficult. For one thing, she never gave me a key to her apartment, so I had to have the superintendent break the lock when she fell on the floor one night and couldn't get up.

"My aunt also would go to great lengths to protect her public persona. Because she lied so much about her age, I had trouble getting her Social Security benefits. They couldn't match their records with the year she said she was born. People in the senate had to pull strings so she could get her benefits.

"Because she was so vain, she would introduce me as her cousin. She didn't want people to think she had a niece as old as I am." Although Lipman's obituary said she was sixty-seven when she died, family members—who also remain in the dark about her age or would rather not comment—believe she was several years older.

During the last year of her life, Lipman was in and out of University Hospital in Newark. "She knew she was dying, but she was still very funny, making jokes about all the politicians she knew," said Lois Hull, a friend from Montclair who visited Lipman daily as the hospital's director of special projects. "She was very brave, not a difficult patient at all."

Lipman also was back and forth to Kessler Institute, a world-renowned rehabilitation center in West Orange, New Jersey. At Kessler, she worked exceptionally hard at her rehabilitation. She wanted to be able to walk again because she had a singular goal in mind: to return to Trenton to finish her term in the senate. "That's all she talked about," DeGeneste said. "Although it was clear to others that she was very sick, I think she convinced herself that she would go back to Trenton and be as good as new."

Most of all, she wanted to see her needle-exchange bill become law. Despite her failing health and the tremendous opposition to the measure, the Steel Magnolia still thought she could gain her colleagues' approval of the legislation. Lipman took her last trip to Trenton in the spring of 1999, just weeks before she died. "She was weak, but she was in her glory," said Ron Rice, her senate colleague. "As the first African-American woman elected to the senate, she had made history. No one could deny that."

In tribute to Lipman's many years of service in the senate, the entire legislature rose to applaud her that day. No longer was she Mrs. Lipman. At that point in time—on that day, at that moment—after twenty-seven years of service to the people of Newark and her adopted state of New Jersey—she was Senator Wynona Lipman.

Lipman died on May 9, 1999. More than five years later, on October 26, 2004, New Jersey Governor James E. McGreevey signed an executive order to allow three unspecified communities to operate needle-exchange pilot programs. Because the governor was leaving office in a matter of days, the order was the subject of much debate. Lipman's hard-fought effort to legalize a needle-exchange program got no mention in news accounts about the governor's action. Again, Rice was the most vocal opponent, joining forces with three other legislators to file suit, claiming that McGreevey had overstepped his legal limits as governor.

Through the years, Lipman has been lovingly remembered by her friends and colleagues. In October 2000, the Wynona Lipman Child Advocacy Center was dedicated in her memory at Children's Hospital of New Jersey at Newark–Beth Israel Medical Center in Newark. It serves troubled children who have been shuffled from agency to agency.

Later that month, former Congresswoman Shirley Chisholm, the first African-American woman to serve in the U.S. House of Representatives, became the first occupant of the Senator Wynona Lipman Chair in Women's Political Leadership at Rutgers University. The chair is endowed by the Center for American Women and Politics, an arm of the university's Eagleton Institute of Politics. Former Labor Secretary Alexis Herman was a later occupant.

In March 2001, Lipman was one of twenty-seven Newark achievers, past and present, chosen by Mayor Sharpe James as the first recipients of the Newark Citizen Recognition Awards. "We are what we are because of those who have come before us," dentist George Jenkins, one of the youngest recipients, told the crowd at City Hall that night. "My aunt would have liked that," said DeGeneste.

In July 2001, on the site where the crime-ridden, drug-infested projects known as Columbus Homes once stood, the Newark Housing Authority unveiled fifty-one units of attractive brickfront townhouses: the Wynona Lipman Gardens.

MARY BEASLEY BURCH

Beloved Philanthropist | 1906–2001

Mary Beasley Burch had no children of her own. Yet as the founder of an advocacy group for black youth, she was Ma Burch to thousands of Newark young people. With the help of her husband, Dr. Reynold E. (Buster) Burch, a beloved obstetrician, she was one of Newark's greatest philanthropists, managing to operate The Leaguers—one of Newark's largest social service agencies—without benefit of grants or public assistance for many years.

To all who knew her, she was a visionary, implementing social programs for young people decades before the federal government's conception of such programs. "She got us assistance for school long before college grants and loans became possible," said Donald Payne. "She taught us that being black and poor had nothing to do with our dignity and respect." Payne, who became New Jersey's first black congressman and is a former president of the Black Congressional Caucus, is one of The Leaguers' proudest products. In 1951 he received the organization's first college scholarship.

Founded in 1949 in the Burches' Newark home, The Leaguers has produced hundreds of doctors, dentists, educators, and other professionals. Some, like singer Dionne Warwick or Hazel O'Leary, energy secretary under Bill Clinton, have recognizable names. Hundreds of other graduates simply are better men and women, better parents, and better citizens because of the influence Mary and Buster Burch had on their development.

When Mary Burch died on August 8, 2001, at age ninety-five, black Newark was in mourning. "Losing Ma Burch was like losing another mother," said Robert Mobley, a retired Newark vice principal and former chairman of The Leaguers' board. "Whatever I am, whatever I've achieved, I owe to her. She meant everything to me."

"She didn't just help us," said Sesser Peoples, a retired Primerica Financial executive. "She knew everything about us. She knew our needs. She knew our parents. She knew if we were telling the truth or lying. That's why we always tried to live up to her expectations. We are what we are because we didn't want to let her down."

In the early days of The Leaguers, Mrs. Burch had no idea that the small group of teenagers she invited to gather in her apartment on South Fourteenth Street would become one of Newark's most respected youth groups. All she wanted to do was keep young people on track. "We had too many ruffians in the neighborhood," she said. "We didn't need more."

Soon, however, the group began taking on a life of its own. Word quickly spread that something good was happening on South Fourteenth Street. Other teenagers joined. A name was chosen: The Junior Leaguers. Officers were elected. In a matter of months, a larger space was needed. "In the early days, we met all over," said Peoples. "Sometimes we got together at the Jones Street Y or at Monmouth Street School. At other times, we'd meet at one of the churches. When we began having our cotillions, our big event of the year, we'd rehearse downtown at places like the Terrace Ballroom or Wideaway Hall."

The need for a permanent headquarters prompted Burch to start a fund-raising effort to buy a house Dr. Burch was eyeing for office space at 750 Clinton Avenue in Newark's South Ward. "Buster always provided Mary strong support," said their friend Helen Johnson. "If The Leaguers needed the house, he was all for the idea."

Pushing her ingenuity into overdrive, Mary Burch came up with a novel idea for raising the money needed to buy the house and the corner lot that went with it: Let the community buy it, brick by brick. Although it was a tedious fund-raising campaign, it was a success, as she recruited every living soul—from teenage members of The Leaguers to her corporate friends—to donate to the cause at the nominal cost of one dollar per brick.

Years later, when the program outgrew the building, The Leaguers bought a shuttered supermarket opposite the original building on Clinton Avenue. Today the agency serves two thousand people of all ages at ten sites in Newark and Irvington. Services have expanded too, ranging from day care, educational programs, and recreational activities to meals and activities for senior citizens.

The Leaguers' commitment to young people remains much the same as it was more than a half-century ago, but the world itself is a far different place. "Today's youngsters, despite all their material possessions, often are much more in need of our services," said Veronica Ray, the agency's executive director. "Many of the children we serve come from homes where there is no father. Their mothers are their sole support. Others have no parents at all and are being raised by grandparents who struggle to keep them in school, off the streets, and out of trouble. Years ago, things were very different. While many of The Leaguers had little in the way of material things, most had strong family support systems."

"Most of us came from homes where both our parents worked," said Yvonne Lowen, longtime board chairperson. "But our neighborhoods were very close. We were very close. Everybody knew everybody, and everybody watched out for one another." Burch was one of those people. As a woman of great distinction in the Newark community, she was able to provide her young charges with social, recreational, and educational opportunities far beyond their families' means. She also recruited many influential friends to provide scholarship assistance. One of those friends, Monsignor James McNulty, was president of Seton Hall University.

"When we were about to graduate from West Side High School, Ma Burch took my friend Dave Snead and me to Seton Hall, where we had an audience with Monsignor McNulty," Bob Mobley recalled. "By the time we left, Dave and I had full scholarships. What a wonderful thing that was. How many kids have the opportunity to know a college president?" Mobley became an educator, Snead a pediatrician.

Having such an influential woman as Mary Burch in their lives was particularly gratifying for Donald Payne, a former Newark councilman and Essex County legislator, and his older brother, William (Bill), a New Jersey state assemblyman. After their mother died, the brothers and their sister, Katherine, were raised by their grandmother while their father was away working on the railroad.

"Ma Burch's concern for us was apparent from the start," the congressman said. "That's why so many of us gravitated to her and to The Leaguers." Reflecting on his youth, he recalled how Mary Burch was always there in his times of need. "Without the scholarship I received to Seton Hall, I probably wouldn't have been able to attend college," he commented. When he needed a job during the holidays, she managed to get him one wrapping gifts at Hahne's, Newark's most exclusive department store. "The only other black employee at the time was the elevator operator," Payne remembered. "I was very appreciative of what Mrs. Burch did for me, so I bought her a Christmas gift and wrapped it myself, topping it with a big red bow. Later that day, I delivered it to her. It was one of those things that made me feel really good about myself as a young man."

"For all of us, Mrs. Burch was like another mother," Bill Payne said. Although he was not a member of The Leaguers as a teenager, devoting his youthful energies instead to a stint as national youth president of the NAACP, his close ties to the organization made that point a technicality. "My first affiliation with The Leaguers was through my ex-wife, Kay Thompson Payne, and her sister, Pat [Joyner]," Payne noted. "Because they were members, I started going to cotillions."

After he went to work for Prudential as an assistant public relations manager, Burch tapped him to be chairman of The Leaguers' alumni. "She asked me to take the position because she saw Prudential and the city's other major companies as a source of support," Payne said. "That led us to form the Friends of The Leaguers." Many of Newark's corporate bigwigs were Friends. They included Robert Harvey, an executive vice president at Prudential; Bob Lilley, the president and CEO of New Jersey Bell Telephone; David Kislak, who ran one of the city's largest real estate firms; and attorney William Wachenfeld.

As The Leaguers' chief fund-raisers, Payne and George Haney, another high-ranking corporate administrator, served as chairmen of the organization's annual dinners. One of the most memorable events was a dinner in 1964, when the Reverend Martin Luther King, Jr., was the speaker. "At first, Dr. King said he was too tired to come to Newark," Payne recalled. "When I told him about The Leaguers, what a wonderful organization it was, he changed his mind. All he asked us to do was to pay for his airfare." Prudential provided a limousine to bring Dr. King and Bayard Rustin, the civil rights activist, from the Carlyle Hotel in New York. Upon their arrival in Newark, Dominick Spina, the police director, provided a police escort to the Terrace Ballroom.

At the dinner, King was introduced by Rabbi Joachim Prinz of Temple B'nai Abraham, who told the crowd that it was the first time "a King had been introduced by a Prinz [Prince]."

From the time she was a young girl, Mary Allison Beasley Burch yearned to be a teacher. Born on August 5, 1906, a date that may or may not be accurate because of her penchant in later years for fudging her age, she was the only child of Charles Henry Beasley, a cabinetmaker from Virginia, and Elsie Amelia Williams Beasley, the daughter of a middle-class family from Lewiston, Pennsylvania.

Burch's maternal grandmother, Alice Williams, was Amish. Her maternal grandfather was African American. "My understanding is that they met while he was passing through their small town while he was working," said Burch's friend Helen Johnson. "They had at least four children, including Mary's mother; her sister, Mary; and two boys who stayed in Lewiston and ran a barbershop." Burch's uncle Joe, her mother's brother, was a World War I veteran. Everyone in the family, including Mary, was light-skinned, very fair," Johnson said. "Joe had blond hair."

When Mary was a girl, her parents divorced. Soon after, her mother, a stunning-looking woman, went to work as a governess for a family in Philadelphia. Mary, who was just twelve, stayed on in Lewiston with her maternal grandmother, who encouraged her interest in becoming a teacher. Her father, who died in 1918, remarried and lived in Lewiston with his second wife.

Following her graduation from Lewiston's public schools, she enrolled at Shippensburg State College in Pennsylvania. At the time, she was one of the school's few black students and the only African American in her class, which often made for a lonely existence. At lunchtime, for example, she had to sit by herself on the back steps. But she persevered and, after graduating from college, she rejoined her mother in Philadelphia.

For the next several years she taught school in Camden. Then one night, on a blind date in Philadelphia, she met Reynold E. (Buster) Burch, a charming young medical resident at Harlem Hospital who was five years her junior. "Mary began coming to Harlem on the weekends to see Buster," said her friend Irma (Pete) Dryden, who was a nursing student at the hospital. "With another couple, we would get together socially or go out to dinner. Mary was teaching then and had many wonderful stories to tell about her students. They were her main topic of conversation."

After Mary and Buster Burch married in 1944, he completed his training as an Air Force flight physician and was assigned to Tuskegee Air Force Base in Alabama. Dryden, who decided to join the military after the Pearl Harbor bombing on December 7, 1941, was stationed there as an Army Air Force nurse.

At the time, Tuskegee was the answer to the military's rampant racism. Although African Americans have served in all of our nation's wars, they generally have been relegated, despite their competence, to all-black units that suffered from inferior training. The pioneering black pilots of the 99th Squadron who trained at Tuskegee changed all that by forcing the federal government to reassess its separatist policies. Their noble service paved the way for the eventual integration of the Air Force.

Mary and Buster Burch arrived at Tuskegee the same week Pete and Charlie Dryden married. Charlie Dryden, a career officer in two wars, eventually rose to the rank of colonel. His book, *A Train: Memoirs of a Tuskegee Man*, recounts the squadron's stunning victories against enemy aircraft in Germany and Italy. Just as important, it captures the essence of the airmen's spirit: their ability to triumph above the daily slights they endured because of their race. Pete and Charlie Dryden met the day she arrived at Tuskegee. They married months later, just before he shipped out.

Soon after, Dr. Burch became a flight surgeon for the 744th Bomber Squadron, an elite position in an elite unit.

As the wife of a military man, Mary Burch was separated for the first time from her work with children, a labor of love she resumed after the war by founding The Leaguers. After they moved to Newark, she began recruiting friends like Pete Dryden to help shape the organization, which started out as The Junior Leaguers and later became The Leaguers, Inc.

From the time the Payne brothers and their contemporaries were growing up in Newark through the early 1980s, The Leaguers' annual cotillion, always a grand affair, was the centerpiece of all activities. Early on, the formal dances took place at the Terrace Ballroom in Newark and East Orange Armory. Later, they were held at places like the Robert Treat Hotel in downtown Newark. The young people who participated—the debutantes, their escorts, and male members of their families who took part with them in a special dance—spent months fine-tuning their routines.

Elizabeth Bell Edwards, a fifth-generation Newarker and the city's first African-American supervisor of school nurses, was among the many professional women Burch enlisted as role models for the debutantes and their escorts. Their mission was to help groom the teenagers in the social graces. "We were known as Leaguer sponsors," Edwards said. Some of the other women who were involved included Thomy Joyner, a reading specialist in the public schools; Lillian Thomas, the principal at Fifteenth Avenue School; Jeanette Pearsall, a businesswoman; and Jeanne Heningburg, a teacher. All of these women were at the forefront of their professions," Edwards said. "They were women who were expected to give something back to the community and who wanted to do so."

Through the years, Burch could always count on her friend Connie Woodruff for assistance. As city editor of the *New Jersey Herald News,* Woodruff gave The Leaguers a considerable amount of ink in the well-read black weekly. Because she and Burch were such close friends, she also served as mistress of ceremonies for the organization's dinners and commentator for fashion shows and other fund-raisers. Ever grateful, Burch wrote a 1975 thank-you note to Woodruff, saying, "I have always had and will continue to have until my dying days a very special place in my heart for you. You've always been there when we have needed you. I just couldn't have continued without you, especially in the early years when no one else gave a damn about black kids."

Millicent Fenwick, who became a highly respected congresswoman from New Jersey, also was very much a part of The Leaguers. At cotillion time she would drive to Newark from her estate in Bernardsville, New Jersey, to talk with the Newark teenagers about their aspirations and provide them with incentives to achieve their goals.

"Ma Burch had us out front," said Sesser Peoples. "She wanted people of influence to meet us and get to know us, and she wanted us to know how to act on any occasion. Meeting people like Mrs. Fenwick and Mrs. Hutchinson, whose husband worked for the Ford Motor Company, gave us those opportunities. I can still see Mrs. Fenwick in her white blouse and Black Watch plaid skirt and blazer. Like Mrs. Burch, she was a very classy lady, very stately."

Everything about the cotillion was first class. Each of the girls who danced the night away to the strains of waltz music wore a white gown. The subdebs and predebs wore pastels. The young men wore tails. "You had to be a senior in high school to be a debutante," said Yvonne Counts Lowen, who took part in the organization's first cotillion in 1951 as a senior at Arts High School.

The subdebs were juniors and the predebs were freshmen and sophomores. For the first few years, there was a program only. Later, a dinner was added. At times, a soloist performed before the cotillion began. One of them was Elaine Jones, whose brother, LeRoi Jones, also was a Leaguer. He became Amiri Baraka, the writer.

Practice for the cotillion, which was presented annually in June, generally began in January. In addition to rehearsing the dances, the students learned everything about the finer points of etiquette, from knowing how to set a table to mastering the art of proper behavior in various social situations. All of this led up to the big night. For Lowen and her friends, the long hours preparing for the cotillion were great fun. "We loved it because we loved getting together," she said. "We loved standing outside and talking before the rehearsals began."

Burch always was anxious before the program started, Lowen recalled. "She'd be yelling at all of us, telling us how terrible it would be if we didn't do our best. Afterward, she was brimming with pride, so happy that everything went so well." After the program, the debutantes, seated at the back of the room, would come forward, escorted by their father or some other important male figure in their lives, to do a short dance together. The boys danced next. "They were always a favorite with the audience because they looked so nice in tails," Lowen said. Eventually, they also wore top hats and carried canes. After dances by the subdebs and predebs, the debutantes danced alone and then with their escorts. "All of the songs were waltzes," said Lowen. "The one many of us remember is 'Now Is the Hour.'"

Over the years, Burch hired several choreographers to help the teenagers prepare for this monumental event. For many years, that assignment fell to a man from Philadelphia whose name has been lost to time. In the 1980s she enlisted the aid of Ada Jones, the wife of a dentist who was her husband's friend at Harlem Hospital.

"Mrs. Jones was a beautiful society woman who lived in a house that became a historic landmark on Striver's Row, in Harlem," said Sheila Oliver, a former executive director of The Leaguers. "Like Mrs. Burch, she was dedicated to helping others, especially children. Our teenagers had never met anyone like Mrs. Jones before," Oliver said. "Her diction and speech were perfect, which meant she would correct them when they used bad English. She was quite precise and demanding, but they loved her."

Cherished memories of those days and the cotillion abound, particularly among members of The Leaguers, who formed an alumni group out of their love for Burch and all she did for them in their youth. "I still treasure the pictures that were taken when I got all dressed up for the debutante ball," said Carolyn Ryan Reed, director of the East Orange Public Library. "The cotillion was more about education than the ball itself. The preparation that went into it—learning the social graces and learning to work as a team—provided us valuable lessons that helped us later on in life."

Carole Anderson Graves joined The Leaguers when she was fourteen and going into her sophomore year at Arts High School. "My first cotillion was in 1955, when I was sixteen," said Graves, register of mortgages and deeds for Essex County. "My mother made my dress. It was pink tulle and net with a crinoline under it. My parents didn't let me date, so my father drove me to the cotillion in a 1947 Pontiac we called the Purple Chariot. I think it was at Graham Hall on Belmont Avenue [now Irvine Turner Boulevard]. It was very elegant, and I enjoyed it, but I still felt like a sixteen-year-old."

Arthur Salley, a retired drug educator for the Newark Public Schools, said his interest in the cotillion stemmed from the fact that "so many pretty girls" were members. "I became involved through my uncle, Dr. Ulysses Campbell, a fraternity brother of Dr. Burch," he said. "At first, it seemed like a corny, high-society thing to me. But I had my eye on a girl named Betty Stancil, so I joined. I never dated Betty, but Yvonne Counts [Lowen] was my dance partner at the first cotillion."

Because of Burch's encouragement and support, most of the teenagers who participated in activities sponsored by The Leaguers were college bound. Carolyn Ryan and Yvonne Counts were headed for Howard University. Like Payne, Bob Mobley and Dave Snead were bound for Seton Hall University. Sesser Peoples wound up at Jersey City State College.

Peoples, a former teacher, and his wife, Irma, who met as students at Barringer High School, were encouraged by friends to join the group in 1950. "My family was living in public housing at the Felix Fuld Homes, what everyone calls Little Bricks," Peoples said. "In those days, I was a member of a group of guys called the Cavaliers. Amiri Baraka was in it too. Irma belonged to a girls' group called the Charmaines. We heard about The Leaguers from some of the girls in my neighborhood. Soon we started going to all the meetings and taking part in the cotillion."

Because of The Leaguers' strong focus on preparing students for college, Burch developed a well-structured academic component. Mobley and Richard Cooke, his Alpha Phi Alpha fraternity brother, became student mentors for The Leaguers in 1959, teaching afterschool courses for the next eight years until rioting ripped Newark.

Two years after the 1967 rebellion, Mobley started The Leaguers' summer day camp at 750 Clinton Avenue. As the first camp director, his objective was "to get kids off the streets" through a diversified program that included classes, field trips, and other activities.

Burch was in charge of the organization, but after several directors came and went, she asked Mobley to serve as interim director. "My job was to stay the ship," he said. "We were very small at the time. We didn't have much of a staff." After a new director was hired, Mobley stayed on as a board member.

"Like Yvonne Lowen, the current president of the board, Mrs. Burch asked me to serve one year," Mobley recounted. "But we've both been here ever since. From the time I was a student at West Side High School, I always felt I had an obligation to Mrs. Burch. I never wanted to let her down."

One of Burch's dearest friends in her later years was Jewel Smith. She was not a Leaguer, but her husband, Teddy Smith was part of a small group of Leaguers, including Betty Harris Neals and Bob Mobley, who watched over Burch as she grew older. Jewel Smith lived in Newark from 1967 to 1986 while she was employed by the Prudential Insurance Company. She met Burch through her husband-to-be, The Leaguers' board chairman.

"Teddy was very close to her as a boy," Smith said. "He went to college on a scholarship given by The Leaguers. When we met in 1976, he was helping with the cotillion. One of the first things he wanted me to do was meet Mrs. Burch." The two women became close friends, a relationship that was strengthened after Burch appealed to Bob Beck, the president and CEO at Prudential, for help with The Leaguers. Beck did more than comply. He assigned Smith to work with The Leaguers on a daily basis, even though his company was going through a rough period financially and he was cutting back on many programs. Prudential paid Smith's salary with The Leaguers for an entire year.

Because the organization was growing so rapidly, Burch was eyeing the Foodtown supermarket at 725–31 Clinton Avenue, opposite The Leaguers' headquarters, as a second site. Smith's goal was to raise enough to cover the owner's $100,000 asking price. "Lots of money came rolling in, which made Mrs. Burch very happy," she said. "Within two weeks, we'd received $50,000 each from the Turrell and Victoria Foundations. Then the owner, after considerable negotiations, dropped the price to $40,000."

This course of events proved to be an embarrassment of riches, Smith said. "We'd also received a personal check of $5,000 from Jane Engelhard," a well-known socialite and philanthropist, "so I had to call the foundations to tell them we had raised more than enough money to buy the building. Everyone told us to keep their checks, which allowed us to significantly expand our programs."

After Ted Smith's death, in March 1986, Jewel Smith moved to Florida, where she taught school until 1994 while studying for her doctorate. She and Burch visited each other and often talked by telephone. "A few years before his death, Mary and Da Da, my name for Dr. Burch, came to stay with me," Smith said. "She loved to talk about her dear friend from Philadelphia, a woman we called Aunt Gladys, and about her Grand M'am, who raised her. From what I understand, a cast iron pot she gave me—which I still have—came from Grand Ma'm's Grand M'am."

When Ernestine (Tina) Howell, an early executive director of The Leaguers, left the organization in the late 1970s, Burch began a search for a new director. Three finalists emerged: Sheila Oliver, who grew up in Newark; Al Bundy, a Leaguers board member; and an assistant director from New York whose name has been forgotten.

Oliver got the job, spending eight years at the helm before leaving to become director of career and tutorial services at Caldwell College. She later was elected to the Essex County freeholder board, which sets government policy at the county level. Currently she is the county's assistant administrator. "I really didn't apply for the job at The Leaguers," Oliver said. "I was working at City Hall in Newark and liked what I was doing as director of the Office of Youth Services and Special Programs."

Nevertheless, she was being scouted by Burch. When a City Hall colleague who was on The Leaguers' board suggested that she meet Burch, she agreed, and accompanied him one lunch hour to The Leaguers' headquarters on Clinton Avenue. "We spent about an hour and a half with Mrs. Burch that day," Oliver said. "Two months later I got a letter from The Leaguers thanking me for my application and inviting me back. I wasn't seeking a job at the time, but my parents suggested that I go, so I did." Oliver decided to take the executive director's job because she was "impressed with what The Leaguers were doing and wanted to do for the community. The hardest thing about it was telling my boss, Harry Wheeler, director of the Mayor's Office on Employment and Training."

When Oliver joined The Leaguers in October 1980, the organization was days away from its major fund-raising event of the year, a dinner at which civil rights activist Andrew Young was to speak. But Young had to cancel. Federal court Judge Leon Higgenbotham, who flew to Newark from Atlanta for the benefit, took his place.

"That night, while we were in the ladies' room, Mrs. Burch told me some things about serving the public that I will never forget," Oliver said. " 'It's tough work,' she said. 'If you're going to succeed, you have to develop skin like an alligator.' That's why I think of her today whenever I have a problem. Whatever it is rolls right off me."

Oliver felt at home at The Leaguers, in part because Dr. Burch was the physician who delivered her. "Not only was I very happy with my job," she said. "I was very happy that he took a great deal of pride in me as executive director of The Leaguers." At the beginning of Oliver's tenure, The Leaguers operated out of 750 Clinton Avenue. Soon after her appointment, Burch bought the Foodtown building across the street, refurbishing it with a grant Smith secured from the Hayden Foundation.

Burch also began seeking financial assistance from Newark's delegation to the New Jersey state legislature, inviting the elected officials to dinner at the Crescent, the East Orange apartment building where she and Dr. Burch had moved. "Over coffee in the den, she scolded each elected official for doing so little for the community," Oliver said. "She had never asked for help before, she told them, but she needed it now. That little pep talk got the ball rolling," Oliver added. "No one could ever say 'no' to Ma Burch," said Sesser Peoples. "I remember going with her one time to see Hugh Addonizio [Newark's mayor in the 1960s]. I can't remember the details, just that she came away with whatever it was she wanted. She had that kind of appeal."

After Burch met with the Essex legislators, Senator Wynona Lipman introduced a bill to provide $50,000 a year each to The Leaguers and two other Newark-based organizations, the North Ward Center and the Ironbound Educational and Cultural Center. "For the next five or six years, we got $50,000 in state funding," Oliver said. Burch made a similar appeal to Newark's mayor and council, winning a $174,000 Community Development Block Grant that was used to renovate the supermarket building and support new programs. After the building was refitted, the city of Newark began leasing space at the center for the South Ward Center, the organization's first tenant.

Burch's involvement in Newark civic and social life extended far beyond The Leaguers. On the social side, she was active in the Girlfriends, an elite group of black women whose husbands were all professionals. Their ranks included Annis Freeman, whose husband was a dentist; Rebecca Kingslow, whose husband was a doctor; and Jean Walton, whose husband was a psychiatrist. "It wasn't my shtick, but Mary recruited me, just like she did other friends, to help with The Leaguers," said Claire Williams, whose husband interned under Dr. Burch at Sydenham Hospital in New York and shared a practice with him in Newark.

Because of her background and interest in young people, Burch was appointed to the Newark Board of Education, which led to her election as board president in 1950. She also was on the board of governors of the Women's State Republican Club and was the first African American appointed to the parole board at New Jersey's Clinton Reformatory.

In 1949 her belief in community-wide political participation on a nonpartisan basis led her to form the United Women's League of Newark. Members participated in a two-week School of Practical Politics to learn how government works. They also were encouraged to take an active interest in state and local politics. Soon they began promoting programs designed to attain better housing and foster neighborhood development. As chairman of the league's Housing Committee, a woman named Armalee Lewis spearheaded an in-depth investigation of housing problems throughout the city. Members also supported programs designed to eliminate discrimination, assisted charities and community causes, and instituted an inspection program at state institutions.

In a *Herald News* article about the organization, Connie Woodruff, who taught some of the classes on politics, concluded, "Mrs. Burch can be credited with developing leadership among Negro women through this group. She has, for many years, been a credit, not only to this community, but to the cities of Philadelphia and Camden, New Jersey, where she has lived and taught school."

In the mid-1960s, Burch was appointed to the Davis Commission, a group of community leaders charged with studying the need for a county college. After months of discussions, the commission, named for Malcolm Davis, then the president and CEO of the New Jersey Bell Telephone Company, found a clear need for a two-year college to serve Essex County residents. They thought the college should be headquartered in Newark because it was the county seat, easily accessible by bus and the hub of all major activities.

One of the commission's first tasks was finding a suitable building for the college. Because of Burch's connections to Seton Hall University, a high-rise office building the university owned at 40 Clinton Street in Newark's downtown business district became the first official home of Essex County College. The trustees chose Robert Ferguson, president of National Newark & Essex Bank, as their president. Burch was another prominent member, as was Dr. Edwin Albano, the state medical examiner. Robert McCabe, a pioneer among leaders of two-year educational institutions, came from Miami-Dade Community College in Florida to serve as Essex County College's first president.

McCabe welcomed Essex County College's first students at a convocation at Newark Symphony Hall in September 1968 as he and his staff worked to get the kinks out of the new institution. At the start, there was mass confusion in the financial office, bookstore, and classrooms. Students could be found wandering the hallways at Clinton Street in search of staff members who could help resolve their problems. One girl who had paid her bill cried when there was no record of it and she was not allowed to buy books or attend classes. The students also had a hard time getting to classes because the elevators, run by a matronly operator, were slow and old. During the first week of school, McCabe took charge, counting off the number of students on each car before sending it on its way upstairs.

Because America was entrenched in a protracted war in Vietnam, not all students went to Essex County College to get an education. For many male students, attending college—any college—was a way of legally dodging the draft. With the Students for a Democratic Society, a group that opposed the war in Vietnam, at the height of its power, pickets decrying the bloodletting soon appeared outside 40 Clinton Street.

One of the regulars in the community room at the college, where young people gathered to discuss their thoughts about the war, was a young man named Tom Hayden. One of the most outspoken and well-known student radicals of his era, Hayden went on to serve eighteen years in the California legislature and run unsuccessfully for the U.S. Senate. He was famous, too, for his sixteen-year marriage to actress Jane Fonda, a comrade in the 1960s antiwar movement.

Although there was no more than general turmoil at Essex County College, a continuing series of student protests and the simple fact that the institution was located in Newark rankled more conservative suburbanites. Before long, a movement to relocate the college to Verona, a less threatening suburban setting, began gathering momentum. "Mary Burch wouldn't let that happen," said A. Zachary Yamba, the college president for twenty-five years. "She fought vigorously against the move to Verona. Because of her struggle, it never happened. The college stayed right here in Newark," Yamba added. "If it hadn't been for Mrs. Burch, we'd be up there in Verona," said Dr. Robert Spellman, who worked closely with Burch as one of the college's vice presidents. "From my perspective, keeping the college in Newark was one of her greatest contributions to our city."

When the struggle ended, the college remained in Newark and Essex County College began branching out. Soon a new $10 million megastructure, a handsome six-story building that runs downhill from Martin Luther King Boulevard east to University Avenue along West Market Street, was up and running. Soon, too, the college began establishing neighborhood learning centers throughout Newark, fulfilling the Davis Commission's mandate to become an institution that was truly reflective of the community.

"That's when Mrs. Burch and I became extremely close," said Spellman, who knew Burch from Fourteenth Street, where they were neighbors while he was growing up. Because of his family's limited financial means, however, he never got to be a Leaguer. "My brother Jim was a Junior Leaguer, but I never got to go to the cotillion because my family couldn't afford the expense," Spellman said. "At the college, I had the chance to help Mrs. Burch and help The Leaguers. I was responsible for a program that brought the college into the neighborhoods. The Leaguers was one of our sites."

Like his wife, Dr. Reynold E. Burch was an important part of Newark's civic life. He served also in several leadership positions, breaking racial ground at the corporate level by becoming the first African-American board member at Public Service Electric & Gas (PSE&G), New Jersey's major utility company.

As a member of the medical staff at the University of Medicine and Dentistry of New Jersey, Dr. Burch was revered by his colleagues. The same could be said in the community, where he practiced privately for four decades. "Buster was a wonderful man and a wonderful physician," said Helen Johnson, whose husband, Dr. Robert Johnson, had been Dr. Burch's roommate at Bates College in Lewiston, Maine. "Like Robert, he considered his patients his extended family," said Johnson. "No matter how late it was at night, my husband would make house calls if one of his patients was sick," Burch said. "Most of his patients were poor. Some couldn't afford to pay anything. So they'd give him things like food to bring home."

Because of their prominence in the community, the couple attended most of the major social functions sponsored by Newark's movers and shakers. Whenever there was a dinner or dance to raise funds for a worthy cause, they were there. They also were world travelers, making frequent trips to places like China when it opened to tourism.

In the mid-1970s, Dr. Burch began showing signs of dementia. "Buster diagnosed himself," his wife told friends. "He came home from the hospital one day and said, 'Mary, something is wrong. I can't remember the simplest things.'" Days later, Dr. Burch became confused when they were out for a drive. He could not find his way home. The next day he resigned from the hospital. He was in the beginning stages of Alzheimer's disease. Although still tall, charming, and strikingly handsome, Dr. Burch was on a rapid downslide. No longer could he take part in his many civic endeavors, including his tenure at Public Service. No longer could he treat his patients or make his rounds at the hospital.

Soon after, Mary Burch moved from the Crescent in East Orange to an apartment on Gates Avenue in Montclair, where Dr. Burch's cousin Eula and her husband, William, lived directly below them. By that time, Dr. Burch needed more assistance than his wife could possibly provide at home. Heartbroken, she signed him into a small nursing home close to where they lived.

For a while, things were fine. Then one day the doorbell rang. Standing before her in his pajamas was Dr. Burch, accompanied by a man she knew from the neighborhood. "Dr. Burch was lost," the man told her. "I found him on the corner. He didn't know where he was." Buster Burch had wandered away from the nursing home. Thanking the Good Samaritan, Burch brought her husband inside. She was furious. How could this have happened? How long would it be before it happened again?

Before long, she decided it would be best for both of them to move to a safer place. Both she and her husband were growing older, and his condition was deteriorating rapidly. Although most of their friends still lived in the Newark area, she chose Silver Spring, Maryland, as their new home, partly because Buster's niece lived there, partly because there were many nursing home facilities in the area she felt satisfied his needs. She was elated, too, because the nursing home she selected also owned a classy new assisted-living facility where she went to live. At Aspenwood, Burch had everything from a beauty shop and ice cream parlor to an apartment with full maid service at her disposal. "I liked it because you could join in the activities or, if you preferred, stay to yourself," she told friends. "Also because it was close to Buster's nursing home."

Fortunately, she was able to provide the best of care for her husband and herself because they had entrusted their assets years before to Eric Williams, the son of Buster's medical partner, Eric S. Williams, Sr. To the younger Williams, a financial adviser for American Express, they were Aunt Mary and Uncle Buster. "I can still remember the night Uncle Buster became my client," he said. "It was during the cocktail hour at a fundraiser in West Orange for the Republican Progressive Association. They were at a critical time in their lives, and they were getting some bad financial advice. Entrusting me with all they had made me feel really good because I couldn't have been more than twenty-five at the time."

As the years passed, the bond between Williams and the Burches strengthened, prompting him to continue to watch over their economic interests long after he took a management position with American Express. When Dr. Burch's health began to fail, Williams was Mary Burch's closest confidant and adviser. "Aunt Mary was like my surrogate mother. She was feisty and fiercely independent, yet she'd call me anytime she had a problem," Williams said. "If she could have, I think Mary would have adopted Eric," said Claire Williams, his mother.

When Burch arrived at Aspenwood, the facility was so new a model apartment was still open to the public. After signing her contract, she was given a first-floor apartment not far from the main dining hall. At mealtime, the residents could order standard fare or anything else they wanted, from steak to lobster tails, for an additional charge. Anything Burch wanted was available.

At the time, she was still driving an older model Mercedes. Never a skilled driver, she wound up one day on a median on New Hampshire Avenue on her daily trip to the nursing home. Fortunately, she was not hurt. Nor was she deterred from getting in the car again the next day to go to see her husband. As always, Buster was her priority. Soon after, however, she had another near miss, which convinced her it was time to give up driving.

For a time, she went to live with Dr. Burch's niece, Patty Bekele, and her family, which included three young children. But she soon tired of the trips to the nursing home. And she was growing dissatisfied, rightly or wrongly, about her husband's care. She wanted him at home with her. And so she set in motion her plan to take Dr. Burch out of the nursing home: She moved to her own apartment and hired a young woman named Connie Thompson, an Aspenwood employee, as his caregiver. Although their first apartment on Stewart Lane in Silver Spring was nothing to brag about, Mary Burch was in heaven. Once again, she and Dr. Burch were together. "I am feeling fine, especially since I have Buster home with me to stay," she wrote to a friend in March 1993. "He is doing fine and looks good. We go out every day. He's slowed down, but that's to be expected, the doctor says."

Although she was growing frail, she was convinced that it would be good for both of them to spend part of the summer in the lakefront cottage they owned in Gardiner, Maine, where Buster grew up. "She didn't want to fly. That would have been too strenuous for Dr. Burch," said her friend Bob Spellman. "I had a motor home, so my family came too, and we drove to Maine. The setting was absolutely pristine. From the road, you went down a lane to a beautiful cottage at the edge of a lake. You could see the lake from the dining room and the porch."

For Mary Burch, the trip to Maine was a joyous time, a reminder of the many summers she and Buster had spent vacationing there with their friends Robert and Helen Johnson and the Johnsons' children—Karen, who became a school social worker in Newark and was their goddaughter, and Robert, who, like Buster Burch and his father, became a physician. "We always [had] so much fun together because Mary had such a great sense of humor," Helen Johnson said. "She was always very thoughtful and grateful to everyone who helped her. People were attracted to her because she was so warm and friendly."

Connie Thompson, who devoted herself to the couple's every need, also made the trip. From the day she went to live with the Burches on Stewart Lane, Thompson gave her all to her job. Even though she worked seven days a week for long stretches and rarely got home to nearby Sandy Spring, she had no complaints. She loved what she was doing. "We became a family," said Thompson, whose affable manner and concern for others made her a natural caregiver. "I'd take Doc everywhere. We went shopping. I took him to picnics and playgrounds. We loved to eat hot dogs together."

Soon Thompson began calling Burch "Granny." "She was like a mother and a grandmother to me," said Thompson. "When she'd get upset with me, she'd tell me, 'You better not do that, or I'll take you out of my will.' 'That's O.K., I'd say. I'm going to take you out of my will too.' That gave her a good laugh."

After Buster Burch's death in 1993, Mary Burch decided to move to a building further up Stewart Lane. Not only was her two-bedroom apartment there much larger; it was much nicer, furnished with many of the treasures she and her husband had collected during their world travels.

To get some rest and keep her mind off her husband's death, she decided to travel to Mobile, Alabama, to visit her friend Jewel Smith. After earning her doctorate, Smith had returned home to become campus director, the equivalent of provost, at Bishop State Community College. In Mobile, Mary Burch and Connie Thompson stayed with Smith more than a month. "We had a great time," Thompson said. "We even went to the Mardi Gras."

"Mary was starting to slow down, yet in many ways she was still very youthful," Smith recalled. "Into her nineties, she was full of vitality and as tenacious as the bulldog she owned when she and Dr. Burch lived on Meeker Avenue in Newark. She was a brilliant woman, far ahead of her time."

In 1998, when Smith married the Reverend Dr. Cain Hope Felder, a professor of New Testament Language and Literature at Howard University, Burch was front and center at the wedding in Mobile. So was Connie Thompson.

By that time, however, it was evident to all that Burch's health was failing. Her health, in fact, had been a lifelong problem. As a young woman she had had a mastectomy, followed by several other serious operations. But she had always bounced back, almost as good as new no matter what the disease or ailment.

Now her hospital stays were more frequent. More often than not, she was in the hospital rather than at home. In her stubborn way she believed that, despite having had two heart attacks, her faltering health had nothing to do with her age. Instead, she convinced herself she was not getting better because of the ineptitude of the doctors who were treating her. If one doctor did not please her, she would search for another—and another. In spite of her poor health, Burchie, as some friends called her, never lost her sense of humor. "I'm getting uglier every day," she wrote to me in September 1996, adding a trademark frown face for emphasis. "I look like one of the witches from *Macbeth*."

After Dr. Burch's death, Connie Thompson turned her complete attention to Mary Burch, helping her bathe and dress each day. Each time Burch went to the hospital, Thompson went too. "I know what goes on in hospitals," Thompson said. "If you can't advocate for yourself, someone else has to do it for you. Granny was my family, my friend. I wanted to be sure she was O.K."

During one period of hospitalization at Adventist Hospital in Washington, Burch's memory appeared to be failing. But her problem was medical, not mental. Her electrolytes were out of whack, making her seem senile. Soon after she returned home, a worker for the Maryland Board of Overseers appeared at her door to check on her mental state and the condition in which she was living. Someone she knew had filed a report with the board, suggesting that she was unable to live on her own anymore. "By the time I got done with him, he knew I had all my marbles," she said afterward, furious at the intrusion into her affairs. "That was the end of that. They thought I should be in a nursing home. What nerve!"

By then she was sticking close to home, paying fewer visits to Newark. Her final visit to the city came in January 2000, when she was invited to launch The Leaguers' fiftieth anniversary celebration. Worn out from all the activity, she did not get to the evening's culminating event, a spring gala at a hotel at the airport where the alumni replicated the cotillion.

During this last visit to her adopted city, Burch was honored at a luncheon at the Newark Club, a private restaurant atop one of Newark's tallest office towers that offers a spectacular view of New York and New Jersey. That night, the Essex County Board of Chosen Freeholders paid tribute to her at their meeting.

In August 2000, scores of Leaguer alumni gathered one night in the garden of the Newark Museum to celebrate her birthday, but she was too ill to travel to Newark. She was in the hospital again. This time, however, she did not come out. She had suffered the first of a series of strokes that gradually left her completely incapacitated. Until her death the next year, three days after her ninety-fifth birthday, she remained bedridden at the Adventist Nursing Home in Silver Spring. She died on August 9, 2001.

Although she remembered friends and loved ones in her will, the bulk of her estate went to the institutions she loved best—Essex County College, where she had established a scholarship fund; Kean College in Union, New Jersey, where she had served on the board of trustees and a dormitory was named for her; Shippensburg State College in Pennsylvania, her alma mater; and Bates College in Maine and Howard University Medical School, her husband's alma maters.

In mid-September 2001, friends, family, and Leaguers past and present gathered in the Mary B. Burch Theater at Essex County College for a memorial service celebrating the life and legend of the organization's founder. The event was coordinated by poet Betty Harris Neals, who recited an original piece in tribute to Burch. Janice Harris Jackson, a professor at Kean College in Union Township, where the Mary B. Burch dormitory stands, was the mistress of ceremonies.

Donald Payne and Hazel O'Leary, two of The Leaguers' most famous alumni, came from Washington to participate. Poet Amiri Baraka was there too. The highlight of the tribute came when Sesser Peoples and Shirley Jenkins, joined by another couple, danced to "Now Is the Hour," bringing new meaning to the cotillions of their youth.

As a special tribute, a children's dance ensemble performed against a backdrop of hundreds of photos of Ma Burch, a display that included many images of the young men and women who had passed through The Leaguers over the years. There, on the screen, sporting a 1970s-style Afro was Al Bundy, who went on to head a program for black medical students at Seton Hall University. There, too, was Connie Woodruff, in her youth, presenting seventeen-year-old Donald Payne his scholarship to attend Seton Hall. There, front and center, were scores of young debutantes and their escorts preparing for their cotillions.

For those in attendance, the program was far more than a memorial. It was a reunion of the minds, a flashback to the days when they too were young, idealistic, and about to take their places in the world with the support of Mary and Buster Burch.

MARION A.
BOLDEN

Champion of Children | 1946–

No one in Marion Bolden's family was at home the night a huge rock came crashing through her living room window. So the question remains whether this was simply a random act of violence or a crime meant to intimidate Newark's most innovative educator in decades. Whatever the reality, to friends, colleagues, and Bolden herself, the incident was a sign that, after three years of guiding New Jersey's largest school system without interference, her job—perhaps even her well-being—was under siege. New Jersey's largest newspaper, the *Star-Ledger,* wrote about the attack. Police responded by patrolling Bolden's street.

One thing was certain, however: With $1.6 billion in school construction funds bound for the Newark Public Schools and a $723 million annual budget for school operations at stake, there were many people who wanted Bolden out. The jousting to gain control of funding for contracts and jobs was revving into high gear, as was one of the most hard-fought mayoral races in years. At the same time, the politicos who controlled the district before a 1995 state takeover amid charges of corruption had regrouped and were now in charge of the superintendent's advisory board.

Whatever danger might lie ahead, Bolden was not scared. Fear was never a part of her psychological makeup. When threatened or pushed to the wall, she simply dug in harder, mustering tremendous strength and exhibiting an unwavering sense of resolve. "No one is going to push me out," she asserted. "When I go, I will go on my own terms." No one perhaps except Bolden knew how right she was.

For the first three years under her leadership, Newark's public schools had made tremendous strides. With nothing major at stake politically, she had been left to do what she wanted, building strong support for her administration among educators, parents, students, the clergy, and the business community. Now, seasoned political forces reaching from Newark to the state capital in Trenton appeared to be working overtime to oust her. For the next ten months, from the summer of 2002 to the spring of 2003, a contentious struggle ensued, one that left the superintendent's job hanging by a thread.

"Our battle to retain Marion as superintendent was never about education," said the Reverend Dr. David Jefferson, Jr., pastor of Metropolitan Baptist Church, Newark's largest African-American house of worship. "It was about politics, and politics only." Despite this enormous distraction to Bolden's work and the staggering costs to her time and health, she kept plugging away, day and night, to put Newark's failing schools back on track after more than three decades of decline.

By the time Bolden became the district's second state-appointed superintendent, in mid-1999, city schools had practically bottomed out. Student test scores were at an all-time low. Many of the district's seventy-five schools, constructed more than a century before, were falling apart. The district was in fiscal chaos. These problems, coupled with the belief that the state Education Department could turn the district around, even though its higher-ups were mostly suburban educators with little urban experience, led the state to take over Newark's public schools in 1995.

But there was little improvement under state control. Bolden's predecessor, who had arrived to a $56 million surplus, had left behind a $123 million shortfall four years later. Despite charges of rife patronage and mismanagement under the old system, the Newark public schools, once among the nation's best, were in more pitiful shape than ever. "A lot of people said I was crazy to accept the superintendent's position," said Bolden, who was promoted from associate superintendent. "They were convinced there was little anyone could do to turn things around. I thought otherwise."

As a proud product of Newark schools, Bolden believed that she could be the catalyst for change. Born and raised in Newark, she was a skilled educator. She knew the turf. No time would be wasted in on-the-job training. Above all else, Bolden believed in the people of her city, especially its children. In them she saw herself—capable, with the proper guidance, of achieving whatever they wanted.

Bolden's appointment gave Newark's African-American community a tremendous lift. As the first black woman from the city to head the school system, she was pioneering a path begun nearly fifty years before by E. Alma Flagg, the district's first black principal of an integrated school. Convinced that great expectations could be turned into great achievements, Bolden began making sweeping changes, instituting new reading and writing initiatives while realigning the curriculum to better meet student needs in a changing society. At the same time, she set about stabilizing her shaky budget.

At the classroom level, Bolden's forceful attack on the social and educational ills restricting the achievement of Newark children began with an increased emphasis on character-building values. At the community level, she encouraged all stakeholders—students, parents, the clergy, and business leaders—to buy into her vision for change. Creating all-encompassing support for all students was paramount to their success, she argued.

From the start, Bolden dedicated herself to changing the status quo, a trait that defined her three decades as an urban educator. Two years into her tenure, signs that she was making progress were clearly evident. Not only had she brought fiscal stability to the district for the first time in three decades; she had removed disruptive students from classes and created ambitious school to career and college initiatives for all students. In short order, she had turned a hefty budget deficit into a sizable surplus, a fiscal feat that won a first-ever national citation of excellence for the district from a prestigious organization of school board auditors.

"What happened was phenomenal," said Bessie White, a former budget director for the district who became Bolden's chief of staff. "In a very short time, she dug the district out of a hole that was swallowing it up financially."

Although Bolden was proud of her administration's accomplishments, a turnabout remained a work in progress after so many years of neglect. At the heart of her master plan for awakening the city's public school students from their long sleep was a corps of skilled, competent, and caring teachers. To rectify the dire need for a capable teaching staff, she began recruitment drives and made scholarships available to Newark students who promised to return home to teach for at least four years after graduating from college. The superintendent also began recognizing the city's top teachers at start-of-the-year convocations. At the same time she made absolutely clear the need for academic improvement.

Early on, there was plenty to celebrate. Abington Avenue School, an average elementary school, was now at the top in all subjects on the state-mandated test for fourth graders. Newark also catapulted into the news when President Bill Clinton named Ann Street School one of the nation's few Blue Ribbon schools. (In 2004 Branch Brook School achieved a similar status, courtesy of President George W. Bush.)

From the start, Bolden's colleagues viewed her as industrious and innovative. From the day she began teaching at Barringer High School in 1968, "it was evident that Marion was a visionary," said Gloria Royster, a retired business teacher. "She was very focused, an excellent teacher full of creative ideas who spent her free time sharing her ideas with others."

At Arts High, where Bolden became chairman of the Mathematics Department in 1982, she came up with the idea of suspending all activities for a few minutes each day so that all students could do math problems. "The kids went crazy trying to see who could solve them," said Hilton Otero, her principal. In 1989, after becoming the first director of mathematics for all of Newark's public schools, she instituted an algebra initiative for all eighth graders. "By the time our students were sophomores and juniors, they already had four years of high school math," said Doris Culver, then principal at University High School. "This was Marion's response to complaints by parents about the poor quality of the math program."

Bolden did not stop there. As district math director, she started a student Math Fair and Olympics. As associate superintendent, she created the Benjamin Banneker Science Center, the only school-based facility of its kind statewide. As superintendent, she bought the old New Jersey Historical Society building for use as a student media center. "Marion's always had a huge vision," said Lannie Paschall, her assistant director of mathematics. "Once she gets going, there is no stopping her. She has an undying love of children and learning that no one can deny."

Despite her upward mobility, Bolden stayed close to her students. "From my freshman year at Arts High, when I was sent to her office after a fight, she kept me out of trouble," said Darren Hawthorne, who became a Newark math and science teacher. "She nurtured my intellect by introducing me to chess and video games."

Born April 28, 1946, at St. Barnabas Hospital in Newark, Marion Alexander was one of three daughters of Bernice Murray Alexander and William Alexander. An older brother, Leonard Moore, is a retired Newark educator. Marion's parents worked hard to support their family. For forty years, William Alexander was a tanner. His wife worked for General Electric.

Bolden's older sister, Cathy Watson, an East Orange teacher called Bubbles by the family, was like their father. "When he went somewhere, I went too," she said. "Marion was our mother's child, quiet and very industrious." Their sister, Sheila Manigault, six years Bolden's junior, credits Bubbles with running interference with their father. "Not that I got in that much trouble," she said, "but my father was very strict."

Nicknamed Bebe by her family, Marion admittedly lacked self-confidence until she discovered her aptitude for math in the fifth grade at Bergen Street School. "Until then I had been told I was a promising student, nothing exceptional," she recalled. Suddenly she blossomed. Now she was the first in her class to correctly solve intricate math problems. She also began asking compelling questions, some that stumped her teachers.

In their South Ward neighborhood, Marion's older sister was considered the family protector. "I was a fighter," said Bubbles. "If anyone looked at Bebe wrong, I'd be on them. All the girls liked her, but a lot of them were afraid to become her friend because they were scared of me." Nevertheless, Marion was voted class president at Clinton Place Junior High School, a sign of her emerging leadership skills.

She also came under the influence of two encouraging teachers who fueled her academic interests, Mr. Schumann and Mr. Adler. But it was Ruth Ringel, her math teacher at South Side High, who influenced her most. "She pushed me," Bolden said. "I went beyond what she expected of others, so she gave me more challenging work."

As a sophomore at South Side, she began dating LaMont Bolden, one of the smartest boys in her class. They were practically mirror images—serious, scholarly, and focused on the future. Eventually they would marry. Like peas in a pod, they studied together, challenging each other's intellect at every turn. Both were class leaders. She was president of the National Honor Society and a member of the class executive committee and yearbook staff. He was class president and vice president of the honor society.

Both of them also were at the top of their class. "A Jewish girl named Rita Levine was the top student," said Dr. Alfred Gaymon, a gastrointestinal cancer specialist who finished fourth academically in South Side's class of January 1964. "What we used to call the Big Three—Franklin, Alexander, and Gaymon—finished second, third, and fourth. I think LaMont finished fifth."

When it came time for college, Al Gaymon, a product of the Stella Wright housing projects, set his sights on becoming a doctor. Ronald Franklin, who became comptroller of the Corning Corporation, sought a career in business. Marion Alexander dreamed of becoming an architect. "But girls weren't encouraged to aspire to things like that in those days," she reflected. "Not only was I not encouraged; I was discouraged."

And so she enrolled at Montclair State College to become a teacher. LaMont started going to school nights at Rutgers University and then was drafted into the army. Unfortunately, college life was not what Marion expected it to be, especially the social aspects. "It was disappointing because there were so few minority students and, therefore, so little social interaction," she said. "When we entered Montclair State in 1964 there were just thirteen of us [African Americans] in a class of thirteen hundred," said Eleta Caldwell, who succeeded Otero as principal at Arts High School. "Only seven graduated."

In their senior year, some of their friends organized an association of black students. But Marion was not part of it. One summer night between her freshman and sophomore years, her mother, who was just forty-one, died of a stroke. Marion's entire world crumbled. Jackie King, who lived down the street from the family and was in the same class in school as Sheila, still remembers that day. "It was the first time any of us had experienced the death of a parent," said King. "I remember it so well that it hurts even now. Mrs. Alexander was one of the mothers in the neighborhood we all loved. She had high standards, but she was always there for you."

With Bubbles married and out of the house, Marion became the head of the household. At nineteen she had a house to tend; college studies to complete; and her thirteen-year-old sister, Sheila, to care for, awesome responsibilities for someone so young. "It was a huge responsibility," said Sheila, a career employee of the U.S. Department of Labor. "Not only did Bebe lose her mother; she had to make sure her little sister stayed on the straight and narrow at a time when young people can be very vulnerable. Thankfully, I was an easy child to manage."

"Bebe had a tremendous amount of responsibility for a young girl," said Sheila's husband, attorney Sam Manigault. "In a very real sense, she served as a surrogate mother to Sheila. People would talk about how strong their mother was. Bebe had that same drive and sense of resolve." As a teenager, Sam Manigault became part of the Alexanders' extended family when he began dating Sheila. "I was always at their house because of Sheila," he said. "When I heard Bebe calling out Sheila's name, I knew by the tone of her voice that it was time to go home."

Until Bernice Alexander's death, life at 127 Ridgewood Avenue was full of activity. In the summer, the couple took their girls to Owego in upstate New York to visit her relatives. "My grandparents, Harold and Clarice Murray, were one of two black families in Owego," Bolden said. "They came from Barbados, but all of their children were born here. My grandfather went to Owego because of the promise of employment as a chef. He worked in one of the hotels."

The family also made occasional trips to South Hill, Virginia, where her paternal grandparents, Robert and Fannie Alexander, had a farm. Bolden's father and paternal grandparents went north in the late 1930s, when he was thirteen. "He didn't graduate from high school, but he was very bright," she said. "He was the one who helped me with my math."

After graduating from Montclair State, Bolden began teaching at Barringer High. "From the day I met her, Marion's honesty was apparent. Her integrity was impeccable. She was very loyal and trustworthy, everything you could possibly want in a friend," said Gloria Royster. "All of us at Barringer were close," said Franotie Washington, retired director of music and art for Newark schools. "We liked to go to parties together and hold cookouts as a group. Marion was very giving. When I subbed in math one summer, she was a great help."

At twenty-three, after her first year of teaching, Marion Alexander and LaMont Bolden, her childhood sweetheart, married at Bethany Baptist Church in Newark. He was out of the army, working as analyst for an insurance company while continuing his education part time at Rutgers. Theirs was a fairly large wedding. Al Gaymon, Ronald Franklin, and Claude Breitenbach, friends from South Side, were in the bridal party, along with LaMont's two brothers. Marion's sister Sheila was her maid of honor. Bubbles and several girlfriends also took part.

Soon after, during their early days in college, Sheila and Sam Manigault married. "Because we were so young, I think Bebe thought she'd somehow failed us," Sheila said. "Years later, when our older daughter, Simone, graduated from medical school, we gave a dinner and everyone in the family gave a toast. Everyone else spoke of Simone's accomplishments, but Bebe had a different spin. She talked about how proud she was of Sam and me. In a sense, that was validating for her too."

In 1974 the Boldens' first daughter, LaMar, came along. Three years later Marion gave birth to another daughter, Reagan. Unfortunately, the marriage did not last. By the time Reagan entered elementary school, Marion and LaMont Bolden had divorced. The trauma of the family breakup was magnified when LaMont died of cancer several years later.

"Mommy loved classroom teaching, but I'm sure she left it to go into administration because she had to pay for the house and support us," said

LaMar, who holds a master's degree in occupational therapy and works for a health care agency. "She did everything for us," said Reagan, who teaches third grade in Newark. "Ours was the smallest yard on the block, but we had an aboveground pool that all the kids swam in during the summer. Mommy turned our basement into Barbie Land. We had a Barbie dining room and a Barbie living room where all the girls in our neighborhood came to play. She was our Girl Scout leader too."

Wertley Dotson, Bolden's neighbor, was the troop co-leader. "We used to meet at Heywood Avenue School in Orange, where the cookies were delivered," Dotson said. "One time, all the cookies—rooms full—came to my house by mistake. Within minutes, Marion was right there, sorting them. You could always count on her because she was determined to get the job done."

Despite her demanding career, Bolden spent every moment possible with her children. Although she loved having family fun, she also was bent on properly guiding the girls' education, even in public. "No matter what we did, there always was something educational to it," said LaMar. "While waiting for dinner, we'd have to answer math questions. The one that I remember best is 'In how many years will you be exactly half my age?' Reagan figured it out. All I wanted to do was eat. Another time, we went on a trip to Williamsburg, Virginia," LaMar recalled. "Reagan and I were anxious to go to Busch Gardens. We did, but first we had to tour all these plantations. Somehow, Mommy always made it fun."

Bolden's niece, Shannon Manigault, a Harvard Law School graduate and practicing attorney, often shared the good times at Bolden's house. "I was a Girl Scout too, so every summer I'd stay with Bebe and go to day camp with my cousins," she said. "Even then, I was impressed by Bebe's work ethic. She did everything thoroughly, even arts and crafts." Shannon's older sister, Simone Alexander Manigault, credits their aunt with providing the drive she needed to become a pediatrician. "My mother and aunts were beside themselves after I graduated from Johns Hopkins University and didn't get into medical school," she said.

At Bolden's insistence, Simone subbed at Newark schools and then applied to the University of Medicine and Dentistry of New Jersey, where she eventually became chief resident in pediatrics. "Through my experience as a sub, I found that I love teaching, especially in Newark because our roots are here," she said. "With all due respect to my father, I would use my middle name and call myself Dr. Alexander, if I could, because I come from a family of such strong women."

In 1982, after Bolden completed her master's degree at Montclair State College and gained certification as a supervisor and principal, Hilton Otero appointed her chairman of the Mathematics Department at Arts High. "Marion had the kind of personality I was looking for," Otero said. "She never lost her cool. She took care of things in a very organized manner. And she would never retreat, no matter what the issue."

From the time Bolden stepped foot into Arts High until she left seven years later to become director of mathematics for the entire district, she displayed exceptional leadership skills. "I depended on Marion a great deal," Otero said. "While she was a department chairman, she really acted as a vice principal. Because she was a talented leader, she had a very loyal staff. Because she worked very hard, her staff followed suit."

Although he would have preferred that Bolden stay on at Arts, Otero applauded her promotion to director of mathematics for the district "because she was so capable and because that was what she wanted." Bolden was not the only candidate for the post. "Powerful political forces were pushing for another candidate," said Dr. Raymond Lindgren, who met Bolden early in his career as a math teacher and served as her first chief of staff. "Marion wasn't thirsting for the position, but there was a tremendous groundswell of support for her. People were saying she was the one needed for the job. That's been symbolic of her career. She hasn't gone after any of the positions she's held, but when an opportunity arises to benefit Newark children, she's willing to accept it."

In her new position, Bolden moved quickly to improve the math curriculum, establishing what Lindgren called "a template for urban education" that could be applied to other disciplines. To that end, she pushed for the formation of a directors' association to ensure the coordination of all aspects of the curriculum, reestablished the Newark Association of Math Educators, and revamped the entire math curriculum, focusing on all students, from the brightest to those functioning below grade level.

"Getting basic skills students back on level was a big part of it," Lindgren said.

"When the state took over the Newark schools in 1995, the Math Department was the only one they left alone and didn't find fault with," said Lannie Paschall, Bolden's project coordinator. Under Dr. Beverly Hall, the district's first state-appointed superintendent, he became a school principal. Bolden was named associate superintendent.

Hall was appointed superintendent by State Education Commissioner Leo Klagholz, the mastermind behind the move to make Newark the third district under state control. Paterson and Jersey City were first. "Leo really wanted to go into Newark first," said Bob Braun, former education editor for the *Star-Ledger*. "He chose Paterson and Jersey City instead because they were smaller and more manageable. He also was testing the waters because of the complex political problems he would face in Newark."

Because Newark was such a political hotbed, control of the school system was always a battle between those in power and those seeking to be in power. At a school board meeting in the mid-1980s when Saul Cooperman was state education commissioner, police ringed the room one night in April as three new members of the board were about to take office.

Teachers and trade unionists who supported the winners, labor leaders Edgar Brown and Fred Stecher and the Reverend Oliver Brown, a Presbyterian minister, packed the room. To their surprise, the board attorney declared Edgar Brown ineligible to hold office. When the attorney announced plans to swear in a losing candidate on the spot, all hell broke loose. With police in tow, Charles Bell, the board president, began chasing the attorney, who was still clinging to the Bible, around the room. Wilnora Holman, another angry board member, swept mountains of papers onto the floor. Senator Ronald Rice, the city's West Ward councilman, climbed atop a table, demanding order.

In a matter of minutes, two hundred disgruntled Newarkers began marching up Warren Street to Rutgers-Newark to voice their objections to Cooperman, who was at the college to deliver an address on urban education. Knowing nothing about the cause of the ruckus, the commissioner tried at first to calm the crowd. After a meeting in his Trenton office the next day with a small contingent from Newark that included attorney Junius Williams, Cooperman sent the case to an administrative law judge. The decision was clear. The duly elected board members must be sworn into office.

A decade later the Newark schools were under state jurisdiction. A report commissioned by Klagholz charged systemic mismanagement and rampant cronyism. Student scores on state proficiency tests were abysmal. Buildings were in disrepair. Fiscal controls were either lacking or inadequate. Klagholz was convinced the state could do a better job, a contention that incensed many Newarkers, who faulted the state for taking away their right to elect board members. Others simply dreaded the day when their power to control jobs and contracts would end.

Klagholz was right on some counts, but his prediction that the Newark schools would improve as a state-operated district under Hall proved dismally wrong. By early 1999, Hall's $56 million surplus had turned into an even bigger deficit. Soon she left Newark to head the Atlanta, Georgia, school system.

On July 20, 1999, Bolden became superintendent of schools. In effect, she also became Newark's first African-American CEO, taking charge of what was then the equivalent of a $650 million corporation with more than seventy-five hundred full-time employees. Given her many years of experience as a Newark educator at all levels, she was well suited for the job.

"Marion's appointment was right on target to people who know how competent she is," said Bolden's friend, Alfred Gaymon. "She has always been very diligent. Nevertheless, I thought it nothing less than a miracle for the state to choose the most worthy person from Newark to head the school system. That's generally not the case."

Outside the educational community, however, Bolden was virtually unknown. "Many community leaders wanted to know who she was," said Maria Vizcarrondo-DeSoto, president of the United Way. "I had heard fabulous things about her but never met her before. Very quickly we found that she was a no-nonsense, straight-ahead person, strictly for the kids."

Until the superintendent's responsibility was fully hers, Bolden did not realize how wearying and thankless would be the task at hand. In addition to getting out from under a mountain of debt and improving scores that found most Newark students failing standardized tests, she had to comply with a legion of burdensome state mandates. Under a state supreme court order, the district was under the gun to design thirty-three new schools as part of a $1.6 billion construction project. Whole School Reform, a school-by-school improvement plan based on different and often conflicting models, had to be implemented on a strict timetable. Another new mandate required her administration to create a full-scale educational program for the city's eight thousand three- and four-year-olds.

Bolden found herself running a troubled urban district far different from the one she knew as a girl growing up in Newark, far different from what she had seen as a teacher at Barringer High School or encountered as department chairperson at Arts High School. School safety was a critical issue. Gangs were on the rise. Disruptive students made the school experience miserable. Hundreds of children whose parents had to scrounge for a living or who were lost to drugs and alcoholism were being raised by their grandparents.

The city itself was changing. Just as it had become more black than white after the 1967 riots, the city's most burgeoning ethnic group was now Hispanics. New students were coming to Newark from all over the world. Whatever the challenges, Bolden's sense of resolve was in high gear. Nothing and no one would stop her from doing her best to resurrect the Newark public schools.

Newarkers got another bonus when Anzella K. Nelms, a beloved teacher and former principal at Camden Middle School with years of experience as a top administrator, became Bolden's deputy superintendent. Born in Raleigh, North Carolina, Nelms graduated from Saint Augustine's College, where she was a stellar student. After teaching in Raleigh for a year, she arrived in Newark in 1965 as a fourth-grade teacher at the Harriet Tubman Elementary School. "Anzella's leadership skills as an educator were immediately apparent," said retired principal Geraldine Sims. "Very quickly, she began moving up the ranks," serving as a Title I project coordinator and elementary vice principal at South Tenth Street (now Harriet Tubman) School and at Chancellor Avenue School.

After serving as principal at Camden Middle from 1979 to 1989, Nelms became assistant executive superintendent in July 1993, responsible for supervising the day-to-day operations of all elementary schools. As second in command, Nelms was perfect for Bolden. Both of them knew Newark. Both of them loved Newark children and had nothing but the highest expectations of their students. Both were committed to the highest educational principles. And both were willing to pour unrelenting energy into their mission to improve the city's schools.

Just as important, their experiences as educators complemented each other. Bolden was the visionary, the one whose bold ideas set the tone for the new administration. Nelms was the expert administrator. Immediately, Bolden began making changes that far exceeded any mandate set by the state's Department of Education. Nelms began setting the Newark Public Schools' house in order, making sure that all reports and mandates were completed efficiently and on time.

Working practically around the clock, Bolden began rebuilding student spirit in the schools, on the athletic field, and in the community. "Students have to want to come to school," she said. "If they don't, no academic plan will work." Bolden's leadership style was inviting. Her door remained open to anyone who wanted to enter. Her e-mail address was available to everyone. No matter what the problem or who had it, she made time to deal with it.

As Newark's No. 1 educator, Bolden was everywhere, meeting with staff members, principals, teachers, board members, parents, and community groups; speaking at dinners and educational conferences; working with state and local officials; going to funerals and football games. If she was not at a school or at some community event, she was ensconced in her office, often deep into the night.

On one of those nights in late 2001, she stayed on with Assistant Superintendent Doris Culver to sign more than one thousand Whole School Reform documents due in the state commissioner's office the next day. It was Christmastime. Other people were out shopping. But Bolden was where she always was—at work. "There's never a day when Mrs. Bolden doesn't have a full schedule," said Claudette Yarbrough, her executive secretary. "She has appointments from eight in the morning until eight at night, often thirty or more a day. And she works just about every weekend. Holidays too."

Bolden's most immediate challenge was reversing the district's dire fiscal situation. "It was exasperating," she said. "We were millions of dollars in the hole." Moreover, the books were a mess. The district lacked budgetary controls. The budget was in disarray, making it impossible to track expenditures. The payroll system was hit or miss, causing problems with employees' paychecks and threats of suits from unionized workers.

Newark's financial problems were systemic. For years before Hall became superintendent, accounting firms hired to reconcile the books had routinely issued disclaimers with their reports. In the early 1980s, for example, an outside auditor cited poor or nonexistent record keeping as a reason for unaccounted funds at many school cafeterias. Because district records were so shoddy, the firm's reports were inconclusive. Year after year, unaccounted funds continued to mount.

Bolden put a stop to such practices. Days into her administration, her business administrator began putting the district's house in order. Two years later, Bolden's administration was able to do what no other administration had done in decades: offer the state a clean bill of financial health. The *Star-Ledger* applauded the district in an editorial titled "Turning a Corner in Newark." Crediting the superintendent for "plugging the $73 million hole left by Hall through the appropriation of state funds and district spending cuts," it concluded that "the district now can turn more attention to the education of 40,000 Newark school kids."

Turning Newark's academic failures around was an entirely different matter, complicated by a myriad of mind-boggling social ills of everyday life that affect children. In winter, many students had no coats or boots, forcing them to skip school. Some ate barely one decent meal each day. Others, albeit decent and resilient, came from homes where physical and mental abuse was commonplace. Whatever the directives and expectations from on high, Bolden was the one who had to deal with the real issues—decades-old problems that could not be fixed by issuing simplistic demands.

Continuity of purpose also was a problem. Given an ever-changing political climate at the state level, she had reported to three different education commissioners less than three years into her tenure. To complicate matters, members of the state board of education, who had the final say on educational issues, often offered conflicting ideas about how urban schools should operate.

"People outside of Newark, including many in high positions that affect how we operate, think you just snap your fingers and problems that took years to surface will vanish," said the United Way's Vizcarrondo-DeSoto. "The depth of the problems Marion faces will take generations to correct." Bolden agreed. "The commissioners and state board members can demand change, but that doesn't make it happen," she said. "I can't wave a magic wand and change everything that's happened over the years at once. We have a well-thought-out educational plan, and we are implementing it. But there is no quick fix." Despite such staggering problems, Bolden remained committed to providing Newark children with every possible chance for success. Her motto: "All children *will* learn."

At the high schools, she developed themes for each school, similar to a program begun at the elementary level. Because of its proximity to the New Jersey Institute of Technology, Central High School's theme was engineering. Barringer's focus became aviation and tourism. "We created the themes to stem the tide of students dropping out of high school or deciding to go to schools outside of Newark," Bolden said. "It made more students want to come to school and stay in school, and it offered them chances for good jobs after they graduated."

Meeting regularly with parents, she felt, was key to academic improvement. To publicize the academies and help students make appropriate selections, she invited eighth graders and their parents to a program at Arts High School one Saturday morning. Hundreds of parents showed up with their children. "This is just the beginning," Bolden told the parents "Eventually, all of our incoming high school students will select secondary schools that suit their interests."

During her first year on the job, Bolden removed nearly three hundred troubled students from high school classrooms and instituted the Twilight Program. This venture allowed students considered disruptive to work in the morning, attend school later in the day, and improve their behavior. The goal was to eventually return them to their regular schools. As it turned out, so many students loved having their own program and their own time and space that they did not want to return.

Bolden also instituted a district-wide writing initiative to improve over-all academic performance. Within a year, writing scores at the city's high schools were up 11 percent. In cooperation with the National Urban Alliance and the International Reading Association, she renewed emphasis on reading at all schools, achieving a slight increase in test scores the first year. Building on a program she started years before as associate superintendent, she got the Newark Public Library to keep its branches open citywide on Saturdays.

Under her leadership, students also were introduced to new music programs created by William May, the district's director of performing arts. In partnership with Cablevision and the VH1 Save the Music Foundation, May brought former President Bill Clinton and teenage idols Mariah Carey and India.Arie to the Louise A. Spencer School in the spring of 2001. The big announcement that day was VH1's gift of $500,000 worth of musical instruments to Newark schools. No stranger to Newark, Clinton had visited Malcolm X Shabazz High School the year before to promote a partnership created by the school district and the city with the New Jersey Nets.

With the superintendent's encouragement, May also formed a sixteen-member jazz band composed of Newark music teachers that made its debut at Newark Symphony Hall in December 2001. The free program for parents and children, sponsored by the city of Newark, featured the Dizzy Gillespie Band. James Moody, the well-known jazz saxophonist from Newark, was the guest artist.

Two years later, after the music program was rebuilt, marching bands from seven schools proudly sported their new band uniforms at the district's first band festival at the new athletic complex. "Music is a wonderful way to generate school spirit and have fun at the same time," said Bolden. "It is nourishment for the soul. Our children deserve the chance to hear all forms of music. They also should have the chance to learn to play an instrument, as most of us did when we were children."

The linchpin of Bolden's school reform plan was her school to career and college initiatives effort. Because so many students were not college bound, she created partnerships with area businesses to train and employ them after graduation. PSE&G pitched in first, providing state-of-the-art equipment to train students at Technology High School in heating and air-conditioning repair. "The program is a two-way partnership," said PSE&G's Shirley Ward. "Newark's high school graduates need jobs, and we need highly trained people to service our equipment." With $1.6 billion in state construction funds promised to Newark, a construction trades apprenticeship program was started to give students a chance for employment when new schools were built and others replaced or renovated.

To keep students off the streets after school, Bolden revamped the district's afterschool program. The director, Elnardo Webster, soon shaped it into one of the nation's best, adding components that included drama, golf, soccer, and music. Because of its success at the elementary level, Bolden expanded to the high schools a program called Newark Do Something. With the help of teachers serving as community coaches, students engaged in projects of their choosing, such as community cleanups and voter registration drives. Another program, Newark Best Friends, which stresses teenage abstinence from drugs, alcohol, and sex, also became part of the superintendent's focus on character building.

When the still stately but vacant New Jersey Historical Society building in Newark's North Ward went up for sale, Bolden bought it for $600,000. Once renovated, it will house a student media center, replete with a state-of-the-art recording studio for teenagers who want to study broadcasting.

Bolden's support among the business community also was building. At a news conference in early 2001, practically every CEO in Newark praised her administration. "We are very fortunate here in Newark to have a strong leader like Marion Bolden who is knowledgeable about the community and is more than willing to partner," said Arthur Ryan, chairman and CEO of Prudential Financial, a key corporate partner. As a testament to his belief in Bolden's leadership, Ryan bought $1 million worth of computers for Newark high school students and provided millions more in technical support to the district.

Support for Bolden's administration also came from Catherine McFarland, executive director of the Victoria Foundation, a major Newark philanthropy. "Despite the lack of support she receives from the state, the tremendous bureaucracy she faces each day, and the friction that often comes from within, she's functioned better than any other superintendent

I've seen," said McFarland, whose ties to the district date to 1971. "When I go into the classroom, I can see steady improvement, which shows that test scores are not everything. That's because Marion knows and understands the kids and really cares about them." After a rough start, Bolden also won over the local newspaper, which created an $80,000-a-year scholarship program for performing arts students in conjunction with the district and the New Jersey Performing Arts Center.

Strong praise for her leadership came also from the Newark Teachers Union, for years an adversary of the administration. After working for months without a contract, members negotiated a generous three-year pact. Critics faulted the deal, but Bolden ardently defended it. "If we want to attract and retain good teachers," she said, "we have got to reward them." To support that belief, she gave each new teacher a $500 grant for the 1999–2000 school year and then found money in the budget to reward veteran teachers who developed innovative classroom programs.

Joseph Del Grosso, the teachers union president, had nothing but praise for the superintendent. "With Marion, we know where we stand," Del Grosso said. "She is from Newark. She was a Newark teacher. And she knows the district." As an ardent opponent of state control, Del Grosso had nothing nice to say about the state's involvement in Newark. "The last time anyone from Trenton was in a classroom was when the trolleys were running," he charged.

The teachers union further demonstrated its respect for Bolden by naming a new science center at the West Ward Cultural Center for her. Another honor was bestowed on her in May 2001 in the form of an honorary degree from Essex County College in Newark.

Despite many conflicting demands as an administrator, Bolden remained in close touch with Newark students. At school performances, she was the first to rise to applaud. At monthly board meetings, she regularly recognized the city's young people for their achievements. At sports events she was in the stands, cheering on the athletes.

"We love Mrs. Bolden because she was always there for us when we needed her. She has a great community focus," said Merissa Munford, a University High alumna. "When I was in the band at Shabazz, I think she went to every game," said Gary Dennis, his school's 2001 valedictorian. "Other educators talked about what they were going to do. Mrs. Bolden kept every promise."

"That's one of the few times I get to see her [at the games]," said Bolden's younger sister, Sheila. "Bebe's too busy for me to just call her and talk." Nevertheless, Bolden's family supports her mission. Even her children, who maintain busy schedules of their own, appreciate her focus. "Mommy is doing for other children what she did for us," said LaMar. Not all of Bolden's holidays are spent at work. "My sisters take turns cooking for the entire family at Thanksgiving and Christmas. Last Christmas it was Marion's turn," said Leonard Moore. "That's when we all get together."

Bolden is at ease with her family, but she has worked hard to develop her public persona. She credits the late Gladys Hillman-Jones, a dynamic Newark educator, with prying her out of her shell. "Gladys told me very candidly that I would have to develop personally if I wanted to put my abilities into play," she said. "So I did."

These days, her outgoing nature in public, especially before large numbers of people, comes as no surprise to her friends. "I think Marion is comfortable in public because she has grown so much over the years," said her friend and former colleague Gloria Royster. "We all grow. She feels comfortable before a crowd because she is a leader, because of the many different kinds of responsibilities she has had as an educator, because of the many people she has met in high places, and because of the extensive traveling she has done as her career advanced."

At school functions, Bolden is always on duty, no matter how much she may be enjoying herself. At one football game, for example, she was out of the stands in search of her security director to better direct fans leaving the stadium. At a basketball game, she was the first to respond when she saw a fight brewing. "We were at a state championship basketball game at the Rutgers Athletic Center when Marion spotted two girls from Newark arguing with girls from another team," said Lannie Paschall. "She sent the vice principal to break it up."

That was hardly the end of the incident. That Monday, the two Newark girls had to report to Bolden's office at 2 Cedar Street. At the next game in Elizabeth, there she was arm-in-arm with the two of them. She had picked them up, driven them to the game, and was taking them home. "Marion's interest was not in the fight," said Paschall. "It was in changing lives. It was about the kids. That's always her focus."

One of Bolden's most thrilling moments came on October 5, 2001, when she presided over the opening of the new $12.6 million Shabazz Athletic Field. To those who know her best, the tremendous pride she felt that day went far beyond her role as superintendent of Newark schools. Before the school became Shabazz, it was South Side—her school, her alma mater. This was her neighborhood, her town. Her home from birth through college, the house on Ridgewood Avenue, was right up the street from the new complex. Now, because of her tenacity and belief that Newark children deserved the best of everything, the stadium was theirs.

Eighteen months later, with a new governor in office and a new state education commissioner over her, Bolden abruptly found herself on a collision course with the state Department of Education. Instead of being rewarded for her good work, she was a candidate for removal. The rock thrown through her window, whether an intentional act or not, was a portent of things to come.

Until the 1995 state takeover, Newark schools were the domain of a small group of Newark politicians who had come to power in 1970, when Kenneth A. Gibson became the East Coast's first African-American mayor. At that time, all nine school board members were appointed by the mayor. The elected board came into being a decade later, after it was revealed one night at a board meeting that Gibson required letters of resignation from his appointees before they were sworn in.

Over the years, Gibson and his successor, Sharpe James, along with Steve Adubato, a powerful North Ward strategist, controlled the city's three major entities—City Hall, the Newark Housing Authority, and the public schools. Adubato also had a strong say in county government. James, who succeeded Gibson as mayor in 1986, was in the middle of his fourth four-year term when Bolden became superintendent. He ran City Hall and controlled housing authority appointments. Gibson and Adubato, dubbed "Newark's white mayor," acting individually or together, had a lock on the schools.

Gibson's chief allies were Central Ward Councilman Charles Bell (a school board member from 1970 to 1995, when the state stripped the board of its policy-making powers) and union leaders John (JJ) Johnson and James Benjamin. Johnson was the president of powerful Local 617 of the International Service Employees and vice president of New Jersey's American Federation of Labor and Congress of Industrial Organizations (AFL-CIO). Until he was sent to prison for skimming $500,000 in union funds, Benjamin headed Local 3, which represented the district's cafeteria workers. Eventually he became a get-out-the-vote expert for former Governor James E. McGreevey. After resuming his role in school politics, Benjamin also worked feverishly behind the scenes to help Gibson gradually regain control of the board.

Although the state removed all nine board members in July 1995, the takeover law called for staggered elections and an eventual return of the district to the voters once certain academic benchmarks were met. The distinct difference was that the new board was strictly an advisory body, lacking policy-making powers. The superintendent could veto any vote. The law also gave the state education commissioner the authority to select the superintendent of a takeover district. His recommendation, however, required approval by the state board of education.

In the summer of 2002, William Librera—just seven months on the job as McGreevey's education commissioner—astonished the Newark community by ordering a national search for Bolden's job nearly a year before her contract was up. Just as surprisingly, Librera put the selection process in the hands of Bolden's advisory board, promising to take the members' choice to the state board of education for approval. In doing so, he gave the board, which had no say whatsoever in hiring practices, the power to name the superintendent. The board members were now Librera's as well as Bolden's chief advisers.

By that time the board was split 5–4 against Bolden. Gibson-backed candidates, who ran on a ticket called the Home Team, constituted the majority. After the search narrowed the field of thirty-five candidates to Bolden and David Snead, superintendent of schools in Waterbury, Connecticut, the members voted twice to hire Snead. The clamor for Snead's approval was led by Evelyn Williams, board president, when the state arrived in Newark. Williams had resurfaced, winning election to Bolden's advisory team on the Home Team slate. Her motion was seconded by Jimmy Parrillo, Ken Gibson's self-described "best friend."

Because of Benjamin's and Johnson's close ties to McGreevey, the Gibsonites were more powerful than ever, bolstered by Gibson's renewed ties to James. That May, Benjamin also was instrumental in James's quest for a record fifth term as Newark's mayor. James's opponent was Cory Booker, considered by many old-timers to be a carpetbagger sent to the city by wealthy outsiders. A nasty campaign ensued. As the darling of the national media, Booker, the Central Ward councilman, was pictured as a young and vibrant political hopeful, possibly of presidential timber. James was characterized as over-the-hill and vindictive, quick to pounce politically on anyone who mentioned Booker's name.

For the first time since running against Gibson in 1986, James faced a real challenge. Booker not only was building widespread support locally; his national clout put $3 million in his campaign till. Young and enthusiastic, Booker's camp seemed sure of an upset. But his supporters proved no match for the solid base of political support crafted by James during thirty-two years in office, half as a city councilman. James won, carrying 52.9 percent of the vote to Booker's 46.5 percent. Nevertheless, the margin was considerably less than the mayor's lopsided victories of the past.

Until Librera's announcement that Bolden's job was in jeopardy, Bolden and James appeared on friendly enough terms. Behind the scenes, their relationship was changing. Bolden thought James was miffed because she refused to fire a longtime employee whose son was deeply involved in Booker's campaign. James denied the charge, distancing himself from Bolden at public events while denying claims by her supporters that he was the chief conspirator behind the move to oust her.

Bolden, however, had substantial community support. A petition drive to save her job, spearheaded by churches, parents, and educators, was soon underway, urging McGreevey and Librera to reverse course and reappoint her. With Jefferson, Metropolitan's pastor, and the Reverend M. William Howard, Jr., pastor of Bethany Baptist Church, at the forefront of a mushrooming pro-education movement, three thousand petitions were sent to the state capital. A rally at Metropolitan drew six hundred people.

Days later, many of the same people marched down Broad Street, the city's major artery, to City Hall, urging James to speak out on Bolden's behalf. He did not.

A *Star-Ledger* editorial bearing the headline "Newark Needs Bolden" called for the superintendent's retention, concluding, "The state Board of Education still holds legal responsibility for running the Newark district and hiring its superintendent. It must now exercise the authority Librera had no right to surrender. The state board should keep Bolden in Newark." But Librera and McGreevey were unyielding, and James said nothing. The commissioner's only concession was to include Bolden in the candidates' pool rather than force her to apply for her job.

Admittedly, Snead was no fiscal expert. What's more, his record as former superintendent in Detroit was marred by alleged fiscal irregularities. Conversely, Bolden had turned around the fiscal mess that predated her four years on the job. "The very fact that strong support was in place for Mrs. Bolden meant that a vote to keep her should have occurred," said the Reverend Reginald Jackson, president of the New Jersey Black Ministers Council. "The fact that there was a search sent the message that she was on the way out—that it was a done deal. It was not about children, it was about contracts and jobs—to go back to the way things were [before the state takeover]."

Librera's argument that he was preparing the Newark Public Schools for a return to local control appeared weak, especially because the academic benchmarks set by his department were nowhere near being achieved. Another irony was that Evelyn Williams and Tina Cruz, two board members who voted for Snead, were members of the 1995 board dissolved by the state.

Behind the scenes, Congressman Donald Payne, Senator Ronald Rice, Assemblyman Craig Stanley, and other powerful Bolden supporters worked furiously to get McGreevey to call off the search. Added pressure came from a community support group called Save Our Children, whose members protested and rallied locally before marching on the state capital.

After months of delay, Librera was about to bring Snead's name before the state board. But he did not, delaying his recommendation in March and again in early April 2003. Instead, he decided to wait until after Newark's April 15 school board election, promising to abide by the results. If the board remained 5–4 in favor of Snead, he would urge Snead's appointment. If Bolden's supporters tipped the balance in her favor, she would be his nominee.

Consequently, Bolden's fate became a political joust for the three open board seats, including those held by Williams and Parrillo—a battle that pitted the pro-Bolden For Us Kids candidates against the anti-Bolden Home Team. Board chairwoman Maryam Bey wanted Bolden replaced because of her alleged failure to include parents in decision-making processes. Despite Bolden's brief tenure, Bey, who was elected by the Home Team, maintained that test scores had not improved significantly enough.

Bolden's support was concentrated largely in the city's heavily Hispanic North and East wards, where the For Us Kids team was backed by Adubato, North Ward Councilman Hector Corchado, and Booker. Community-wide support came from the Newark Teachers Union, churches, and parents. "From the start, the overwhelming sentiment of our teachers and staff members was in support of Mrs. Bolden," said Newark Teachers Union chief Del Grosso.

With James Benjamin at the helm as campaign manager, the Home Team ticket, led by Williams and Parrillo, operated out of Ken Gibson's downtown offices. Confidently, Benjamin predicted a clean sweep. Phil Alagia, an Adubato protégé who ran the For Us Kids campaign, was more cautious, at least publicly. The primary goal, he said, was to take control of the board by winning at least two seats.

Election day dawned bright and sunny, attracting 15 percent of the city's voters to the polls—three times the usual Newark turnout and significantly better than the 10 percent average statewide. Bolden's supporters, despite disparate interests, swept all three seats by huge margins—3–1 for Dana Rone, the top vote-getter, and more than 2–1 for Anibal Ramos, who became the new board chairman, and Tony Machado, their running mate.

Their victory was Bolden's victory. On Wednesday, May 7, 2003, the state board of education, by unanimous vote, reappointed Marion

Alexander Bolden state district superintendent of the Newark Public Schools. For Bolden, winning the election was far more than a personal triumph. "Wherever I went, even shopping at Pathmark, I was approached by people who urged me to stay on for the children's sake—so that we could continue the progress," she said. "That's what I did because that's what all this really was about for me."

APPENDIX: PROFILES

Arts/Entertainment

Lisa Attles, a soloist with the Dance Theater of Harlem from 1982 to 1995, toured with the company throughout the United States, Europe, Africa, Asia, and South America. She has performed leading roles in *Medea, Dougla,* and *John Henry.* Attles began her training at the Newark School of the Arts and furthered her studies under Fred Danieli at the Garden State Ballet and Alfred Gallman at Gallman's Dance Theatre. She became the director of the Covenant Life Ministries' Dance and Drama Ministries in River Edge, New Jersey.

Amina Baraka is a well-known Newark poet who appears regularly with BluArk, a group that combines expressions of the written word with African musical forms. With her husband, poet and playwright Amiri Baraka, she edited *Confirmation: An Anthology of African-American Women* (Quill, 1983). In 1998 their ensemble presented a program on the life of jazz legend Willie (the Lion) Smith at the New Jersey Performing Arts Center in Newark. A cultural space in their home is called Kimako's Blues People.

Dolores Collins Tillery Benjamin founded and directed the North Jersey Philharmonic Glee Club, the nation's oldest African-American male chorus. Begun in 1939, the chorus presented an acclaimed program at Town Hall in New York City in 1948. A native of Norfolk, Virginia, Benjamin graduated from Virginia State University in Petersburg, Virginia. Before her retirement, she was a teacher in East Orange, New Jersey.

Daphne Haygood Benyard, a faculty member at Essex County College in Newark, has penned three volumes of poetry and written more than two hundred poems and essays. Her poems have appeared in many anthologies, and her profile is included in *Afro-American Women Writers of New Jersey.* She holds a master's degree in public administration from Rutgers University and studied at the University of Bristol in England.

Salome, Geraldine, and Andy Bey were known as Andy Bey and the Bey Sisters. Duke Ellington described their distinctive approach to ensemble singing, which incorporated jazz, blues, gospel, R&B, Broadway, and pop, as "beyond category." The trio made two albums for Prestige, *Now! Hear!* in 1964 and *'Round Midnight* in 1965. Geraldine is deceased. Salome and her brother, Andy, who is one of the most highly respected names in jazz, continued their careers as solo artists. Their niece is singer Ronnell Bey.

Chakaia Booker, who was born in Newark in 1953, transforms found objects into works of art. Her sculptures are produced by recycling tires into abstract African designs. She earned a bachelor's degree in sociology from Rutgers University and a master of fine arts degree from City College of New York. Her commissions include works for the Laumeier Sculpture Park in St. Louis, the National Aeronautics and Space Administration Art Program, and the Neuberger Museum of Art at Purchase College in New York.

Nellie Johnson Boone taught special education and English in the Newark schools for thirty-five years. A contralto soloist, she appeared in concerts at the First Presbyterian Church and Carnegie Hall in New York, singing seventeenth-century songs, arias, and spirituals. After graduating from Benedict College in Columbia, South Carolina, and earning a master's degree at New York University, she taught at Morris College in Sumter, South Carolina. She subsequently taught at Kean and Rutgers Universities. Her father was the Reverend B. F. Johnson, Sr., pastor of Metropolitan Baptist Church and dean of Newark's Baptist ministry.

Eleta J. Caldwell, a former art teacher, retired in 2003 as principal of Newark's Arts High School. As an artist, she has exhibited her work at the Newark Museum, Studio Museum of Harlem, Jersey City Museum, various galleries, and public and corporate sites. Her mixed media pieces are in several private and corporate collections. Born in Chapel Hill, North Carolina, and educated in the Newark Public Schools, she is a graduate of Arts High School and Montclair State University. She also studied at the Rhode Island School of Design, Seton Hall University, and The Art Students League of New York.

Tisha Campbell-Martin, a graduate of Arts High School, costars in the ABC-TV sit-com *My Wife and Kids.* She previously starred as Gina in the long-running comedy series *Martin*. She made her show business debut at age three, singing Billie Holiday's "Them There Eyes" at a tribute to Newark singer Viola Wells (Miss Rhapsody) and went on to appear on television in *Big Blue Marble* and *Captain Kangaroo* and on Broadway in *Really Rosie*. At fifteen she appeared in the film *Little House of Horrors* and then moved to Hollywood to appear on the television series *Rags to Riches*. Other film roles include Spike Lee's *School Daze*, *House Party (I, II, and III)*, *Another 48 Hours*, *Homeward Bound II*, *Boomerang*, and *Sprung*.

Berenice Maxwell Cross, a coloratura soprano, studied under Cora Wynn Alexander of Newark. Born in Newark, she is a graduate of Weequahic High School, studied at Dana College, and took business courses at the Essex County Vocational School. As a teenager she began singing in the choir at Thirteenth Avenue Presbyterian Church in Newark. Her first recital was at Arts High School. She also sang at the Bermuda Opera House and in the choir of Basilica Cathedral of the Sacred Heart in Newark. She was employed for sixty-five years at the *Star-Ledger,* where her father was the first black editor. In 1929 her brother, Jocko, became the nation's first black sports announcer.

Hisani DuBose has worked in the entertainment industry since graduating from Seton Hall University, where she wrote, choreographed, and performed in her first musical, *A Different Kinda Blues*. After seeing her perform, Arthur Mitchell, founder of New York's Dance Theatre of Harlem, offered her a scholarship to study music and dance at the company's school. She has written a musical, cable TV show, several shorts, and a feature-length film, and she ran the production company of jazz great Jimmy Scott. As a singer-songwriter, she performed with Angela Bofill, Bernard Wright, and Danny Madden. She is the founder of the NJ Moviemakers Network.

Gloria Gaynor, dubbed the Queen of Disco was born Gloria Fowles in Newark, New Jersey, where she graduated from South Side High School. Discovered by Arista founder Clive Davis, she recorded an album every year from 1973 to 1981. Every one went Top 40. Her anthem, "I Will Survive," recorded in 1979, won a Grammy Award for best disco song. During a countdown of the 100 Best Dance Records in 2000, it topped the charts. She has performed in more than eighty countries and was featured on VH1's *Behind the Music*.

Yvette Glover is a jazz and pop singer whose worldwide performances include an appearance before the king of Morocco. A favorite at local clubs, she is a graduate of Essex County College, where she was president of the Student Government Association. She also serves on the board of International Women in Jazz. Her parents, Anna Mae Lundy Lewis and Billy Lewis, were key figures on Newark's jazz scene during the Swing Era. She is the mother of tap-dancing sensation Savion Glover.

Gladys Barker Grauer is a graduate of the Art Institute of Chicago. In the early 1970s she founded the AARD Studio Gallery in her South Ward neighborhood, offering African Americans a chance to meet area artists and purchase paintings for as little as a dollar a week. With Newark artists Eleta Caldwell, Nettie Thomas, and Janet Pickett, she founded Black Women in Visual Perspective. Her work has been exhibited in museums and galleries in New Jersey, New York, and Dakar, Senegal. She is a former artist-in-residence at the Newark Museum.

Evelyn L. Greene, a coloratura soprano, taught music for many years at Rutgers University in Newark and was a soloist in many church and community concerts. As a child, she and Sarah Vaughan sang in the choir at First Mount Zion Church in Newark. She is a former president of the Newark Club of the National Association of Negro Musicians.

Gwen Guthrie, singer and songwriter, contributed to dozens of albums as a composer, lead singer, and disco star. As a child, she studied classical music and piano. She began her professional career singing background vocals for Aretha Franklin. Later she worked with Roberta Flack and Luther Vandross and recorded with Kenny Loggins and Steely Dan. She is best known for her 1980s R&B dance hit, "Ain't Nothing Goin' on But the Rent." She died of uterine cancer in 1999 at age forty-eight.

Delora Elizabeth Jones-Hicks, who died on January 4, 1996, at age fifty-eight, was manager of the Division of Concerts and Lectures at Rutgers University in Newark, where she was responsible for bringing diverse artists such as Sarah Vaughan, Yehudi Menuhin, and the Count Basie Orchestra to perform on campus. She also served as chairwoman of the Organization of Black Faculty and Staff at Rutgers-Newark. Educated in the fields of social science and health administration at Rutgers University, she also studied alcohol and drug abuse at several colleges. She was a co-founder of the New Well, one of New Jersey's first treatment centers for drug addicts.

Emily (Cissy) Houston began singing as a child with the Drinkard Four, a family gospel group. She later sang with the Drinkard Singers and

Sweet Inspirations, a backup group for singers that included Aretha Franklin. During the 1970s and 1980s she sang regularly at Freddie's, Mikell's, and the Horn of Plenty, New York nightclubs. Her film roles include an appearance with her daughter, Whitney Houston, in the movie *The Preacher's Wife*. She serves as president and CEO of the Whitney Houston Foundation for Children and is the choir director at Newark's New Hope Baptist Church. Her biography, *How Sweet the Sound*, was published by Doubleday in 1998.

Whitney Houston, whose records have sold millions, is a household name the world over. Born in Newark on August 9, 1963, she graduated from Mount St. Dominic Academy in Caldwell. Before the release of her first hit record, *Whitney Houston*, on Arista in 1985, she sang background for her mother, Cissy Houston. She made her first nightclub appearance as a solo artist at Sweetwater's in New York City. Her first Grammy was for "Saving All My Love for You." Other hits include "Greatest Love of All," "You Give Good Love," and "How Will I Know?" Her screen credits include *The Bodyguard, Waiting to Exhale,* and *The Preacher's Wife*.

Carrie Jackson, a well-known singer on Newark's current jazz scene, is the leader of Carrie Jackson and her Jazzin' All Stars. She also heads her own recording company and books many area singers and musicians. Her husband is Gil (Bop) Benson, a master interpreter of bop.

Lillette Jenkins, music director and jazz pianist for the off-Broadway hit *One Mo' Time,* served for many years as minister of music at Mount Zion Baptist Church in Newark. A native of Harlem, she graduated from the New York College of Music at New York University and attended Westminster Choir College in Princeton, New Jersey. Her movie credits include *The Cotton Club* and *Coming to America.* On television, she has appeared in *All My Children.* A prolific recording artist for more than fifty years, she has appeared at jazz festivals in Europe and the United States and on world cruises.

Dorthaan Kirk, a founder of WBGO Jazz 88, is the National Public Radio station's director of community relations and special events and curator of its art gallery. She runs the WBGO Children's Jazz Festival and the Jazz Vespers program at Bethany Baptist Church in Newark. Until his death in 1977, she accompanied her husband, jazz saxophonist Rahsaan Roland Kirk, on worldwide tours. She continues to manage his music and guide his publishing company. She is a native of Houston, Texas.

Queen Latifah was born Dana Owens in Newark on March 18, 1970. This versatile singer, composer, actress, and producer gained fame as the first lady of hip-hop. She has appeared in starring roles on television as Khadijah James on *In Living Color* and in films, including *House Party 2*, *Jungle Fever*, and *Chicago*, for which she was nominated for an Academy Award for Best Supporting Actress in 2003. As a producer, her work includes *Beauty Shop* and *The Cookout*. Her mother, Rita Owens, is a teacher at Irvington (New Jersey) High School.

Anna Mae Lundy Lewis, organist and pianist, was a fixture at Newark nightclubs in the 1940s. She later became minister of music at Newark's New Point Baptist Church, serving in that position for sixty years. Born in Jacksonville, Florida, in 1916, she was the daughter of Dick Lundy, a star of the Negro Baseball League and manager of the Newark Eagles. She was the mother of singer Yvette Glover and the grandmother of tap dancer Savion Glover. She died on June 2, 2002, at age eighty-five.

Benilde Little is the author of the best-selling novel *Good Hair* (Simon & Schuster, 1996), which examines class distinctions among African Americans. Selected as one of the ten best books of 1996 by the *Los Angeles Times*, *Good Hair* spent six months at number one on the Blackboard Bestseller list. She was nominated for an NAACP Image Award for her work and was named Best New Author by the Go on Girl Book Club, a nationwide reading group. She has written subsequent novels, including *The Itch* (Simon & Schuster, 1998) and *Acting Out* (Free Press, 2003). A former senior editor at *Essence* and a contributing editor at *Heart and Soul*, Little has been a reporter for *People*, the *Cleveland Plain Dealer,* and the *Star-Ledger.* Born and raised in Newark, she received a bachelor's degree in journalism from Howard University and did graduate work at Northwestern University.

Inez McClendon teaches music at the Newark School of the Arts and directs the South Side High School Alumni Chorus. A graduate of South Side, she holds a bachelor's degree in music education and a master's degree in speech and theater from Montclair State University. She is the star of a one-woman traveling show, *The Many Faces of Inez.*

Deborah Mitchell is the artistic director of the New Jersey Tap Ensemble, which she founded in 1994. She is a protégé of Leslie (Bubba) Gaines of the Copasetics and a student of tap masters including choreographer Henry Le Tang. She appeared in the film *Cotton Club* and in the Broadway and Paris productions of *Black and Blue*. She is a principal affiliate with the New Jersey Performing Arts Center and taught in the NJPAC Dance Academy residency program for six years. A former social worker, she holds a master's degree in social work and psychology.

Melba Moore won a Tony for her role in *Purlie* on Broadway, where she also appeared in other musicals, including *Timbuktu*. A graduate of Arts High School and Montclair State College, she has enjoyed a diverse career in show business that has included starring in her own TV show and recording extensively. She is a former Newark teacher. Her parents, Bonnie Davis and Clem Moorman, were among Newark's most popular entertainers during the 1940s.

Thelma Moorman, a jazz pianist, was a popular figure at Newark nightclubs in the 1930s and 1940s. Born in Newark, she came from a musical family that included her brothers, Clem and Mixie; a sister, Hazel; and a niece, Melba Moore.

Gwen Moten appeared with Melba Moore and Eartha Kitt on Broadway in *Timbuktu* and also served as the show's assistant choral conductor. She toured North America and Europe with Harry Belafonte in 1983 and nationally in a revival of *Guys and Dolls*. As the only African-American woman to operate a music service business, she wrote music for Broadway artists and orchestras. In 1993 and 1994, she was a cultural ambassador for the U.S. Information Agency, assigned to Botswana. From 1988 to 1996, she was director of the Newark Boys Chorus School and its chorus. Subsequently she became director of cultural affairs for the city of Newark. In 2003 she was appointed director of Newark Symphony Hall. She also serves as minister of music at St. James African Methodist Episcopalian Church in Newark.

Betty H. Neals, a Newark native, is known internationally for her spirited and moving poetry, which focuses on African-American experiences. She retired as a teacher after thirty-seven years in the East Orange school system. In 1973 she was listed in *Outstanding Elementary Teachers of America*. A performing artist, she appears at schools and churches and before community groups. Her books include *Spirit Weaving* (Sesame Press, 1977) and *Move the Air* (Stonechat Press, 1980). She also was a lyricist for jazz musicians, including John Coltrane and Rahsaan Roland Kirk.

Henrietta S. Parker is the recipient of five Emmy Awards from the National Academy of Television Arts and Sciences for her work as coordinating producer of *Due Process* for NJN, New Jersey Public Television and Radio. She also has produced two movies: *Sweet Inspiration* (about singer Cissy Houston), and *Peg Leg Bates: The Dancing Man*. For NJN she produced *The Cholesterol Challenge: Can You Cut It?* and *The Chase Lincoln-Douglass Debates*. Born in Newark, she is a graduate of South Side High School and Newark State College, where she received a bachelor's degree in elementary education.

Rhoda Scott, a prolific recording artist who has lived outside Paris for the past three decades, is a master of the Hammond B3 organ. She gained popularity appearing with saxophonist Joe Thomas and drummer Bill Elliot at Len & Len's in Newark and at the old Key Club, where Charles (the Mighty Burner) Earland, Captain Jack McDuff, and Jimmy McGriff also performed regularly. She is known as the Barefoot Organist because she wears no shoes when she plays.

Gladys Black Sherman, who developed the art of batik, blended fabric with wax and dye in her designs. She graduated from the Newark School of Fine and Industrial Arts, where she taught at the college level for twenty years. She was the school's registrar, consultant, and faculty coordinator when she retired in 1991. In 1965 her work was exhibited at the World's Fair Pavilion in New York City under the pseudonym Gadem. She died in 1995.

Carrie Smith, an internationally known blues singer who has carried on the tradition of southern folk blues made famous by Bessie Smith, first performed in church at age seven. Her musical training took shape at two Baptist churches in Newark, Greater Abyssinian Baptist and Greater Harvest. She made her professional debut in the 1960s at New York's Town Hall and then toured with Big Tiny Little, Al Hirt, and the Cab Calloway bands. She has appeared at nightclubs and jazz festivals worldwide and was a mainstay of George Wein's Grande Parade du Jazz in Nice. In 1989 she appeared on Broadway in the musical *Black and Blue*. She is a native of Fort Gaines, Georgia.

Connie Pitts Speed, a highly regarded jazz singer, performed both sacred and secular music. In her youth, she was the lead singer of the Pitts Sisters, a group that included her siblings, Eloise and Edith. The sisters' home was True Love Baptist Church in Newark, where their father, the late Reverend William H. Pitts, was the pastor. Connie also was a soloist with the Youth Cavalcade, a group of Newark's finest young gospel singers established by radio personality Bernice Bass. She was minister of music at First Baptist Church of Nutley, where she sang in the choir with heiress Doris Duke. She died in October 1996 at age sixty-five.

Sarah Vaughan, who was born March 27, 1924, in Newark, was one of the jazz world's most famous names. Known as Sassy to her friends and the Divine One to her fans, she was a musical legend whose distinctive style and rich contralto voice influenced many singers of popular music. Born and raised in Newark, she sang in the choir at Newark's Old First Mount Zion Baptist Church, where she became the organist at age twelve. In 1942 she won the Amateur Night contest at Harlem's Apollo Theater and then joined the bands of Earl Hines and Billy Eckstine. Her first hit was "Tenderly," on the Musicraft label (1947). Her complete output for Mercury was 263 cuts, including her signature songs, "Misty" and "Send in the Clowns." She died on April 3, 1990, at her home in Hidden Hills, California.

Valerie Wilson Wesley is the author of the Tamara Hayle mystery series (G.P. Putnam's Sons) about a female detective from Newark. Her adult novels include *Ain't Nobody's Business If I Do* (Avon, 1999), a Blackboard Bestseller that won the 2000 award for adult fiction from the Black Caucus of the American Library Association, and *Always True to You in My Fashion* (Avon, 2002), an *Essence* bestseller. She also writes children's books, and her short stories and essays have been included in anthologies. A former executive editor of *Essence,* she is a graduate of Howard University and holds master's degrees from the Bank Street College of Education and the Columbia Graduate School of Journalism. Her husband is the noted playwright and screenwriter Richard Wesley.

Princess White, a dynamic performer, was the star of the Silas Green from New Orleans minstrel show from 1900 to 1917. Born in Philadelphia in 1880, she was recruited at age four to travel with a troupe bound for Australia. In later years she was a member of Irvin C. Miller's Brownskin Models. After a long retirement, she began singing again at age ninety-four with the Harlem Blues and Jazz Band, cutting two records with the band. A year later, on March 21, 1976, she collapsed and died in the wings of the Emelin Theater in Mamaroneck, New York.

Business

Carol E. Boyd is the owner of Branford Press, the only African-American union-operated print shop in New Jersey. A graduate of West Side

High School, she was appointed by Mayor Sharpe James to serve on the Newark Workforce Investment Board. She also is active with the A. Philip Randolph Institute and the African-American Heritage Parade Committee.

Edith C. Churchman is the director of the James E. Churchman, Jr., Funeral Home of Newark, the fourth generation of her family to run the family business, which was founded in 1899. A graduate of Arts High School in Newark, she earned a bachelor's degree from Heidelberg College in Tiffin, Ohio, a master's degree from Emerson College in Boston, and a doctorate from Bowling Green University in Ohio. After graduating from the New England Institute of Funeral Service Education, she taught school before joining the family enterprise.

Eugenia (Jeanne) Dawkins owned the Key Club, a popular Newark jazz club that attracted stars such as Sarah Vaughan and was Home of the Hammond B3 Organ to musicians such as Rhoda Scott and Jimmy McGriff. Founded on West Street in Newark, the club later moved to William and Halsey Streets, where it gained a reputation as the Jazz Corner of the World. Born in Belleville, New Jersey, and educated in the nearby Bloomfield schools, Dawkins ran the club alone after her husband Walter's death. In 1976 she was named Newark's Woman of the Year. She died in 1978 at age fifty-two.

Josephine Belle Janifer, a former executive director of the Newark Preschool Council, became administrator of the city's Private Industry Council, a job training and development agency for the disadvantaged, in 1979. A native of Montclair, New Jersey, she holds a bachelor's degree in history from Upsala College in East Orange and a master's degree in economics from the University of Pittsburgh. Her father-in-law, Dr. Clarence Janifer, was a well-known Newark physician.

Marilyn (Penny) Joseph is general manager of recruiting and outreach programs for Panasonic (Matsushita Electric Corporation of America). Previously she was the company's assistant general manager of corporate contributions, helping direct more than $50 million in donations to nonprofit organizations. Before joining Panasonic, she was manager of public affairs at Mutual Benefit Life Insurance Company in Newark and a planning analyst for the city of Newark. She is a 1976 graduate of Spelman College.

Effa Manley, who owned the Brooklyn Eagles and the Newark Eagles of the Negro Baseball League from 1935 to 1948 with her husband, Abe, was considered the First Lady of Black Baseball. In 1946 the Eagles won the league championship and the Black World Series, led by Monte Irvin,

Larry Doby, and Don Newcombe. A generous woman, Manley often arranged musical entertainment for the troops at Fort Dix during World War II.

Ella Moncur, who owned the popular Theatrical Beauty Salon in Newark, was born in Newark on May 6, 1919, and educated in city schools. Many important women, including singer Sarah Vaughan, were her customers. After retiring to Miami, she studied at Miami-Dade Community College and became a vocational teacher. She was the wife of Grachan (Brother) Moncur, bassist with the Savoy Sultans, and the mother of jazz trombonist Grachan Moncur III. Her stepfather, Bishop Allen W. Hamilton, was the pastor of the Church of God and Saints in Christ in Newark. She died on April 15, 1999, in Miami.

Gabriella Morris is corporate vice president of community resources for Prudential Financial and president of the Prudential Foundation. She is charged with oversight of the foundation's grant making and the company's social investment programs. Before joining Prudential, she was an attorney with the law firm of Baker & Botts, based in Houston, Texas, where she specialized in corporate and real estate law. She served as vice chairman of the Kean University board of trustees. She has a bachelor's degree in architecture and urban planning from Princeton University and a law degree from the University of Texas Law School.

Mae Muldrow, who owned La Vogue Beauty Salon in Newark, was at the forefront of her profession nationally. During the early years of her business, Algine Ray, who subsequently opened a shop of her own, was her partner. Muldrow was responsible for the Cordelia Green Johnson Foundation, which provided scholarships for aspiring black beauticians and cosmetologists. She died in a car accident in Newark on September 16, 1977.

Marjorie (Marge) Perry is president and CEO of the MZM Construction Company. After participating in the New Jersey Institute of Technology Business Incubator Program in 1997, she landed an excavation and landscaping job at the New Jersey Performing Arts Center in Newark. She counts among her clients the Port Authority of New York and New Jersey, New Jersey Transit, the New Jersey Department of Transportation, and the city and state of New York.

Virginia A. Perry, president and owner of Perry's Funeral Home in Newark, is a native of Bassett, Virginia, and the oldest of ten children. A graduate of the University of Maryland–Eastern Shore, she majored in business education and taught for eleven years in Roselle and Newark before enrolling at the American Academy McAllister Institute of Funeral Services in New York City.

Michele T. Ralph is director of human resource information services for Merck, the giant pharmaceutical company. She is a former director of the Newark Mayor's Office on Employment and Training and former director of personnel for Schering-Plough. She serves on the board of the Essex County College Foundation. She holds a bachelor's degree in French from St. Peter's College and a master's degree in business administration from Fairleigh Dickinson University.

Eurlee Reeves, who operated the Nest Club nightclub on Warren Street in Newark, was the only female owner of a Newark nightclub during the Swing Era. A shrewd businesswoman, she focused on developing local talent and presenting full-scale weekly musical revues that packed the house. Born in Pelham, New York, in 1898, she died on February 1, 1990, in the New Community Nursing Home in Newark.

Louise Scott, a domestic-turned-businesswoman, became a self-made millionaire, reigning over a chain of Newark beauty shops. Born in Florence, South Carolina, she enrolled at the Apex Beauty Culture School in New York City after graduating from high school. She moved to Newark in 1938 and opened her first beauty salon on Barclay Street in 1944. Eventually she owned five beauty salons, a guest house, and a hotel. In 1958 she bought a forty-three-room mansion at Court and High Streets in Newark that had been built by beer baron Gottfried Krueger in 1888 at a cost of $100,000. Soon after her death, on April 21, 1983, the city of Newark seized the Krueger-Scott Mansion for unpaid taxes. After spending nearly $10 million to restore it, the city's plans for an African-American museum never materialized.

Linda Spradley-Dunn is the founder and CEO of the Newark-based Idamar Enterprises, a marketing and communications firm cited in 2001 by INC. magazine as one of the nation's three fastest-growing companies. She serves as vice chairperson of the Essex County College Foundation and is a member of the New Jersey Small Business Development Center's Statewide Advisory Board and the Women's Board of the New Jersey Performing Arts Center.

Amealia Steward was a self-made millionaire whose wealth came from her investments and interest in the restaurant business. Steward's

Restaurant, which specialized in African-American food, began on Prince Street with just four tables. Later it moved to a larger spot on Avon Avenue, eventually winding up on Lyons Avenue in Newark. Her son John later established, and still runs, John's Place, another popular Newark restaurant. Steward's Restaurant is now run by her grandson Darryl. Amealia Steward was born in Albany, Georgia, on March 15, 1917, and died on September 23, 2001, at age eighty-four.

Diane Sutton, who owned and operated Je's restaurant with her husband, Harry, and their sons, Harry, Chad, and Jason, was one of Newark's most successful businesswomen. Born in Warren County, North Carolina, on November 3, 1941, she was the daughter of a sharecropper. In the mid-1960s, she and her husband were the first people of color to open a restaurant in downtown Newark, Je's Coffee Shop on William Street. In 1985 they moved to larger quarters at William and Halsey Streets, where Je's became a regional landmark for southern cuisine, attracting celebrities from the world over. Sutton, who supported many community causes, died suddenly on August 11, 2000, at age fifty-eight.

Shirley M. Ward, an administrator with PSE&G of Newark since 1979, has been manager of the company's Strategic Urban Development/Diversity program since December 1998. Her urban model for strong public-private partnerships was recognized in 1988 at a White House ceremony. From 1991 to 1996, she was the utility's manager of community affairs. She holds a bachelor's degree in business administration from Montclair State University and several certificates in corporate and urban management.

Carolyn. M. Whigham was a successful real estate property management consultant in Los Angeles when she bowed out of the business to return to her native Newark in 1985. She enrolled at the American Academy McAllister School of Mortuary Science in New York City, where, at graduation, she received the Thomas M. Quinn Award for Outstanding Achievement. Upon his retirement, her father, Charles L. Whigham, founder of the Whigham Funeral Home, appointed her manager and president of the family business. A graduate of Virginia State College with a bachelor's degree in business administration, she studied ancient methods of embalming and preservation in Egypt.

Janet White spent twenty years as operations manager at Merrill Lynch, one of the country's top financial services firms, serving as a troubleshooter for offices around the nation until her retirement in 1986. A GOP County Committee member in West Orange and Newark, she was a member of the New Jersey Black Republicans, New Jersey Advisory Commission on the Status of Women, and National Association of Negro Business and Professional Women's Clubs, which named her Business Woman of the Year. She died on October 21, 2004, at age eighty-three.

Church

The Reverend Alexina Brown coordinated a 1990s tutorial program for Newark students run by twenty-four churches in cooperation with the Newark Public Schools. She was chairman of the Education Committee of the Newark–North Jersey Committee of Black Churchmen and tenant association president at Court Towers, a Newark senior citizens apartment building.

Elder Anna Cooper is the pastor of Mother's Foundation Holiness Church in Newark, which she founded in 1973 in the basement of her home. Born in Hemingway, South Carolina, on September 3, 1925, she raised nine children as a single parent. Her second-oldest daughter, Elder Shirley Polite, is her assistant pastor. Mother Cooper, who grew up in the Pentecostal religion, joined Daniels Temple Holiness Church after moving to Newark in 1967. Before starting her own church, she was assistant pastor at Daniels Temple and St. Luke's Holiness Church in Newark.

The Reverend Martha A. Daniels was, until her death in the mid-1990s, pastor of the Community Baptist Church in Newark. She was ordained by her husband in 1953. In 1975 she became the first female member of the Committee of Black Churchmen of Newark and Vicinity. A former choir director, church organist, and Bible school director, she earned her doctor of divinity degree after completing graduate studies at Columbia Teacher's College and Seton Hall University.

Dr. Leah Gaskin Fitchue became president of Payne Theological Seminary at Wilberforce University in Ohio in November 2004, making her the first woman to preside over a black seminary. She is a former associate professor of urban ministry and director of urban ministry studies at Eastern Baptist Theological Seminary in Philadelphia and former associate minister at Philadelphia's Mother Bethel AME Church. In 1997 *Ebony* magazine named her to its Honor Roll of Great Black Women Preachers. From

1999 to 2003, she was executive vice president of academic services and academic development at Atlanta's Interdenominational Theological Center. A graduate of South Side High School, she holds a bachelor's degree from Rutgers University and a master's degree in speech pathology from the University of Michigan. She earned her master of divinity degree from Princeton Theological Seminary and a doctorate from Harvard University.

Rosetta Lee, a missionary at St. James African Methodist Episcopalian Church in Newark, helped establish a church in Haiti and a health clinic in Botswana, South Africa. Born in Iron City, Georgia, she completed religious classes while working as a nurse's aide at city hospitals. During fifty years of world travel, she led the effort to erect five buildings in Dumarney, Haiti, including the church, which is named for her, and a school that serves 175 children. At St. James, she was the first chairperson of the credit union education program. She died in 2003 at age ninety-two.

Mattie Lee Hodge Moore, assistant pastor at Newark's Union Chapel, grew up on a farm in Empire, Georgia, where she worked days as a practical nurse and ran a sewing service at night to support her family after her husband died. Before moving to Newark in 1967, she attended Maryland Bible School in Aberdeen for two years. She completed an additional eight years of study with the American Methodist Conference and the African Methodist Episcopal Institute. She later earned a bachelor's degree at Rutgers University and a teacher's certificate at Kean College and then became a substitute teacher in the Newark Public Schools. In 1978 she ran for mayor of Newark, finishing third.

Ann L. Drinkard Moss was born into a musical family in Newark on April 16, 1927. With her sister, Cissy Houston, and their brothers, Larry and Nick, she formed the Drinkard Four. Renamed the Drinkard Singers, the group became the first gospel ensemble to sing at the Newport Jazz Festival and record on the RCA label. She later formed the Drinkard Ensemble, the on-the-road opening act for her niece, Dionne Warwick. She joined New Hope Baptist Church in Newark in 1953, becoming choir president and directress and assistant minister of music. She was the recipient of a Pioneer of Gospel Music Award. She died on January 1, 2003, at age seventy-five.

The Reverend Joan S. Parrott is vice president of leadership and spiritual renewal programs for the Children's Defense Fund at the former Alex Haley Farm in Clinton, Tennessee. A native of Newark, she graduated from Montclair State University and completed further studies at Union Theological Seminary; Bossy, the Ecumenical Institute in Switzerland; United Theological Seminary; and Harvard University's Community Builder Fellowship Program. She is a former East Orange, New Jersey, teacher; former Peace Corps volunteer in Niger, West Africa; and former executive director of the Lighthouse Community Services Homeless Shelter in Newark, founded by her father, the late Bishop James Parrott. She also has served as deputy general secretary for the American Baptist Churches in the United States. She made history as a U.S. Baptist minister when she became the first woman in 129 years to be ordained at Bethany Baptist Church in Newark.

Lila Mae Ralph received the Pro Ecclesia et Pontifice Medal, the highest honor given to a lay person in the Catholic Church, from Pope John Paul II in 1986, symbolizing years of work to combat racism through the recruitment of African-American parishioners. She was one of the most active members of Blessed Sacrament Church in Newark's South Ward, where her eight children attended grammar school, serving as chaplain of the Rosary Society and singing in the Adult Inspirational Choir. At the *Star-Ledger,* she was the matriarch of the Classified Advertising Department, winning awards for telemarketing. She died on July 6, 2000, at age seventy-four.

Margaret Simpson, a well-known gospel singer, grew up on a farm in Ridgeville, South Carolina. After moving to Newark in 1948, she sang in the choir at Abyssinian Baptist Church, turning to gospel singing full time after she lost her eyesight a decade later. Known as Madame Margaret Simpson, the Golden Lady, she appeared at hundreds of concerts at churches, senior citizens centers, and schools. She is deceased.

Grace Lambert Spellman served as national recording secretary of the Church of Our Lord Jesus Christ of the Apostolic Faith. Born in 1915 near Sylvania, Georgia, she received her early religious training at the Industrial Union of America, later renamed the R. C. Lawson Institute, in Southern Pines, South Carolina. As a child, she went to live with the Lawsons in Harlem, headquarters of the Beloved Refuge Church. In 1939, following her marriage to the Reverend Harry T. Spellman, she moved to Newark. At Macedonia Church of Christ, where her husband became bishop and her son, Robert, is now the pastor, she was president of the Missionary Society. Mother Spellman died on March 5, 1997, at the age of eighty-two.

Communications ⌐

Bernice Bass was host of radio station WNJR's Sunday night community news program *News and Views* for many years. Gospel greats, including the Reverend James Cleveland, the Dixie Hummingbirds, and Mahalia Jackson, were her friends. She interviewed every major figure of the civil rights movement, including Martin Luther King and Malcolm X a week before his assassination. She also founded the Youth Cavalcade, a group of young gospel singers who sang on WHBI radio. Until her retirement in 1983, she was director of the Administrative Division of the U.S. Customs Service for Newark Area Region II. Bass died in early January 2000.

Gloria Bryant founded The Writing Company in 1986, drawing on her extensive experience as a top-level public relations executive for the United Negro College Fund, where she worked on the theme "A Mind Is a Terrible Thing to Waste." She previously worked for Medgar Evers College and Bell Labs and is a former public relations director of the Newark School District. Her company's campaign for the Newark Office of Recycling won a 1990 Big Apple Award for marketing communications from the New York City Chapter of the Public Relations Society of America. A product of Newark schools, she holds a bachelor's degree from Kean College in Union, New Jersey, and did postgraduate work in communications and marketing at New York University and the New School of Social Research.

Dr. Gwendolyn Goldsby Grant is a private consultant, media psychologist, certified counselor, and sex education advocate. She writes a monthly column for *Essence* magazine titled "Between Us" and has worked as a consultant for several Fortune 500 companies. Her book, *The Best Kind of Loving* (HarperCollins, 1996), is about healing male-female relationships. She has hosted a radio talk show on mental health and has appeared on television on *The Montel Williams Show, Oprah, The MacNeil/Lehrer News Hour,* and CNN. She was nominated for an Emmy for a segment on the *Sally Jessy Raphael Show.* She received the Bobby E. Wright Community Service Award from the Association of Black Psychologists for her life's work in mental health.

Jan Edgerton M. Johnson, co-founder of City News Publishing Company and YES Communications, is president and CEO of both companies. She also serves as editor in chief of the publishing group, which established *City News* in 1983 and publishes several other weeklies serving black communities. Johnson also created the City News 100 Most Influential, a tribute to New Jersey residents who have had a significant impact on black life. Originally from Kansas City, Missouri, she attended Michigan State University on a scholarship, earning bachelor's and master's degrees in television and radio with an emphasis on television production.

Carol Patterson is director of community outreach for the Newark Public Schools and president and founder of Correct Communications, a multicultural marketing agency. Her clients include Allstate Insurance Company, Colgate-Palmolive, the Gillette Company, and Maybelline. She previously served as a director at the Mingo Group Plus, a New York City advertising agency, and as public relations director for *Essence* magazine. Business News NJ named her one of the state's top twenty African Americans.

Joan Whitlow joined the editorial board of the *Star-Ledger* in April 1995. Drawing on more than twenty years of experience as a medical editor and a columnist for the newspaper, she has written editorials on a broad range of subjects, focusing on health, education, social issues, and legal issues. She currently writes a column called "Under the Big Top," covering Newark City Hall. She has won awards for editorial writing from the New Jersey Chapter of the Society of Professional Journalists, the Deadline Club, the New York Chapter of the Society of Professional Journalists, the New Jersey Press Association, and the Garden State Association of Black Journalists. Born in Cleveland, Ohio, she attended public schools there and graduated from the University of Pennsylvania.

Sally Cooke Young wrote a society column, "Sally's Chatterings," for the *New Jersey Herald News*, a Newark black weekly, and for *Club World*, a magazine she created that chronicled black social life. The magazine provided a register of social affairs sponsored by black organizations, including fraternity and sorority events, which helped prevent overlapping schedules. She also reported on social events in Newark's African-American community. Writing was her avocation: by day she worked for the federal government.

Community Service/Volunteerism

Maggie C. Beckett served as president of the New Jersey State Federation of Colored Women's Clubs in 1947. The Newark businesswoman was founder of the Bella Becketta Women's Club at Bethany Baptist Church in Newark.

Fredrica Bey is a founder and executive director of Women in Support of the Million Man March, a nonprofit organization devoted to providing child care, spurring economic development, increasing health awareness, and supporting programs and events for the betterment of the Greater Newark community. After joining the Nation of Islam in 1965, she became a volunteer at the Sister Clara Muhammad University. As a single mother, she left the world of welfare behind to take a job in the Title I program at the Newark Board of Education, buy her own home, and dedicate herself to uplifting others.

Gloria Butler, a founding member of the first community board of the United Community Corporation, the city's antipoverty agency, was a longtime volunteer in Newark's Central Ward. She was a Girl Scout leader, a member of the Eastern Star, and an Essex County Democratic committee member instrumental in electing many black officials. A member of Greater Phillip's Metropolitan Christian Methodist Church of Newark, she was secretary of the North Jersey Usher's Union for thirty years. She died on September 15, 1998, at Columbus Hospital in Newark. She was sixty-six.

Barbara Bell Coleman is president of BBC Associates, serving as a consultant and adviser to nonprofit and corporate entities. She is former president of the Amelior Foundation, which has provided millions of dollars for Newark improvement projects, including the New Jersey Performing Arts Center, and a former executive director of the Newark Boys and Girls Clubs. With philanthropist Ray Chambers, she was co-architect of the READY Foundation (Rigorous Educational Assistance for Deserving Youth), which provides inner-city youngsters with tuition assistance and educational support. She holds a bachelor's degree from Rutgers University and a master's degree in public health from Columbia University. She is the daughter of the late Dr. Nathan Wright, an Episcopal priest, a scholar, and a civil rights leader.

Mae B. Cooke, a past president of the Newark Branch of the National Council of Negro Women, was a longtime associate of Mary McLeod Bethune, founder of the national organization, and Bethune's successor, Dorothy Height. For her service, she received the council's Outstanding Service Award, the Mary McLeod Bethune Achievement Award, and the Bicentennial Achievement Award. She also received the Negro Business and Professional Women's Clubs' highest honor, the Sojourner Truth Award. She was a charter board member of the Newark Community

School of the Arts and sponsor of the Friends of the Newark Community School of the Arts. In 1969 she served on the White House Conference on Food, Nutrition and Health in Washington, D.C. She and her husband, Joseph H. Cooke, ran Esquire Ticket Service, in East Orange. Both are deceased.

Kandice Ruth Dickinson had a passion for helping people and putting the needs of others before her own. Born in St. Albans, New York, she relocated to Newark in 1965 as a single mother of three children. In 1970 she was a member of the first graduating class at Essex County College, where she became a faculty member and professor of Spanish and English as a Second Language. She gave freely of her time to the women's center at the college, the Essex County Commission on Women, which she served as a president and adviser, and the New Jersey Performing Arts Center, where she accumulated one thousand hours of volunteer service and established a volunteer training program. She died on May 8, 2000, at the age of sixty.

Rebecca Doggett is an independent consultant and project director of the Essex County Construction Careers Program. From 1995 to 2000 she was special assistant for community development for the Newark Public Schools. She also has been director of the office of Business and Job Opportunities for the Port Authority of New York and New Jersey, auditor general of the Newark Public Schools, manager of the Division of Human Resource Planning for the Port Authority, director of the Essex County Department of Citizen Services, and executive director of the Tri-City Citizens Union for Progress of Newark. A founder of the Newark Preschool Council, she served that agency as executive director from 1965 to 1971. She holds a bachelor's degree from Upsala College in East Orange and a master's degree from the New York University School of Education.

Louise Epperson served as patient relations director at the University of Medicine and Dentistry of New Jersey, where she was a founder of the Board of Concerned Citizens. Before the hospital was built, she was a key opponent of the takeover of her Thirteenth Avenue neighborhood, a protest that led officials to scale down construction plans. Born in Waynesboro, Georgia, she grew up in West Palm Beach, Florida, and moved to Newark in the 1930s. She received the first honorary degree given by Essex County College and was a member of the Newark Women's Hall of Fame. She died on March 8, 2002, in St. Barnabas Medical Center in Livingston, New Jersey, at age ninety-three.

Wilma Grey is the acting director of the Newark Public Library, where she has worked for more than thirty years. Among other positions she has held are assistant director for Community Library Services, supervising librarian for Popular Library Services, principal librarian for Young Adult Services, and manager of the Roseville Branch Library. Born in Newark, she graduated from Arts High School. She holds a bachelor's degree in psychology with minors in math and science from Howard University and a master of library science degree from Rutgers University. She is on the board of trustees of the Newark Literacy Campaign and the board of directors of the Newark Arts Council.

Georgia Henson Hearn, known as Mother Hearn, was active for many years in Essex Temple No. 42 and the auxiliary of Pride of Newark Elks Lodge No. 93. Born in Washington, D.C., she moved to Newark in 1918 and became active in civic affairs soon after. Through Boy Scouting, she became the city's first black den mother. As a member of St. John's United Methodist Church in Newark, she traveled the city by bus to visit the sick and homebound. Born on April 23, 1892, she died on January 11, 1998. She was 105 years old.

Mildred Helms was president of the Clinton Hill Area Redevelopment Corporation (CHARC), a housing development agency that in the early 1970s constructed the $4.6 million Clinton Hill Community Gardens, 151 garden apartment units in Newark's South Ward. Her church, Trinity United Methodist, also sponsored CHARC II, which transformed a vacant South Ward building into a fifty-unit apartment complex. She also brought to the community Mount Calvary Homes—two eight-story structures at separate intersections on Bergen Street. She was a supervisor for the federal government's Office of Dependency Benefits until her retirement in the early 1970s. The former Cooper Memorial Park in Newark is named in her honor. She died on October 21, 2002, at age ninety-five.

Ethel Moore Johnson wrote the column "Jaunts in Jersey" and was a columnist and advertising and sales manager for the *New Jersey Afro-American* (a black weekly serving Newark) from 1942 to 1955. Born in Vauxhall, New Jersey, she went to work for the *Afro-American* after completing her schooling at Newark's Central High School. She was employed by the William Scheer Advertising Agency in Newark from 1955 to 1965. From 1965 to 1978, when she retired, she was with Amalgamated Publishing Company of New York City, the advertising representative for eighty-five black newspapers. She wrote a syndicated column, "Ethel's

Cookery," which appeared in those papers through 1985. A longtime member and past president of the North Jersey Unit of the Negro Business and Professional Women's Clubs, she received a Presidential Award from Lyndon B. Johnson for her contributions to the youth of America.

Maria Johnson, an executive with IBM, is a founder and president of the Reverend B. F. Johnson, Sr., Foundation. Named for her grandfather, the longtime pastor of Newark's Metropolitan Baptist Church, the foundation sponsors an annual golf outing that has provided scholarships for nearly one hundred students. Born March 7, 1958, to Newark educators Evelyn and Charles Johnson, she graduated from Iona College in New Rochelle, New York, where she earned a bachelor's degree in communications and played basketball. She was assistant girls' basketball coach at Georgetown University before returning to New Jersey to work for IBM.

Dorothea Lee is a former president of the North Jersey Unit of the Negro Business and Women's Clubs and governor of the Northeast District of the National Association of Negro Business and Professional Women's Clubs. She is a founding member of the New Jersey Coalition of Black Women, past president of the Ironbound Educational and Cultural Center, life member of the National Council of Negro Women, and president of the Newark Branch of the NAACP. A former U.S. Air Force nurse, she served on active duty with the Air National Guard from 1961 to 1962. She was the first black woman inducted into the New Jersey Air National Guard and the first black woman in New Jersey to serve as commander of an Amvets post. She went on to become the first black second vice commander and the first black first vice commander of the Amvets Department of New Jersey. Until her retirement in January 2004, she was the relocation officer for the Newark Housing Authority.

Lucye Belle Harrington Lee was born in Carthage, North Carolina, graduated from a one-room schoolhouse operated by the Presbyterian Church, and then completed classes at Scotia Women's College in Concord, North Carolina. She also studied for two years at the Cooper Normal School. After completing classes at the Newark Business College, she worked for a black-owned insurance company. She established the Urban League Guild's Golf Classic and helped create a public school program at Chestnut Street School for pregnant girls. A member of the guild for fifty years, she served as president from 1968 to 1970, establishing a breast cancer screening program. She also recruited volunteers to oversee the home care and adoption of abandoned babies for the Community Agencies Corporation. She died on July 28, 2000, in University Hospital in Newark at age ninety-three.

Mary Mathis-Ford has served for twenty years as chairman of the Board of Concerned Citizens of the University of Medicine and Dentistry of New Jersey, representing Planned Parenthood of Metropolitan New Jersey. She is co-founder and organizer of Harmony Day at all six University of Medicine and Dentistry of New Jersey campuses, an event that emphasizes the importance of diversity. She holds a bachelor's degree in radiology technology and a bachelor of science degree in allied health administration and education from Montclair State University. She is the community relations director for Planned Parenthood.

Vera Brantley McMillon was born in Cedar Springs, Georgia, on October 8, 1909, and relocated to Newark in 1922. After graduating from Barringer High School in 1927, she earned a bachelor's degree, cum laude, in 1932 and a master's degree in economics in 1935 from Howard University. During thirty-seven years of employment by the Newark Department of Public Welfare, she developed the Positive Approach to Welfare Program, a predecessor of the Welfare Incentive Program. From 1965 to 1966, she supervised a pilot project known as Rehabilitation of the Hard Core Unemployed, a federally funded $3 million job training program. After her retirement, she became an instructor at Kean College in Union Township, New Jersey. In the late 1950s, she was a founding member of the Tri-City Citizens Union for Progress, a neighborhood service agency. With Dr. Myra Kearse, she co-wrote and produced a weekly radio program on black life in New Jersey. In 1964 the New Jersey Historical Society appointed her to its Committee for Study of Negro Life History and Contributions to New Jersey. She died in February 1987.

Mary Rone is the longtime president of the Newark Tenants Council, the citywide organization that represents public housing residents. Under her leadership, the New Jersey Association of Public and Subsidized Housing Residents received federal grants in excess of $800,000 to advocate for residents of public and subsidized housing. She was the first resident to serve on the New Jersey Chapter of the National Association of Housing and Redevelopment Officers. During the Clinton administration she was a member of the U.S. Department of Housing and Urban Development Ad Hoc Committee of Residents, which developed the Tenants

Opportunity Program to fund resident organizations. She also was on a welfare reform committee that brought about the Work First New Jersey Housing Assistance Program.

Mary Palmer Smith, founder and executive director of Babyland Family Services, received a bachelor's degree in sociology from Rutgers University and a master's degree from Kean College in early childhood education. Founded thirty-five years ago, Babyland Family Services serves fifteen hundred children and families at eleven facilities, including seven child care centers and two twenty-four-hour child and family centers. Smith was named a Paul Harris Fellow for her contributions to society by the Rotary Club of Newark and received the Pro Ecclesia et Pontifice Award from Pope John Paul II. She was the first African-American woman named Mother of Their Village by the Catholic Church. She also was a trustee of the University of Medicine and Dentistry of New Jersey and a member of the Newark Public Schools Advisory Board.

Edna Rainey Thomas pushed for affordable housing, the creation of day-care facilities, drug prevention and treatment programs, and federal funding for AIDS patients during thirty years of community service. Thomas, who died on December 15, 1996, at age fifty-seven, was director of the Addiction Planning and Coordinating Agency in Newark and founder of Soul-O-House, a city drug treatment program. She was a founding board member of the Citywide Public Housing Tenants Association and the Toussaint Urban Renewal Corporation, which constructed Georgia King Village, housing for low-income residents. She also led the Central Ward Coalition of Youth Agencies and was on the board of the Newark Symphony Hall Corporation.

Aneatha Dames Todd, a former teacher, was at the forefront of many controversial issues affecting neighborhood life in Newark. She wrote a community newspaper called *P.A.T.C.H,* which exposed inequities affecting city residents, and, as a member of the University of Medicine and Dentistry of New Jersey's Review Committee, vigorously opposed health experiments that she felt exploited African Americans. She also inspired people to learn about economic development by starting their own businesses and for many years ran the gift shop at United Hospitals in Newark. She was a program aide and consultant to the blind at the Catholic Services Senior Day and Visually Impaired Program in Newark. At St. James African Methodist Episcopal Church in Newark, she was a Cub Scout leader, youth choir director, and charter member of the credit union. She died on July 3, 1998. She was seventy-nine.

Delores Tyson started her career with Planned Parenthood of Metropolitan New Jersey in 1976, working her way up through the ranks to become president and CEO in 2000. Under her leadership, Planned Parenthood expanded from four to six centers in three northern New Jersey counties. She is president of the Family Planning Association of New Jersey and past president of the Planned Parenthood Affiliates of New Jersey. In 2004 she was named by Essex County Executive Joseph N. DiVincenzo, Jr., to a six-member panel charged with creating and enforcing a new code of ethics for the county.

Carolyn B. Thompson Wallace has been the administrator and executive director of the International Youth Organization since its founding as the Brick Towers Youth Association in the early 1970s. Her work with juvenile delinquents was featured on the CBS documentary *Crisis in America: The Vanishing Black Family* and on the TV shows *Straight Talk* and *Currents*. She has testified before U.S. Congressional committees and the Congressional Black Caucus on welfare reform, family values, youth development, and youth and crime. She is the author of a chapter in *The Black Family: Past, Present and Future* (Zondervan Publishing House, 1991). After attending South Side High School in Newark, she gained training in business and human relations skills through the city's Office of Total Employment and Manpower (TEAM) and the New Jersey Department of Civil Service.

Mary Willis, a lifelong resident of Newark, was the area director of the Council for Airport Opportunity, which furthered opportunities for minorities in the airline industry. She was a founder of the Newark Day Care Council and the Springfield Avenue Community School, a facility that was renamed for her after her death. From 1967 to 1976, she worked for the New Jersey Department of Education, developing day-care programs throughout New Jersey, Virginia, Maryland, Mississippi, and Georgia. She received a bachelor's degree in early childhood education from Rutgers University and taught courses in sociology and early childhood education at Newark State Teachers College and at Queens College in New York. She died in May 1987 in Beth Israel Medical Center, Newark.

Education

Marie A. Bagby, one of only a few black teachers in Newark when she started her career in 1944 as a teacher of the disabled at the Girls Trade School, went on to serve as a guidance counselor, vice principal, and principal at Barringer High School. She was principal of West Side High School from 1975 to 1978 and University High School from 1986 to 1990. A business education graduate of New York University, she earned a master's degree in educational psychology there and completed postgraduate work in student personnel services and in supervision and administration at Seton Hall University. A lifelong Newark resident, she served on the advisory board of St. Michael's Medical Center, the Affirmative Action Committee of the Roman Catholic Archdiocese of Newark, and the Executive Committee of the City Administrators and Supervisors Association. She died on April 12, 2003, at age seventy-seven.

Beverly Berry Baker is the longtime director of the Exceptional Educational Opportunities Program at Kean University, where she has worked since 1969. The program provides a wide range of education services and activities for students who are economically and educationally disadvantaged. A native of Newark, she is a graduate of Barringer High School and Winston-Salem State Teachers College. She holds a master's degree in guidance and student personnel services from Seton Hall University. She serves on the board of directors of the Tri-State Consortium of Opportunity Programs in Higher Education. She also is on the board and serves as treasurer of the Union County Community Action Organization.

Katherine Bell Banks, a nonagenarian, concluded her thirty-seven-year career in the Newark Public Schools as chairperson of the Department of Foreign Languages at Vailsburg High School. From 1934 to 1943, she taught at two historically black colleges, Spelman and Talladega. At Talladega she supervised Wynona Lipman's teaching practicum. She received a bachelor's degree in French in 1934 from Montclair State Teachers College and a master's degree in 1936 from Columbia University. She completed postgraduate studies in French and Spanish at McGill University, National University of Mexico, Middlebury College, and the Sorbonne. She was the recipient of a Foreign Exchange Scholarship to France in 1932 and a Fulbright Fellowship in France in 1952.

Tina Eugene Holtzclaw Bohannon was head guidance counselor at Arts High School for thirteen years. Born in Selene, Michigan, she taught briefly in Durham, North Carolina, and was a curriculum specialist for the District of Columbia before moving to Newark, where she taught at Cleveland Junior High School and was a guidance counselor at Robert Treat Junior High School. She was a graduate of Howard University. She headed the Urban League Guild's education and vocational guidance committees and served on the Selection Committee of the National Merit Scholarship awards. She also hosted *Opportunities Unlimited,* a weekly radio program on WNJR. She died on July 14, 1999, at age ninety-four.

Pansy L. Borders, a social worker, was the first director of child guidance for the Newark Board of Education. During a forty-two-year career, she worked at nearly every school in the Newark system, developing one innovative program after another. At South Side High School, her alma mater, she established the Borders Personal Achievement Award, presented annually to the highest student achiever. At West Kinney Junior High School, she developed the model for the district's Title I program. In 1958 Vice President Richard Nixon appointed her to the President's Committee on Government Contracts. In 1967 she was named Social Worker of the Year by the North and South Jersey chapters of the National Association of Social Workers. Born in Buxton, Iowa, she was the daughter of the Reverend Henry T. Borders, pastor of Newark's Hopewell Baptist Church. After graduating from Howard University, she earned a master's degree in speech at Columbia University. She died in December 1972.

Hattie Coppock, the organist at St. James African Methodist Episcopal Church, and her husband, John, made sure their four daughters and two sons had the best education possible. All six—Bernice, Dorothea, Yvette, Evelyn, Bertram, and John—graduated from college and became educators, mostly in the Newark school system. Bertram eventually became the principal at Barringer High School, from which he and his siblings graduated. His brother John taught music at South Side High School in Newark, following the example of his mother, who had given piano lessons to hundreds of Newark children. Bernice Coppock Johnson taught for seventeen years in Newark and was vice principal at Dayton Street School for eighteen years.

Delores E. Cross is a former president of Chicago State University and Morris Brown College in Atlanta, Georgia. She presently teaches at DePaul University in Chicago. Raised in Newark, where her grandfather, the Reverend Thomas T. Tucker, was pastor of Union Baptist Church, she was a working mother of two children when she earned a bachelor's degree in elementary education at Seton Hall University. She holds a master's degree from Hofstra University and a doctorate in education from the University of Michigan. She also is a former vice president of the GE Fund, based in Fairfield, Connecticut.

Theresa Spears David, who was born May 26, 1923, in East Orange, New Jersey, became the first African American hired to teach in a Newark high school in 1946. Over the course of four decades in the Newark school system, she served as a teacher, vice principal, principal, and deputy superintendent. At Arts High School, she was a beloved Spanish teacher for twenty-five years. She later became the school's vice principal and principal. A graduate of Montclair State College, she studied at the University of Mexico as a Margaret Holtz Exchange Scholar. She did postgraduate work at Cornell, Rutgers, and Seton Hall Universities. She retired from the Newark School District in 1988. She died on March 2, 2004.

Linda Caldwell Epps, who is completing her doctoral work in American Studies at Seton Hall University, is director of advancement for the New Jersey Historical Society. She is a former vice president of college relations at Bloomfield College in Bloomfield, New Jersey, and former vice president of institutional relations for the NJN Foundation, an arm of New Jersey Public Television and Radio. She holds a bachelor's degree from Douglass College and a master's degree from Seton Hall University. At Bethany Baptist Church in Newark, she leads the Book Club and classes for members interested in discussing topical issues.

Grace Baxter Fenderson, who taught at Monmouth Street School for forty-two years before her retirement in 1948, was a champion of Negro causes. Born in Newark on November 2, 1882, she was one of five children of James Miller Baxter and Pauline Mars Baxter. Her brother Leroy was New Jersey's third black assemblyman. She was a graduate of the Colored School in Newark, where her father was principal, and the Newark Normal and Training School, which eventually became Kean University. She was president of the Newark Branch of the NAACP and chairman of its executive board, as well as a national NAACP vice president and board member. She died of a cerebral hemorrhage on March 16, 1962, at age seventy-nine in Philadelphia and is buried in Evergreen Cemetery in Hillside, New Jersey.

Gladys Berry Francis, director of elementary education in Newark from 1957 until she retired in 1967, began teaching in Newark in 1936 at Charlton Street School and South Eighth Street School. She was vice principal at South Eighth Street, Oliver Street, and Bragaw elementary schools and was an instructor for several years at William Paterson State College. She received bachelor's and master's degrees in education from Newark

State Teachers College. A past president of the Directors and Supervisors Association, she served on the board of trustees of the Newark Public Library and the Education Committee of the Newark Museum. She died in February 1993 in the Chilton Memorial Hospital in Pompton Plains, New Jersey. She was eighty-two.

Helen Fullilove was president of the Newark Board of Education from 1971 to 1972 after being appointed to the board in 1970 by Mayor Kenneth A. Gibson. She also served with the New Jersey School Boards Association. She was a 1937 graduate of Spelman College, where she received a bachelor's degree. She served on the board of trustees of Planned Parenthood of Essex County, the Urban League of Essex County, the NAACP, Newark Community School of the Arts, and radio station WBGO. Born in Lowell, Massachusetts, she was the wife of Dr. Robert E. Fullilove, Jr. She died in October 1988 at age seventy-two.

Dorothy Gould was assistant executive superintendent of the Newark School District in charge of special education when she retired in 1986 after a forty-three-year career that began as a teacher. Born in 1922, she graduated from South Side High School and Upsala College, where she received her bachelor's degree in mathematics in 1943. Her master's degree in mathematics is from Montclair State College. She was certified to teach special education at Newark State Teachers College. Hampered by discriminatory practices, she subbed for six years at Cleveland School before becoming a regular teacher in the Special Education Department at Montgomery Street School. She taught at Montgomery for sixteen years and remained there for another thirteen years as principal. She also was principal of Morton Street School. A lifelong member of what is now Trinity & St. Philip's Cathedral, she was a founding member of St. Philip's Academy, a private elementary school.

Margaret E. Hayes, a former dean of college development at Bergen Community College in Paramus, New Jersey, holds a master's degree in psychology from the New School for Social Research and a doctorate in counseling psychology from Columbia University. She began her career in special education at Jersey City State College, where she became associate director of black studies. She served as executive director of Jobs for Youth in New York City, which serves underemployed youth, and is a former admissions director of the Borough of Manhattan Community College of the City University of New York. She is principal consultant and president of MEH Associates, a consulting firm that caters to nonprofit and faith-based organizations. She is the founder and past president of the New Jersey Coalition of 100 Black Women and serves on the board of the Liberty State Park Development Corporation and the New Jersey Regional Plan Association.

Gladys Hillman-Jones was executive director of the St. James Preparatory School in Newark at her death in January 1998. Previously she had been a teacher, vice principal, principal, assistant superintendent, and deputy executive superintendent of the Newark School District. She received a bachelor's degree in elementary education from the State University of New York at Oneonta and a master's degree in reading specialization from Newark State College. She was named One in a Million by the University of New York at Oneonta. A former president of the Newark Principals Association, she also was a founder and vice president of the Organization of African-American Administrators and the New Jersey Alliance of Black School Educators and a trustee of Newark Beth Israel Medical Center. Two Newark landmarks, the Gladys Hillman-Jones Auditorium in George Washington Carver School and the Gladys Hillman-Jones Model Middle School, are named for her.

Wilnora Holman, a former president of the Essex County Council of Parent-Teacher Associations, served briefly on the Newark Board of Education. A former aide in the city's public schools, she was a Newark Housing Authority commissioner and president of the James C. White Manor Tenants Association. She received an honorary degree in the humanities from Essex County College in 1987. She was a member of the Newark Human Rights Commission and the New Jersey Association of Black Educators. The Wilnora Holman Scholarship, which benefits Newark students, is named for her. She died on October 3, 1994, at age eighty-two.

Willie Belle Hooper graduated from Newark State College and earned her New Jersey certification as a teacher in 1960 after raising eight children. After teaching first grade at Newark elementary schools, including Robert Treat and Belmont Runyon, she retired. She then began mentoring people preparing for careers as teachers and was a substitute teacher in Newark schools. At eighty-eight, she retired for good. Born in South Carolina, she taught there before moving to Newark in 1935. Her son Arthur was a Newark school principal. Franklyn and Wilbur became Newark teachers; Willie, an engineer; Chester and Ralph, contractors; and Jimmy, an army recruiter. Theresa Marshall, her only daughter, became a teacher, earned a doctorate, and went on to head a White House council charged with monitoring the U.S. Education Department during the Reagan administration. At Mount Zion Baptist Church in Newark, Willie Belle Hooper taught Sunday school and was active with Advocates for Christian Education. She died on July 31, 1999, in Columbus Hospital, Newark. She was ninety-two.

Bessie P. Morize, director of guidance for the Newark Public Schools from 1978 to 1995, began her career as an English teacher at Clinton Place Junior High School in 1960. She received a bachelor's degree from Howard University, earned a master's degree from Seton Hall University, and pursued further credits at Kean University. Through her work, she developed a crisis intervention program in all of the elementary schools and implemented a dropout intervention program for all ninth-grade students. She also started an elementary school guidance program at all of the district's K–8 elementary schools, enhanced services at the secondary level, and developed a career education program for the Essex County Boy Scouts of America at all Newark high schools, a design replicated by Boy Scout councils throughout the United States. She died on September 1, 2001, at age seventy.

Trish Morris-Yamba is executive director of the Newark Day Center, director-coordinator of the Newark Fresh Air Fund, and president and CEO of TRZ Associates, which manages child care centers. As a student at Livingston College in Piscataway, New Jersey, she established an on-campus day-care center when she needed a safe haven for her daughter. After earning a master's degree in education at Rutgers University in New Brunswick, she moved to Newark to head the Council for Higher Education School. She is president of the Newark Public Library board, first vice chairperson of the National Congress of Black Women, and chairwoman of the Newark Mayor's Commission on the Status of Women. She also is on the board of the women's center at Essex County College. Her husband, A. Zachary Yamba, is the college president.

Irene Pataquam Mulford, a graduate of the Colored School run by James Baxter, was the first Negro student to enter the Newark High School. She was the mother of Mae Mulford, a teacher at Morton Street School who retired in 1950.

Anzella King Nelms has served as deputy superintendent of Newark Public Schools since 1999. She has been employed by the district as a teacher, Title I project coordinator, associate superintendent, and assistant executive superintendent for more than thirty-five years. She proved her theory "All Children Can Learn" as principal at Camden Middle School, which became a successful model for inner-city schools under her leadership. From 1995 to 1999, she served as an assistant superintendent of schools, developing sixteen theme schools. One of them, Ann Street School of Mathematics and Science, was deemed a National Blue Ribbon School by President Bill Clinton.

Audrey Potts retired in 2004 as northeast regional vice president of Scott Foresman, an educational publishing company. She began her career as a teacher in the Newark Public Schools after graduating from Newark State Teachers College with a bachelor's degree in elementary education. She holds a certificate in administration and supervision and a master's equivalency in education and behaviorial science. Her master's degree in K–12 reading is from Jersey City State College. She started in publishing in 1979 as a consultant with Ginn and Company, winning promotions that led to her appointment in 1984 as sales manager for New Jersey; Maryland; Washington, D.C.; and all of New England. In 1985 she was named Sales Manager of the Year. After her company merged with Silver Burdett in 1986, she eventually became regional vice president.

Carrie Epps Powell, who taught eighth grade at Central Avenue School for thirty-one years, was the first Negro teacher in the Newark schools appointed to an administrative position as the result of a competitive examination. In 1962 the Newark Board of Education named her vice principal of Hawthorne Avenue School. She ranked No. 18 on the vice principals' eligibility list, the highest of six Negro teachers among fifty-one candidates. Born in Newark, she graduated from East Side High School and joined the school system as a teacher at Lafayette Street School in 1923 after graduating from Newark State Normal School. She received a bachelor's degree from Rutgers University in 1931 and a master's degree from Columbia University in 1935.

La Francis Rodgers-Rose, editor of *The Black Woman* (Sage Publications, 1980), is president of the International Black Women's Congress. She received her doctorate from the University of Iowa in social psychology, after which she served as a visiting professor in Afro-American Studies at Princeton University. She also was a research sociologist at Educational Testing Services and is a past president of the American Association of Black Psychologists.

Geraldine Sims, principal at Maple Avenue School for seventeen years prior to her retirement, is a product of Newark schools. She earned a bachelor's degree in elementary education from New Jersey State Teachers College in Newark and a master's degree from Seton Hall University. In preparation for her certification in administration and supervision, she studied at Kean College, the University of Pennsylvania, and Rutgers University. After twenty-three years of teaching at Roseville Avenue School in Newark, she transferred to Maple Avenue School Annex as a teacher to assist the principal. She became acting principal at Maple Avenue in 1969 and was promoted to principal in 1970. She served on the board of trustees of the Newark-based Education Law Center and on the Bioethics Committee of Newark Beth Israel Medical Center. She also is a past president of the Zonta Club of Essex County.

Rosamond Marrow Stewart was president of the board of trustees of the Booker T. Washington Community Hospital on West Kinney Street in Newark. When the hospital was closed in 1930, she was at the forefront of a movement to raise $300,000 to build a new modern facility at a different site, a plan that did not materialize. A beautician and educator, she established a vocational school program for girls at the North Thirteenth Street Vocational School in Newark. She also was a political activist in Newark's old Third Ward in the 1930s and 1940s.

Dorothy Strickland is the State of New Jersey Professor of Reading at Rutgers University and a former president of the International Reading Association, an organization dedicated to increasing literacy worldwide. Born in Newark, she is a former classroom teacher and was the Arthur I. Gates Professor at Teachers College, Columbia University. She served on the faculties of Kean University and New Jersey City University and taught in New Jersey public schools for eleven years—six as a classroom teacher and five as a reading consultant and learning disabilities specialist. She holds a bachelor's degree from Newark State University and a master's degree and doctorate from New York University. A past president of the Reading Hall of Fame, she has been an educational adviser to three presidents—Carter, Clinton, and Bush.

Franotie Alston Washington, a Newark native, was employed by the Newark School District for thirty-five years, retiring in 1997 as director emerita of the Office of Visual and Performing Arts. As the first African American to serve as director of art education for Newark schools, a position she held from 1988 to 1996, she was responsible for the art, music, home economics, and industrial arts curriculum. In 2001 she received the New Jersey Governor's Award in Art Education. A graduate of Barringer High School, she earned a bachelor's degree in art education and history from Fisk University. At Montclair State University, she was the first African American to earn a master's degree in art education and educational administration. In 1998 she was cited by *City News*, a black weekly, as one of the most influential persons affecting black life in New Jersey. Her mother was Altha Mary Bleach Alston, New Jersey's first female African-American parole officer.

Audrey West served nearly a decade as executive director of the Newark Preschool Council, New Jersey's largest Head Start agency, until her retirement in 2001. Under her leadership, several new facilities were constructed. A native of Trenton, she served from 1978 to 1988 as deputy director and director of the New Jersey Department of Human Services, Division of Public Welfare. From 1968 to 1978, she was director of the Division of Public Welfare for the City of Newark. She was the first African American to hold these positions. She also was special assistant to the commissioner of the New Jersey Department of Personnel from 1988 to 1990. She earned a bachelor's degree from Howard University and a master of public administration degree from Rutgers University. She died on March 17, 2003.

Marion Thompson Wright (1902–1962), the first African-American historian to receive a doctorate from Columbia University, was known for her groundbreaking doctoral dissertation, "The Education of Negroes in New Jersey," in which she documented patterns of school segregation that existed in spite of an 1881 law banning racial discrimination in public schools. Her study helped to provide critical data for the NAACP's court challenge to the "separate but equal" doctrine overturned by the U.S. Supreme Court in 1954 in *Brown v. Board of Education of Topeka, Kansas.*

Fashion

Janet Beadle was a top name in fashion in Newark during the years before and after World War II, following the lead of Emily Miles and Renee Starks. "Along Fifth Avenue" was the theme of her annual fashion show. She designed and created many of the fashions for the show, working without a pattern. Like Miles and Starks, she was a milliner, known for her stylish and unusual hats.

Everee Jimerson Clarke opened the Everee Clarke School, home to the Clarke Models and Dancers, in Newark on March 27, 1960. Her aim was to spotlight new faces and foster new talent by staging fashion shows and special events for leading designers and stores. Her students also participated in beauty and talent contests and appeared on radio and television. Clarke, who was active in the civil rights movement in her native Florida, subsequently relocated her home and business to West Palm Beach.

Brenda McGuire Long is the founder of the LenGuire Institute of Fashions, a nonprofit educational agency that offers participants career opportunities and apprenticeships in the fashion industry. She received a bachelor's degree in elementary education from Seton Hall University and has been a teacher in Newark schools since 1978. She has been the proprietor of the LenGuire Fashion Company since 1977 and has served on the board of the National Association of Fashion and Accessory Designers since 1987, currently holding the position of executive secretary. In 2003 she created and introduced a fashion design and clothing construction curriculum in the Newark Public Schools.

Caryl Renoir Lucas, who heads Renoir Productions, has produced and served as commentator for fashion shows and events for nonprofit organizations, churches, colleges, and malls. She has hosted the Lou Rawls Telethon and shows at the Acapulco Black Film Festival and Newark Festival of People. She is a product of the Emily Miles School of Charm and was Miss Black Teenage New Jersey in 1979. She has written for the *Star-Ledger*, *Today's Black Woman*, and *Essence* and is a regular contributor to *Odyssey Couleur*. She is an alumna of Upsala College in East Orange, New Jersey.

Emily Miles, a Newark fashion legend, was famous for designing hats and staging extravagant shows along the Eastern Seaboard. As a model, she shattered any notion of age as a factor, strutting the runway for six decades. After graduating from Howard University, where her major course of study was physical education, she founded a modeling and charm school and studied millinery design at Pratt Institute, the Fashion Institute of Technology, and the Parsons Schools of Design. More than one thousand young women, including singers and actresses Whitney Houston and Grace Jones, graduated from her school. Her Belle Meade Models were the talk of the town. She died on June 11, 1999, at St. Barnabas Medical Center in Livingston, New Jersey. She was eighty-eight.

Theresa Ross, called T by family and friends, was one of New Jersey's first successful black models. Born in Spartanburg, South Carolina, where she was educated, she appeared in many areas of the country as a fashion, millinery, and hairstyle model. She also appeared at national conventions and was named one of the ten best-dressed women in New Jersey in a statewide contest. She died on September 10, 1999, in Irvington General Hospital at age eighty-four.

Renee Starks was one of Newark's mostly highly regarded fashion designers. Born in Panama City, Florida, she was one of Newark's top black businesswomen for more than five decades, starting out in a tiny beauty shop on Springfield Avenue before opening a designer's studio at 591 High Street. From 1950 to 1952 she studied at the International House of Design in Paris and then opened Renee's School of French Design. Known for her hats and fashion shows, she also ran a school for models and sponsored an annual Black and White Ball. She died on March 23, 1996, in Orange Memorial Hospital.

Sadie Veney was called Pretty Lady by friends because of her style and grace. Always beautifully dressed and coiffed, she was a trendsetter who drove a red car and ran fashion extravaganzas to benefit community organizations. Her fashion shows at churches, schools, and senior citizen centers featured her Solid Gold Models and Golden Nuggets. Born in Durham, North Carolina, she grew up in Newark. She also wrote for *Stuff,* a Newark-based black newspaper. She died on January 28, 1987, in University Hospital in Newark at age seventy-three.

Government

Delores W. Battle served on the Essex County Board of Freeholders from November 1987 until December 1990. A South Ward district leader from 1969 to 1990, she was vice chairperson of the South Ward Democratic Party under the leadership of Congressman Donald Payne. In 1983 she became the first black woman in Essex County commissioned by the governor to serve on the Essex County Board of Elections. She was employed until her 1994 retirement by the Newark Board of Education. She was secretary of the now dissolved Clinton Hill Neighborhood Council and adviser to the South Ward Precinct Community Council.

Pearl Beatty was an Essex County freeholder from 1978 to 1987, serving as board president during her first year in office. From 1971 to 1987 she was chairman of the Newark Housing Authority. Born in Newark, she studied at Arts High School, earned her bachelor's degree at Shaw University in North Carolina, and did graduate work at Fairleigh Dickinson University. Before her election, she was the risk manager of the Newark Insurance Fund Commission and executive secretary of the Urban League of New Jersey. In 1984 she was elected to head the state board of welfare. She later became executive director of the New Jersey Martin Luther King Commemorative Commission.

Mamie Bridgeforth won election to the Newark Municipal Council as the city's West Ward representative in 1998 and was reelected in 2002. She has taught for more than thirty years at Essex County College, where she is chairperson of the Social Service Division. Before that, she was a caseworker with the state division of youth and family services, providing services to needy families. An ordained minister and licensed evangelist, she served on the board of the Metropolitan Ecumenical Ministries and is a founding member of the New Jersey Coalition of Outreach Ministries and the Faith Christian Center Church of Newark. She holds an associate degree in education from Essex County College, bachelor's and master's degrees from Rutgers University (her master's degree is in social work), and a doctorate in religious education from Arkansas Bible College.

Gayle Chaneyfield-Jenkins, a native Newarker, was elected to the Newark Municipal Council in 1995. After graduating from Sister Clara Muhammad High School, she continued her education at Bloomfield College, majoring in business administration. She is a graduate of the Intensive Chef Program of the New York Restaurant School of Cooking. Before her election, she was employed by the New Community Corporation and was director of public relations and marketing for Babyland, a child service agency.

Mildred C. Crump was sworn to a four-year term as Newark's first African-American councilwoman on July 1, 1994. Born and raised in Detroit, Michigan, she graduated from Wayne State University, where she was named the Most Outstanding Female Student for Leadership and Scholarship. She was the first African-American teacher of Braille in Detroit and was employed until her retirement as an educational consultant and Braille teacher with the New Jersey Commission for the Blind and Impaired. She is the founder of the Newark Women's Conference, which seeks to empower Newark-area women. She hosts *Straight Talk*, a community-oriented cable television show.

Adrianne Davis, a graduate of West Side High School and Montclair State College with a bachelor's degree in business education, has served as clerk of the Essex County Freeholder Board since 1989. Prior to that, she spent sixteen years as administrator of the North Ward Center in Newark. She was an Essex County freeholder at-large, an elected position, from 1982 to 1987. She served as chairperson of the board of trustees at Essex County College from 1979 to 1981 and was a consultant to the John Hay Whitney Foundation from 1973 to 1974.

Christy E. Davis, an attorney, is vice president for governmental affairs at the University of Medicine and Dentistry of New Jersey. Before taking on her present position, she was president and CEO of Davis & Partners of Newark, specializing in legislative advocacy, media relations, and governmental lobbying. Early in her career, she was legislative director for the late state Senator Wynona Lipman and state chief of staff for U.S. Senator Frank R. Lautenberg. She also was campaign manager for U.S. Senator Jon Corzine.

Carole A. Graves, a former teacher, became Register of Mortgages and Deeds for Essex County, a statutory office responsible for filing and preserving all property transactions for the twenty-two county municipalities, in 1994. Before that, she was president of the Newark Teachers Union for twenty-seven years. During a protracted strike by the union in 1970, Graves and other Newark Teachers Union members were jailed for six months, an experience she said served to reinforce her Christian fortitude. Born and educated in Newark, she is a graduate of Arts High School and Newark State Teachers College. She also holds certification as a labor relations specialist from the Rutgers Institute of Labor and Management Relations.

Joyce Wilson Harley became the first woman to serve as Essex County administrator in March 2005. She served previously as executive director of the Newark Downtown District, which promotes development in the city's main business area. Before that time she had a private law practice in Newark and was program director for New Jersey Multi-City Local Initiatives Support Corporation, a national group that provides financial support for urban revitalization.

Queen Elizabeth James was a Democratic kingmaker among Newark politicians. Known as Queenie, she worked in the administration of Mayor Kenneth A. Gibson for sixteen years and served as a Democratic County Committee leader in Newark's South Ward for twenty-five years.

As vice chairwoman of the South Ward Democratic Organization, she helped shape the political careers of elected officials, including Gibson, Mayor Sharpe James, and Congressman Donald Payne. As a businesswoman, she operated a beauty salon and ran the Chef Supreme Catering Service. Born in Birmingham, Alabama, she died on January 17, 1998, in Newark at age seventy-three.

Diane J. Johnson is the longtime director of field operations in New Jersey for the U.S. Department of Housing and Urban Development. Born in Jersey City, New Jersey, and educated in the Newark Public Schools, she is active with the St. James African Methodist Episcopal Church in Newark, where she served as cochairperson of the building campaign for St. James Preparatory School.

Jennie L. Lemon, a prominent figure in Essex County politics, was born in Doerun, Georgia, and lived in Newark most of her life. From 1962 to 1969 she was Newark Mayor Hugh Addonizio's liaison to community groups. She worked extensively with elderly and disabled people, organizing voting drives and providing assistance programs. She died in March 1982 at age sixty-nine.

Grace E. Malone was the first African American to serve as director of the Newark Welfare Department, then known as the Newark Local Assistance Board. Appointed to the position in 1942, she served until her retirement in 1969. Malone was active in community affairs, including business and professional women's organizations and the Urban League of Essex County, which she served as treasurer. She is deceased.

Hazel Rollins O'Leary was born in Newport News, Virginia, in 1938 and grew up in Newark, where she attended Arts High School. She graduated Phi Beta Kappa from Fisk University in 1959 and earned a law degree from Rutgers University. She was an Essex County and state prosecutor in New Jersey prior to becoming a senior energy official during the Ford and Carter administrations. From 1993 to 1997, she served as U.S. Energy Secretary in the Clinton administration. In 2000 she was named president and chief operating officer of Blaylock & Partners, a New York City–based investment banking and brokerage firm.

Sheila Yvette Oliver, a member of New Jersey's General Assembly since 2004, is Essex County's assistant administrator. She served on the Essex County Freeholder Board from 1969 to 1999 and is a past vice president of the board. In 1997 she ran for mayor of the city of East Orange, falling short of winning by fifty-one votes. From 1987 to 1992, she was director of the Essex County Division of Community Action and director of the Essex County Division of Consumer and Constituent Services. Prior to that, she was executive director of The Leaguers. A graduate of Weequahic High School in Newark, she holds a bachelor's degree from Lincoln University, where she became director of the Cooperative Education Program, and a master's degree in community organizing, program planning, and administration from Columbia University's School of Social Work.

Mary Singletary was the director of the North Jersey office for Governor Christie Whitman and Acting Governor Donald T. DeFrancesco until Governor James E. McGreevey took office in January 2002. She also was director of the New Jersey Division on Woman under Governor Thomas Kean. A graduate of South Side High School and the St. Agnes Hospital School of Nursing in Raleigh, North Carolina, she is a registered nurse and holds a bachelor's degree in health education from Jersey City State College. She also served as director of Planned Parenthood of Essex County, director of special projects for the Montclair Board of Education, and director of the Sixty-Plus program for the Young Women's Christian Association (YWCA) of Montclair–North Essex. A former president of the National Association of Negro Business and Professional Women's Clubs, she is the group's representative to the United Nations.

Larrie West Stalks was born and raised in Newark, where she became the city's first female department head as director of health and welfare under Newark Mayor Hugh Addonizio. She also was executive secretary of the Newark Central Planning Board. Stalks was elected county register of deeds and mortgages in 1973 and was reelected every four years through 1989. In 1978 she received a three-year presidential appointment as commissioner of the United Nations Educational, Scientific, and Cultural Organization (UNESCO). In 1984 she became the first black female president of the County Officers of the State of New Jersey. She is the founder of Municipal Career Women of Newark and served as its counselor. As president and founder of the Newark Community Housing Corporation, she spearheaded the development of 426 units of Newark housing. She was educated at Rutgers University and New York University, where she matriculated for her master's degree in public administration.

Bessie Walker, who was elected to an at-large position on the Newark Municipal Council in 1998, was raised in Newark, one of twelve children. She attended West Side High School, Essex County College, and Kean University. For twenty-one years she was coordinator of athletics for the Newark Public Schools. Currently she is director of Community Action for Essex County, providing social services for the homeless, seniors, tenants, and persons with HIV/AIDS. She is a co-founder of Project Pride, an organization that provides scholarships and recreational activities for young people.

Blonnie R. Watson was born in Savannah, Georgia, where she studied early childhood development at Savannah State College. After moving to Newark in 1962, she began a career with the postal system, rising from mail room clerk to supervisor and postal systems examiner before retiring as a postal systems compliance analyst. In 1973 she was elected to the board of directors of the High Park Gardens housing development, where she is currently board president. She was elected to the Essex County Freeholder Board in 1996 and won reelection twice, becoming board vice president.

Labor

Clara Elaine Dasher, who taught elementary school in Newark from 1959 to 1973, spent nineteen years as a special assistant to Carole A. Graves, president of the Newark Teachers Union. For fourteen years, until her death on November 13, 1995, at age sixty-five, she was president of the board of trustees of Essex County College. She also was state and county president of the A. Philip Randolph Institute, a social justice organization tied to the labor movement. In 1988 she received the governor's Pride of New Jersey Award as Labor Person of the Year. A founding member of the New Jersey Coalition of 100 Black Women, she also was a member of the New Jersey State Advisory Committee to the Civil Rights Commission, the Governor's Commission on Public Responsibility for Educational Success, and the New Jersey Martin Luther King Commemorative Commission. She received a bachelor's degree in health education from Jersey City State College in 1950, followed by a master's degree from Newark State College.

Mae Massie Eberhard, a top-ranking labor official with the International Union of Electrical Workers, a trade union in which nearly one-third of the members were women, pioneered the way for equal pay for equal work and maternity leave legislation and also served as a mentor to many younger women in the movement. In 1996 she became the first administrative vice president of the New Jersey Industrial Council. She also was a founding member of Black Women United, a group composed of issue-oriented women from the Newark area.

Myrtle L. Hartsfield, the administrative organizer of the National Union of Hospital and Health Care Employees for many years, was the first woman to join the city of Newark's Alcohol Beverage Control Commission in 1981. As director of the hospital union, Hartsfield, a former nurse's aide at Clara Maass Hospital in Belleville, New Jersey, represented service and maintenance workers, housekeepers, dietary employees, nurse's aides, orderlies, and laboratory technicians. She studied at the Institute of Management and Labor Relations at Rutgers University–Newark.

Virginia Morton, a longtime labor leader and community activist in Newark, served eight years as president of the bargaining union for Local 492 of the Newark-based General Electric Lamp Division. A longtime Central Ward Democratic district leader, she has been a volunteer counselor for a church youth retreat program, organized an inmate rehabilitation program, and sponsored events to raise funds for community causes.

Christine (Roz) Samuels, vice-president of the Newark Teachers Union for almost two decades, also is the union's secretary-treasurer, the first woman to hold that position. Born and raised in Newark, she attended Drake Business School, the New York Broadcasting School, Emily Miles' Belle Meade Modeling School, and Ophelia Devore Modeling School. After modeling for several years, she became a fashion commentator. She is vice president of the New Jersey State Federation of Teachers, AFT-CIO (American Federation of Teachers and Congress of Industrial Organizations), and is active with the Essex-West Hudson Labor Council, A. Philip Randolph Institute, and the Coalition of Black Trade Unionists. In 2001 the National Association of Negro Business and Professional Women named her Business Woman of the Year.

Law/Law Enforcement

Altha Mary Bleach Alston, the first black female parole officer in the State of New Jersey, graduated cum laude from Fisk University in 1935 with a bachelor's degree in sociology. She continued her studies at the New School of Social Research in New York, where she earned her master's degree. As a girl, she attended Selden Institute in Brunswick Georgia, where her father, the Reverend Henry A. Bleach, was the principal and a trustee and her mother, Frances M. Bleach, was an instructor and assistant principal. In 1931 she graduated from Asbury Park High School in New Jersey with high honors. As a high school junior, she won a national oratory contest sponsored by the *New York Times*. She and her husband, John H. Alston, were Republican North Ward district leaders. Active with the North Jersey Branch of the National Association of College Women, she helped deserving young women win college scholarships. She died in August 1963.

Marcia Wilson Brown became associate dean and director of the Rutgers-Newark Academic Foundations Center and special adviser to the Rutgers-Newark provost in July 2001. A 1994 graduate of Rutgers University School of Law in Newark, she clerked for the late Robert N. Wilentz, Chief Justice of the New Jersey Supreme Court. Before becoming assistant dean at Rutgers School of Law, she practiced on her own and with several other African-American female attorneys in Newark. She is a former labor relations specialist and manager with the U.S. Department of Housing and Urban Development and philanthropic manager of the Lucent Technologies Foundation, having primary responsibility for the city of Newark. As a co-founder and president of the University Heights Neighborhood Development Corporation, she helped build sixty housing units in the Central Ward for low- and moderate-income families.

Sally G. Carroll became one of Newark's first black female police officers in 1949, working a detail that found her arresting "mashers" who accosted women at Broad Street theaters. In the early 1950s, she went to work for the Essex County Sheriff's Office as a detective and court attendant, a position she held until 1977, when she left to join the state parole board. She retired from the board in 1991. During her tenure as president of the Newark Branch of the NAACP from 1967 to 1974, her administration established a day-care center, a cultural center, and a multipurpose center. She has served on the national board of directors of the NAACP since 1984 and is presently chairperson of its Committee on Branches. She is a charter member of The Batons, a group of law enforcement officers. Born in Roanoke, Virginia, she graduated from South Side High School in Newark and the now-defunct Essex Junior College.

Ruth Crumpton Dargan was a singer and actress who appeared on the road in *Carmen Jones* and *St. Louis Woman* before returning home to

Newark to become a Newark police officer in 1949. After serving on traffic duty, she was assigned to the Youth Aid Bureau. During her thirty-two-year career with the department, she became Newark's first black female detective, assigned to the Homicide Squad, and was the first black female officer to attend the Federal Bureau of Investigation (FBI) Academy. After her retirement in 1980, she became an investigator for the University of Medicine and Dentistry of New Jersey, New Jersey Transit, and the New Jersey Exposition and Sports Authority. For the past ten years she has been an aide to Essex County Freeholder Johnny Jones. She earned a bachelor's degree in criminal justice at Rutgers University when she was fifty-six years old.

Geraldine (GiGi) Foushee was New Jersey's first woman to serve as warden of the Essex County Jail in Newark. Raised in the Scudder Homes, a low-income city housing project, she became a substitute teacher, city police officer, administrator at Essex County College, sheriff's officer, executive secretary to the Newark Alcohol Beverage Control Board, and deputy mayor of Newark. She earned a bachelor's degree, magna cum laude, in political science from Rutgers University. She was a member of the Bronze Shields, an organization of black law enforcement officers, and served in leadership roles with law enforcement groups, including the Police Benevolent Association, the Fraternal Order of the Police Lodge 12, The Batons, and the National Organization of Black Law Enforcement Officers. She died on January 27, 1997, at age forty-nine, after a long struggle with cancer.

Barbara (Cookie) George, who followed her sister, GiGi Foushee, into law enforcement, was the first woman and first African American to attain the rank of captain in the Newark Police Department. Born in Newark, she was the fourth of seven children of the late Clarence and Anna Mae George. She was a graduate of Weequahic High School in Newark and Bloomfield College, where she earned a bachelor's degree in biology. At the Police Academy she was named Outstanding Recruit in her class. After joining the Newark Police Department, she advanced quickly, becoming the department's first female sergeant and first female lieutenant. For a time, she commanded the Sexual Assault Rape Analysis unit. She died of cancer on March 12, 2000. She was forty-seven.

Michelle Hollar-Gregory became a New Jersey Superior Court judge, assigned to Essex County, in November 2000, after serving more than eight years as corporation counsel for the city of Newark—the first black woman to hold the city's top legal post. She began working for the city as assistant corporation counsel in 1987 after working in a general law practice, as an assistant Essex County counsel, and as a teacher at Arts High School in Newark. She is a graduate of Lincoln University and holds a master's degree from the University of Pittsburgh and a law degree from Rutgers University. After graduating from law school, she served as a judicial clerk to state Superior Court Judge David Baime.

Golden E. Johnson, an assistant Essex County prosecutor, holds a bachelor's degree with a major in bacteriology from Douglass College in New Brunswick and a law degree from Rutgers University School of School. When she was a microbiologist for the Veterans Hospital in East Orange, her research was cited for its importance in the search for a vaccine for the cure or prevention of tuberculosis. Turning to law, she became an attorney for Hoffmann-LaRoche in Nutley, New Jersey, specializing in corporate acquisitions before being promoted to general attorney for the corporation. From 1974 to 1977 she was a Newark Municipal Court judge. She is a former municipal court judge in Montclair, New Jersey.

Alison Brown Jones is a New Jersey Superior Court judge and former presiding judge of the Newark Municipal Court. She was appointed to the Newark Municipal Court in 1988 and became chief judge five years later. Before that, she worked for six years as an assistant corporation counsel in Newark's Law Department, serving as a section chief for labor contracts negotiated by the city and disciplinary hearings for municipal agencies. She is a graduate of Newark's Weequahic High School, Jersey City State College, and Rutgers University School of Law. A lifelong resident of Newark, she is one of nine children. Her siblings include a Newark school principal and vice principal, a physician, and a real estate broker.

Jacqueline Jones became the first female member of the Newark Fire Department in 1981. In 1989 she became the department's first female captain, responsible for leading the work of firefighters at the scene. As of 1999, Jones was one of just ten women identified statewide as firefighters in paid departments. She is currently assigned to the Planning and Research Division at fire headquarters.

Betty Lester, a judge of the Superior Court of New Jersey, was the first woman in Newark to head the municipal court system. Before her appointment to the superior court, she was chief presiding judge of the

Newark Municipal Court. She received a bachelor's degree in business administration from Howard University in 1968 and a law degree from Rutgers University in 1971. Her legal experience includes work with the Newark Legal Service Project, the state Public Defender's Office, the state Department of the Public Advocate, and Supermarkets General Corporation. She has served on the State Supreme Court Committee on Probation and the State Supreme Court Committee to Study the Bar Examination.

M. Bernardine Johnson Marshall was a trailblazing Newark attorney who began practicing law in the city in 1949 after she and Martha Belle of Montclair became the first African-American women admitted to the New Jersey Bar Association. Born in Trenton, she graduated from Newark's West Side High School. She attended Howard University, graduating with a bachelor's degree in sociology in 1944. In 1947 she graduated from Rutgers University School of Law and began practicing with her father, the late J. Bernard Johnson, Sr., a former assistant prosecutor in Essex County. From 1955 to 1958 she was associate counsel to a U.S. Senate Judiciary subcommittee investigating juvenile delinquency—the youngest woman lawyer and only black woman practicing law on Capitol Hill. Subsequently she resumed practice with her father and then continued on her own until her retirement in 1988. She was the first female member of the Newark Alcoholic Beverage Control Board, a charter member of the city's Rent Control Board, and a member of the board of directors of Blue Cross and Blue Shield of New Jersey. She died on September 17, 1997, in Mercy Community Hospital in Port Jervis, New York.

Carolyn Ryan Reed, director of the East Orange Public Library, has more than three decades of experience as a librarian in public, school, and college libraries and more than thirty years' experience as an attorney in all phases of legal representation for public entities. She served previously as assistant corporation counsel for the city of East Orange and associate counsel for the Newark Board of Education. In the mid-1960s, she was executive aide to the Newark Executive Superintendent of Schools and associate counsel for the Newark Housing Authority. From 1971 to 1983 she was a library media specialist for the Newark Board of Education. A Newark native, she holds a bachelor's degree from Howard University and a master of library science degree from Rutgers University in New Brunswick. Her law degree is from Seton Hall University.

Vivian Sanks-King, an attorney, became vice president of legal management and general counsel of the University of Medicine and Dentistry of New Jersey in 1994—the first black woman to achieve the rank of vice president. Since 1988 she had been associate director of the university's office for legal management, which handles all legal matters and the management of the university's legal staff for eight schools on five campuses. A native Newarker, she is a graduate of South Side High School, Rutgers University, and Seton Hall Law School. She also served as director of community relations at University Hospital, assistant counsel for the Newark Board of Education, and assistant dean of student services at Seton Hall University. She is a past president of the Seton Hall University School of Law Alumni Association and past chair of the Community Health Law Project, a legal advocacy organization for individuals with disabilities

Karol Corbin Walker made history in 2003 when she became the first African American to serve as president of the New Jersey Bar Association. She is a partner with St. John & Wayne, a Newark law firm. A native of Jersey City, she graduated with honors from Jersey City State College in 1980 and Seton Hall University School of Law in 1986. In 1995 she became the first African-American woman to attain partner status at a major New Jersey law firm. She also performs pro bono services, representing mothers in parental termination cases, and provides free legal services for senior citizens. She has been an adjunct professor at Seton Hall Law School and is past president of the Garden State Bar Association, an organization of African-American lawyers who practice in New Jersey. In 1999 she was recognized by *Business News New Jersey* as one of New Jersey's top twenty African-American achievers and was installed as secretary of the New Jersey State Bar Association, becoming the first African-American officer in the association's one-hundred-year history.

Marilyn Williams was sworn in as a municipal court judge for the city on December 29, 1992. A lifelong resident of Newark, she is a graduate of Eighteenth Avenue Elementary School, where she has established a peer court for students. She earned a bachelor's degree in political science from Montclair State College and a law degree from Rutgers University in 1980. After her admission to the New Jersey State Bar as an attorney in 1986, she joined the city of Newark's Law Department as an assistant corporation counsel and developed a private practice, concentrating on matrimonial law and real estate matters. Now a superior court judge in Essex County, she is a member of the New Jersey Supreme Court's State Domestic Violence Working Group, presiding over mock trials and competitions of the New Jersey State Bar Foundation.

Medicine/Health Services

Alma Beatty is assistant vice president of community affairs at Newark Beth Israel Medical Center, an affiliate of the Saint Barnabas Health Care System. She began her professional career at Beth Israel in 1967 as administrator of the Security Department after receiving her certification from the John Jay College of Criminal Justice in New York. As director of community affairs, she developed and implemented the hospital's Patients Advocacy Department, organized its first Black History Month celebration, and initiated House Calls, a program that allows senior citizens to receive medical and social services at home. She is the hospital's community advocate, internally and externally.

A. Sue Brown became the youngest person and the first woman to head a major teaching hospital when she was named administrator of College Hospital (formerly Martland Hospital) at the age of thirty-three in 1980. She had been the hospital's acting administrator for the previous two years. A native of Meridian, Mississippi, she graduated from Bloomfield College in 1968 with a major in sociology and a minor in psychology. After earning her master's degree from Rutgers University Graduate School of Social Work in 1969, she became director of health for the Urban League of Essex County. A Washington-based management consultant, she assists Head Start officials with the development of special education programs and health-related services for Head Start children.

Ann Byrd Crumidy, who owns the Newark Vision Center, is a pioneering Newark optician. Born and schooled in Newark, she entered the field of optometry in 1951. At that time, the state of New Jersey did not require a license to practice. Years later, when a license was required, her longtime experience in her field allowed her to be grandfathered in as an optician. For ten years, including two as president, she served on the New Jersey State Board of Ophthalmic Dispensers and Technicians, the body that regulates her profession.

Evelyn Boyden Darrell, a clinical psychologist, was the supervisory psychologist at Bellevue Psychiatric Hospital in New York City when she retired in 2000. Born in Spring Lake, New Jersey, she graduated from West Side High School in Newark. After working for a year at the Friendly Neighborhood House in the old Third Ward, she enrolled at New York University, where she earned bachelor's, master's, and doctoral degrees. She was the first black psychologist to train at Bellevue, where she completed her internship and worked for twenty-nine years. In 1997 she was chosen from among five thousand employees as the recipient of the hospital's Black History Award. Since 1978 she has served on the Superior Court of New Jersey Child Placement Review Board. She is a Montclair, New Jersey, resident.

Sharon Johnson, an obstetrician and gynecologist, maintained a private practice in Maplewood for nearly twenty-five years. Born November 11, 1951, in Community Hospital in Newark, she is a graduate of Rensselaer Polytechnic Institute in Troy, New York, where she completed a three-year premedical program, and the University of Medicine and Dentistry of New Jersey, from which she graduated in 1976. After interning at Martland Hospital, she spent three years on the staff of Margaret Hague Hospital in Jersey City before establishing her own practice.

Eloise Rogers Phillips, a Newark cancer and blood disease specialist, has maintained a private practice on West Market Street in Newark for many years. She is the daughter-in-law of another well-known Newark physician, Dr. Algernon Phillips.

Doris Slaughter, who was born in Washington, D.C., moved to New Jersey in 1953. Soon after, she and her husband, James Slaughter, opened one of the first black-owned and black-operated optical centers in the city. In 1971, to reach a broader base of clients in the downtown area, she opened Doris Slaughter Optician, which she still runs on Branford Place. Two of her three children, Denise and Wanda, and her granddaughter, Utenzi, have followed her into the business. Denise Slaughter and her daughter, Utenzi Miller, attained associate degrees and ophthalmic dispensing licenses after completing three-year courses at Essex County College. At age thirty-two, Denise established Elegant Eyes, one of the largest full-scale optical retail centers in Newark. Utenzi, a graduate of Newark's Science High School, continued her education at Rutgers University and works alongside her mother.

Ernestine Watson is assistant vice president for vendor programs at the University of Medicine and Dentistry of New Jersey. Before joining the university's staff, she was chief of purchasing and contracts administrator for the Newark Housing Authority and purchasing manager for the Newark Board of Education. She is a graduate of South Side High School and Shaw University in North Carolina, where she earned a bachelor's degree in business administration with a minor in economics. She is president of New Hope Village, the housing development component of New Hope Baptist Church, and spearheads scholarship efforts by the church and University of Medicine and Dentistry of New Jersey, including fund-raising for a scholarship named for her late sister, J. Lorraine Watson.

Senior Citizen Advocacy

Nellie Grier was the founder of the Emanuel Senior Citizens Day Care Center in Newark, which now bears her name, and an organizer of the Newark Senior Citizens Council. Affectionately known as Mother Grier, she was born in Statesboro, Georgia, in 1900 and moved to Florida in 1919, where she opened the state's first children's day-care center. She moved north to Jersey City in 1947 and then to Newark in 1954. As a matron of the Order of the Eastern Star, she founded the Emanuel center to help provide health, medical, and recreational services for the disabled elderly. She died in 1984 in St. Barnabas Medical Center in Livingston, New Jersey. She was eighty-four.

Margaret E. Cannon Moore was deputy director of the Newark Office of Elderly Affairs at the time of her death on November 29, 1979, at age seventy-three. Born in Bainbridge, Georgia, she graduated from Florida A&M University. Among the many positions she held were director of Senior Citizen Programs for the Friendly Fuld Neighborhood House in Newark, caseworker for the Newark Division of Welfare, director of programming for the Rutgers University Elderly Research Project, and supervisor of the Homemaker Program for the Newark Senior Citizens Commission. She also worked with the Newark Golden Age Project and directed the Senior Citizens Golden Age Choral Group. After her death, the senior citizens building at 1 Court Street in Newark was renamed the Margaret Moore Court Tower Apartments in her honor.

Katherine (Kitty) Kearney Taylor, Newark's Ambassador on Aging, was born in Wake Forest, North Carolina, and moved to Newark at age three. She graduated from South Side High School, where she was on the debate team, and earned a bachelor's degree in social work from Howard University. After her marriage to Willis Taylor, Sr., the couple moved to Oklahoma, where he was in the military, and she established the first Teen Campfire program for girls and was "adopted" by a Native American tribe. From 1967 to 1989, she was senior citizen director for the United Community Corporation, Newark's antipoverty agency. In 1989 she became senior citizen developer specialist for the city of Newark. In 2000 she received a Lifetime Achievement Award from William Paterson University in Wayne, New Jersey. For more than fifty years, she hosted community-based radio programs on WNJR, WHBI, and WOR, focusing on senior citizen issues.

Bessie Walker Williams, the seventh of ten children, was born in 1906 on a turpentine farm in Stillmore, Georgia. While attending the Daytona Normal Institute, she met Mary McLeod Bethune, the school president and founder of the National Council of Negro Women. Bethune made her want to reach for the stars, but Bessie was forced to leave school at twelve after her mother died to care for her siblings. After her first husband's death in 1925, she did domestic work while raising her sister's two children. Fifty years later, she earned her high school equivalency diploma. She received an associate degree from Essex County College in 1977 and earned her bachelor's degree at Rutgers University in 1985 at age seventy-nine. As a community activist, she established a neighborhood health clinic, conducted voter registration drives, and created an award-winning garden with the assistance of the Rutgers Urban Gardening Program. She died on August 10, 1994, at age eighty-eight.

Sports

Effie Brent, who became one of Newark's first black policewomen in 1949, also was a top-flight amateur golfer. Although there were few competitive outlets for women athletes at that time, she and other Newark women—such as Evelyn Johnson, a Newark schoolteacher and playground leader—were first-rate golfers. Johnson also was a champion bowler.

Joetta Clark Diggs, an Olympian runner in 1988, 1992, and 1996, never missed an indoor or outdoor season in more than twenty-five consecutive years, racing in 800- and 1,500-meter events. Indoors, she won national championship races eighteen out of nineteen years, consistently ranking in the top ten worldwide. At age thirty-seven, she was ranked fourth in the world. She is a graduate of the University of Tennessee, where she captured nine collegiate titles (including relays) and earned a bachelor's degree in public relations. In 1997 Governor Christie Whitman appointed her a commissioner of the New Jersey Sports Exhibition Authority. For her work with children, she received the 1998 Visa Humanitarian Award and was named a Hometown Hero by *Sports Illustrated*.

Carla Dunlap, a world-champion bodybuilder, was Ms. Olympia 1983, winning her sport's equivalent of Wimbledon. The same year, she also became one of six women to capture the Grand Slam by winning three major bodybuilding titles. As an all-around athlete, she also competed in gymnastics and in synchronized swimming events, winning a gold metal in the 1977 Junior National Team championships. She is featured in the movie *Pumping Iron II—The Women.*

Althea Gibson, one of America's greatest athletes ever, made history in 1957 when she broke the color barrier in tennis by becoming the first African American to win Wimbledon and the U.S. Nationals title. She repeated that feat in 1958 and won three doubles titles at Wimbledon between 1956 and 1958. Born to sharecroppers on a farm in South Carolina on August 25, 1927, she was considered a natural athlete. She won her first tournament, the New York State black girls' singles, when she was fifteen. A 1953 graduate of Florida A&M, she won the national black women's tennis championships twice in 1950 and became the first black player to appear in the U.S. Nationals. She won her first major title, the French Open, in 1956. Overall, she compiled eleven Grand Slam tournament titles, including five singles. In 1963, after retiring from tennis, she became the first African American on the Ladies Professional Golf Association Tour. She died on September 28, 2003, at age seventy-six. Her accomplishments live on through the work of the Newark-based Althea Gibson Foundation.

Anna Lois Jones, the mother of poet-playwright Amiri Baraka, studied at Tuskegee Institute in Alabama and then earned a bachelor's degree in liberal arts from Shaw University in Raleigh, North Carolina. A star athlete, she was considered the second-fastest woman runner in the world as a teenager, earning an invitation to participate in the 1936 Berlin Olympics. But her father, the Reverend Thomas Everett Russ, would not let her go. In the 1980s, she was elected to the Tuskegee Institute Sports Hall of Fame. Her work life included stints as an administrator at Newark's Community Hospital, community relations specialist at the Newark Housing Authority, and assistant to the director of the Newark Board of Education's Title I program. She died in May 1987.

Carolyn Kelly owns and operates the First Class Championship Development Center on Bergen Street in Newark's South Ward. A onetime bail bondswoman, she was New Jersey's first licensed female boxing promoter and matchmaker. She is a former Newark district leader.

Vanessa Watson, a member of the Newark Athletic Hall of Fame, has been the head girls' basketball coach at Malcolm X Shabazz High School, her alma mater, for more than twenty years. During the 2002–2003 season, she led her team to the Watching Hill Conference Title, Essex County Tournament championship, Group III state championship, and Tournament of Champions title, making the Lady Bulldogs the best team in New Jersey, a first-ever for a Newark school and a feat the team repeated the following year. A stellar player at Shabazz (then South Side), she played on the Essex County championship squad in her senior year and then went on to play at Virginia State University, where she earned her bachelor's degree. She is an assistant supervisor of physical education for the Newark Public Schools.

Lorraine White, an educator in the Newark Public Schools for many years, was the first and only female football coach in the Newark area. She became a drug awareness coordinator at Weequahic High School and is a member of the Newark Athletic Hall of Fame.

Annette Williams, from Greenwood, South Carolina, holds a bachelor's degree in health and physical education from Winthrop College and a master's degree in administration and supervision from Clemson University. In high school and college, she played basketball, softball, and ran track. After arriving in Newark in 1972, she taught health and physical education at Malcolm X Shabazz High School and then became department chairman at West Side High School. At Shabazz, her basketball teams won many Newark City League, county, and Christmas tournaments. In 1983 she led the squad to the state Group III championship. She is supervisor of health and physical education for the Newark Public Schools. A member of the Newark Athletic Hall of Fame, she was a New Jersey State Interscholastic Athletic Association Coach of the Year.

Unsung Heroism

Geraldine Woods Coles is a publicist and consultant to business and professional organizations. She is active with Bethany Baptist Church in Newark, where her service includes a term as cochairperson of the Black College Committee. A former vice president of the Urban League Guild of Essex County, she also was president of the Union Guild and treasurer of the national council. She holds a bachelor's degree from Jersey City State College. After a twenty-year career with the federal government, she retired in 1992 from the Internal Revenue Service as a management analyst.

Elizabeth (Betty) Flood received the President's 1991 Volunteer Action Award, given by President George Bush, after having won an award the previous year from New Jersey Governor Jim Florio for providing Newark children with a safe haven during afterschool hours and on weekends. At Garden Spires, where she lived, she established a game room where children gathered, played, and participated in activities like Boy Scouting. Flood was a telecommunications assistant at PSE&G for twenty years. She died in a car crash in Newark in December 1992 at age fifty-nine.

Annie Moses Rose Johnson, who was born in Waynesboro, Georgia, on December 1, 1911, lost her sight in infancy through a medical mishap. After moving to Newark in 1922, she attended Washington Street School, and with the help of the New Jersey Commission for the Blind, studied at the Perkins School for the Blind in Watertown, Massachusetts, and at Hampton Institute in Virginia, where she earned bachelor's degrees in education and social studies and was class valedictorian in 1939. In the early 1940s, she held a series of jobs as a secretary, home teacher for blind people of color, teacher of the deaf and blind, and factory worker. She also earned her master's degree in secondary education from Hampton Graduate School. After graduating from the Riverton Laboratory in Newark in 1959, she was an X-ray assistant and radiology technology instructor at Martland Medical Center in Newark for thirty-two years until her retirement. She subsequently testified on health and senior issues before two Washington, D.C., legislative committees.

Evelyn Johnson, who taught sixth through eighth grades and computer education at Quitman School for thirty years, is considered the Queen Mother of Newark's Central Ward playgrounds. Born in Iron City, South Carolina, she met her husband, Charles Johnson, also a retired Newark teacher and the son of the late Reverend Dr. B. F. Johnson, Sr., when they were students at Allen University in Columbia, South Carolina. After their marriage in 1951, the couple made Newark their home. She holds a bachelor's degree from Seton Hall University, where she majored in K–8 elementary education with a minor field of study in physical education. After her retirement, she continued working part time in the afterschool program at Quitman Street School.

Florence Johnson, through her outreach work as a customer service representative for the New Jersey Symphony Orchestra, has introduced hundreds of Newark senior citizens to classical music. For twenty-one years, she was a property manager for privately owned senior citizen buildings in the city, managing Court Towers and helping to open

2 Nevada Street, Grace West Manor, and Villa Victoria. She was chairperson of the Newark Senior Citizen Commission under Mayor Kenneth A. Gibson. Born in Newark, she is a graduate of Arts High School and a fifty-year member of Bethany Baptist Church.

Elizabeth King is a charter trustee of the Friends of the Newark Public Library and longtime volunteer for Celebrity Read, an educational program of the United Way of Essex and West Hudson. From 1983 to 1995 she was chairperson and administrator of the Newark Board of Education's United Way–sponsored Public School Employees Charitable Campaign. Since 1995, she has coordinated the employees' annual Christmas Toy Drive sponsored by Newark Emergency Services for Families. A board employee for four decades, she was the first African-American administrative secretary in the district, assisting Harold J. Ashby, the first African-American business administrator. From 1973 to 1985, she was president of the Administrative Employees Association, the bargaining unit for middle managers.

Jeroline Lee, who worked for the Newark Department of Health and Human Services for thirty years before her retirement, was in the forefront of Newark Girl Scouting. Born in Albany, New York, on April 15, 1924, she died on January 27, 2002, at the age of seventy-seven. Her involvement with the Greater Essex Girl Scout Council began in 1959, when she volunteered as her daughters' troop leader at the Friendly Neighborhood House. Eventually she became the council's first African-American vice president, helping to turn a downtown office into the council's first Newark satellite. In the 1960s, she was a founding member of Newark's Crispus Attucks Parade, named for the first black man to die in the Revolutionary War. She was a Eucharistic minister and instructor for the Right of Christian Initiation for Adults at Blessed Sacrament Roman Catholic Church.

Mary Sheard was a Republican district leader in Newark's Central and South Wards for thirty years. With Harold Edwards, she founded the Concerned Black Republicans of New Jersey in 1983. Born in Dawson, Georgia, she moved to Newark in 1934 and graduated from Arts High School and Essex County College. She earned bachelor's and master's degrees in sociology from Rutgers University and was employed as a cosmetologist and hair stylist at the Essex County Hospital in Cedar Grove and at the Newark Girls Vocational High School. After the death of her son, Richard, she began a grassroots group to fight AIDS in his memory. She was a founding member of the Newark Community Project for People with AIDS and served on the Newark Senior Citizens Commission and Saint Michael's Hospital Community Advisory Board. She died on December 24, 1998, at age sixty-nine.

BIBLIOGRAPHY

Note: All interviews were conducted by the author. Locations listed for telephone interviews indicate the location of the interviewee.

Connie Woodruff: Advocate for All

Interviews

Boone, Bea. East Orange, N.J., November 18, 2001.

Byrne, Brendan T. Telephone interview: Livingston, N.J., December 3, 2001.

Dargan, Ruth Crumpton. Telephone interview: East Orange, N.J., November 13, 2001.

Davis, Reita Greenstone. Telephone interview: West Palm Beach, Fla., December 4, 2001.

Hazelwood, Harry. Telephone interview: Newark, N.J., November 12, 2001.

Payne, Donald M. Mary Burch Memorial Tribute. "In Celebration of the Life, Legend and Legacy of Mary Beasley Burch." Burch Theater, Essex County College, Newark, N.J., September 22, 2001.

Singletary, Mary. Telephone interview: Montclair, N.J., November 4, 2001.

Spina, Samuel. Telephone interview: West Orange, N.J., December 5, 2001.

Williams, Frederick I. West Orange, N.J., December 25, 1988.

Woodruff, Connie. Taped interviews: West Orange and Passaic, N.J., 1988–1994.

News Accounts

Beautler, Patty. "Women Impede Other Women: Feminist Leader Says Older Women Becoming 'Good Old Boys.'" *Lincoln Star,* February 2, 1985.

Dreispan, Leslie R. "New Priorities on Vital Issues Goal of Women's Advocate." *Herald News,* April 23, 1975.

Finley, Charles Q. "Jerseyan of the Week: Frankness Wins Admirers for Women's Leader." *Star-Ledger,* June 17, 1984.

Hall, Lawrence. "A Tradition of Service: Newark Native Embodied a Nobility Often Missing in Life." *Star-Ledger,* October 23, 1996.

Harney, James, Jr. "Mrs. Woodruff Honored by 500." *Star-Ledger,* September 12, 1975.

Kukla, Barbara. "Still Spry at 100: West Orange Centenarian Reflects on Living, Luck, Loved Ones." *Star-Ledger,* February 19, 1985.

———. "Veteran Black Leader Dies." *Star-Ledger,* October 21, 1996.

Lamendola, Linda. "Agency Called Unresponsive to Minorities." *Star-Ledger,* April 10, 1980.

Peterson, Lisa. "The Prospects for Women. . . ." *Star-Ledger,* January 25, 1981.

Webber, Harry B. "Connie's Finest Hour." *New Jersey Afro-American,* July 5, 1977.

———. "Connie Woodruff Chairman of N.J. Women's Advisory Board." *New Jersey Afro-American,* February 28, 1975.

Woodruff, Connie. "Connie's Corner: Looking Back." *City News,* June 20, 1987.

Other Sources

Coleman, Leonard S. Connie Woodruff's Eulogy: Messiah Baptist Church, East Orange, N.J., October 23, 1996.

Rodino, Hon. Peter W., Jr. "Tribute to Connie Woodruff." *Congressional Record,* March 30, 1984.

Women's Project of New Jersey. "Constance Oneida Williams Woodruff." In *Past and Promise: Lives of New Jersey Women,* pp. 432–433. Metuchen, N.J.: Scarecrow Press, 1990.

2 Gladys St. John Churchman: Central Ward Savior

Interviews

Churchman, Dr. Edith C. West Orange, N.J., November 13, 2001.

Churchman, James E., Jr. Telephone interview: Montclair, N.J., November 18, 2001.

Churchman, James E., III. Telephone interview: Newark, N.J., November 14, 2001.

Darrell, Dr. Evelyn Boyden. Newark, N.J., December 17, 2001.

Gould, Dorothy. Telephone interviews: Newark, N.J., November 3, 2001, and January 5, 2002.

Latta, Dorothy Foster. Telephone interview: Newark, N.J., January 3, 2002.

Moncur, Grachan. Telephone interview: Newark, N.J., November 6, 2001.

Newby, Cheryl Wright. Telephone interview: Newark, N.J., December 21, 2001.

Payne, Donald M. Newark, N.J., December 27, 2001.

Sauls, Isabell. Telephone interview: Newark, N.J., December 12, 2001.

Sims, Geraldine. Newark, N.J., December 17, 2001.

Wright, Eugene. Telephone interview: Owensboro, Ky., January 13, 2002.

Wright, Mary. Telephone interview: Newark, N.J., December 28, 2001.

News Accounts

Coleman, Chester L. "Fuld House Oriented to Family Needs." *Newark Sunday News,* September 13, 1970.

Finley, Charles Q. "Care, Compassion Lives at Friendly Fuld Houses." *Star-Ledger,* November 17, 1974.

———. "United Way Gifts Benefit Friendly Fuld." *Star-Ledger,* November 7, 1976.

Johnson, Trudy. "Fuld Director Focuses on Jobs for Central Ward Youth. *Star-Ledger,* September 5, 1983.

"Newarker Selected to Head Fuld Center." *Star-Ledger,* August 1, 1971.

"Settlement Houses Will Join Jan. 1." *Star-Ledger,* December 16, 1970.

Williams, Beverly A. "Friendly Fuld Serving Newark since 1905 Faces Finance Crisis." *New Jersey Afro-American,* May 26, 1973.

Other Sources

Dedication program: Gladys E. Churchman Portrait, Weequahic High School Library, Newark, N.J. February 8, 1976.

Women's Project of New Jersey. "Gladys St. John Churchman." In *Past and Promise: Lives of New Jersey Women,* pp. 253–254. Metuchen, N.J.: Scarecrow Press, 1990.

3 Dr. E. Alma Flagg: Pioneering Educator

Interviews

Crutchfield, Evelyn. Telephone interview: Plainfield, N.J., November 18, 2001.

Doggett, Rebecca. Newark, N.J., September 30, 2004.

Flagg, Dr. Thomas L. Telephone interview: Ann Arbor, Mich., December 15, 2001.

Flagg, E. Alma. Newark, N.J., December 7, 2001, and December 11, 2001.

Foley, Luisa. Telephone interview: Cherry Hill, N.J., January 5, 2002.

Hazelwood, Harry. Telephone interview: Newark, N.J., November 7, 2001.

Henderson, Carroll (Timmie). Telephone interview: Lancaster, Va., November 21, 2002.

Henderson, Joan. Telephone interviews: Lancaster, Va., November 19, 2001, and November 21, 2001.

Jackson, Willa. Telephone interview: Newark, N.J., November 18, 2001.

Knauer, Dorothy. Telephone interview: Newark, N.J., December 4, 2001.

Potts, Nathaniel. Telephone interview: Newark, N.J., January 4, 2002.

Seligman, June. Telephone interview: Roseland, N.J., December 3, 2001.

Sims, Geraldine G. Telephone interview: East Orange, N.J., December 1, 2001.

News Accounts

"Flagg Appointed Professor." *New Jersey Afro-American,* August, 2, 1971.

Kukla, Barbara. "Educator Guides LWV Unit in Teaching Voters." *Star-Ledger,* July 26, 1982.

Lucas, Caryl R. "Retired Educator Hailed for 40 Years of Dedication to Youth, Community." *Star-Ledger,* November 4, 1985.

Razen, Nancy. "Dr. Alma Flagg: She's Still Learning." *Sunday Star-Ledger,* August 5, 1964.

Other Sources

Thompson, Marion Wright. "Mr. Baxter's School." *New Jersey Historical Society Quarterly Magazine,* April 1941.

Women's Project of New Jersey. "E. Alma Flagg." In *Past and Promise: Lives of New Jersey Women,* pp. 290–291. Metuchen, N.J.: Scarecrow Press, 1990.

4 Dr. E. Mae McCarroll: Revered Physician

Interviews

Bates, Julia Baxter. Telephone interviews: East Brunswick, N.J., December 2, 2001, and December 6, 2001.

Cooper, Eric. East Orange, N.J., November 9, 2001.

Cooper, Gwendolyn. East Orange, N.J., November 9, 2001.

Cross, Carol V. Telephone interview: San Diego, Calif., November 10, 2001.

Dargan, Ruth Crumpton. Telephone interview: East Orange, N.J., November 14, 2001.

Johnson, Florence. Newark, N.J., July 27, 2003.

Latta, Dorothy Foster. Telephone interview: Newark, N.J., November 12, 2001.

Lee, Jeroline. Telephone interview: Newark, N.J., November 11, 2001.

Lester, Esther. Telephone interview: East Orange, N.J., December 5, 2001.

McCarroll, Dr. E. Mae. Newark, N.J., May 5, 1984.

McGrath, Monsignor Patrick. Telephone interview: Newark, N.J., November 18, 1990.

Moorman, Clem. West Orange, N.J., December 2, 2001.

Roberts, Bill. Newark, N.J., November 30, 1985.

Stoller, Eleanor. Telephone interview: Edison, N.J., December 8, 2001.

Taylor, Kitty Kearney. Telephone interview: Newark, N.J., November 11, 2001.

Way, Lucille. Telephone interviews: Miami, Fla., November 11, 2001, and November 16, 2001.

Woodruff, Connie. West Orange, N.J., March 16, 1995.

News Accounts

"Dr. Kenney Dead at 75." *Newark News,* January 30, 1950.

"Dr. McCarroll Breaks Bar, Joins City Hospital Staff." *New Jersey Herald News,* January 12, 1946.

"Dr. McCarroll Keeps Busy in City's Health Service." *Newark News,* March 20, 1946.

Heyboer, Kelly. "Julia Baxter Bates, Civil Rights Champion." *Star-Ledger,* July 23, 2003.

"Hospital Ends Long Service: Community Board Hopes to Purchase New Quarters." *Newark News,* June 15, 1953.

"Hospital Here Faces Closing." *Newark News,* April 18, 1948.

"Hospital Staff Now Has Negro." *Newark News,* January 4, 1946.

"Hospital Will Close: Temporary Action by Booker T. Washington Unit to Meet State Requirements." *Newark News,* June 13, 1953.

Hunter-Gault, Charlayne. "Black Women MDs: Spirit and Endurance." *New York Times,* November 16, 1977.

"J. A. Kenney Dead: Medical Leader, 75." *New York Times,* January 30, 1950.

"J. A. Kenney, Noted Negro Physician, Dies." *Star-Ledger,* January 30, 1950.

Kukla, Barbara. "Photo Exhibit Salutes Blacks in Medical Field." *Star-Ledger,* February 15, 1993.

"Trustees Seek Funds for New Negro Hospital." *Star-Ledger,* June 10, 1953.

Woodruff, Connie. "Remembering Dr. E. Mae McCarroll." *City News,* February 20, 1990.

Other Sources

Cobb, W. Montague, M.D. "E. Mae McCarroll: First Lady of the NMA." *Journal of the National Medical Association,* November 1973.

"Dr. E. Mae McCarroll." *Ebony,* May 1964, p. 76.

McCarroll, Dr. E. Mae. Speech delivered at dedication of the Haskin-McCarroll Public Health Building, Newark, N.J., May 5, 1982.

McCarroll, Edward B. Letter to Barbara S. Irwin, April 3, 1989.

"Profile" [Dr. E. Mae McCarroll]. *Journal of the National Medical Association,* November 1955.

Program, dedication of Haskin-McCarroll Public Health Building, Newark, N.J., May 5, 1982.

Women's Project of New Jersey. "Earnest Mae McCarroll." In *Past and Promise: Lives of New Jersey Women,* pp. 355–356. Metuchen, N.J.: Scarecrow Press, 1990.

5 Viola Wells (Miss Rhapsody): Newark's No. 1 Brown Gal

Interviews

Bernhardt, Clyde. Newark, N.J., September 18, 1985.

Darrell, Evelyn Boyden. Newark, N.J., December 17, 2001.

Evans, Viola Wells (Miss Rhapsody). Taped interviews: Newark, N.J., and Passaic, N.J., 1975–1984.

Pinckney, C. Theodore. Newark, N.J., March 4, 2002.

Sims, Geraldine. Newark, N.J., December 17, 2001.

White, Princess. Newark, N.J., 1972–1985.

Wright, Fannie. Telephone interview: Clark, N.J., January 15, 1989.

News Accounts

"Blues Singing Mother." *Pittsburgh Courier,* October 13, 1945.

Calvin, Doris. "It's Wrong to Type Blues Singers as Vulgar, Cheap, Cussing Pistol Packin' Mamas, Says Miss Rhapsody." Calvin News Service, *Norfolk Journal and Guide,* December 16, 1944.

Davis, Curt. "On the Town." *New York Post,* August 6, 1981.

Kukla, Barbara. "Fame Again Seeks Out Miss Rhapsody." *Star-Ledger,* May 29, 1975.

———. "Miss Rhap: A 40s Thrush Nests in Newark." *Star-Ledger,* July 18, 1972.

"Pastor Almost Offered Eulogy." *New Jersey Afro-American,* October 1, 1949.

"Slaying of Dad Stirs Daughter." *New Jersey Afro-American,* October 1, 1949.

"Trial for Jackson." *New Jersey Afro-American,* October 1, 1949.

Wilson, John S. "'Miss Rhapsody' Still Sings at 70." *New York Times,* June 7, 1973.

———. "Old Timers Get a New Bandstand." *New York Times,* February 27, 1981.

Woodruff, Connie. "Connie's Corner." *New Jersey Afro-American,* December 14, 1984.

Other Sources

Harris, Sheldon. "Viola Wells and a Dream Come True." *Melody Maker,* August 13, 1972.

Stewart-Baxter, Derrick. "Blues and Views." *Jazz Journal,* January 1974.

———. "Blues Digest." *Jazz Journal,* July 1971.

———. "Ramblin' Around." *Storyville,* March 1975.

Women's Project of New Jersey. "Viola Gertrude Wells." In *Past and Promise: Lives of New Jersey Women,* pp. 417–420. Metuchen, N.J.: Scarecrow Press, 1990.

6 Wynona M. Lipman: The Steel Magnolia

Interviews

Brown, Dr. Jennie. Telephone interview: Montclair, N.J., December 13, 2001.

Brown, Willie. Telephone interview: Newark, N.J., December 18, 2001.

Byrne, Brendan T. Telephone interview: Livingston, N.J., December 4, 2001.

Carr, Kathryn Penn. Telephone interviews: Los Angeles, Calif., November 5, 2001, and November 17, 2001.

DeGeneste, Saundra. West Orange, N.J., November 3, 2001.

Gill, Nia. Telephone interview: Montclair, N.J., December 28, 2001.

Hull, Lois. Telephone interview: Montclair, N.J., December 27, 2001.

Johnson, Ethel Moore. Telephone interview: East Orange, N.J., December 15, 2001.

Lipman, Dr. Matthew. Telephone interview: Montclair, N.J., November 6, 2001.

Miller, Dr. Julia (Judy). Telephone interview: Montclair, N.J., December 14, 2001.

Moore, Dr. Karen. Telephone interview: Atlanta, Ga., January 23, 2002.

Rice, Ronald L. Newark, N.J., December 30, 2001.

Singletary, Mary. Telephone interview: Montclair, N.J., November 4, 2001.

Stebbins, Abbins. Telephone interview: Newark, N.J., May 5, 1999.

Walker, Della Moses. Telephone interview: Newark, N.J., November 6, 2001.

News Accounts

Baird, Christine V. "Newark Phoenix Rises Where Projects Stood." *Star-Ledger,* July 13, 2001.

Carter, Kathy Barrett. "State Senators Pass Bill as Final Tribute to Late Colleague." *Star-Ledger,* May 25, 1999.

Chassan, Alice. "The Steel Magnolia: Wynona Lipman Makes Her Mark." *New Jersey Reporter,* July–August 1988.

"Donald Moore, Early Duke Black Physician, Dies." *Duke Dialogue,* August 9, 1991.

"John W. Moore, Prominent Negro, Succumbs Here." *LaGrange Daily News,* December 26, 1951.

Kukla, Barbara. "City Recognizes Those Who Have Made a Difference." *Star-Ledger,* March 8, 2000.

———. "The Indomitable Senator Taught How to Respect." *Star-Ledger,* May 13, 1999.

Lamendola, Linda. "Lipman Heads Committee in a Senate First." *Star-Ledger,* January 15, 1980.

Marsico, Ron. "Legislator Sees Whitman Isolated from Needy." *Star-Ledger,* August 3, 1995.

Scott, Gale. "Clean Needle Program Quietly Makes Rounds." *Star-Ledger,* September 21, 1995.

Stewart, Angela. "Black Clergy Split Over Officials' Pitch for Needle Exchange to Fight AIDS." *Star-Ledger,* September 16, 1993.

Wald, David. "Sen. Lipman, Trailblazer for Women in Government, Dies at 67." *Star-Ledger,* May 11, 1999.

Walker, Stephen T. "Branch Renews His Call for Needle Distribution." *Star-Ledger,* September 21, 1993.

———. "Rice Remains Critical of Clean Needles Bill." *Star-Ledger,* September 28, 1993.

Other Sources

Jenkins, Dr. George. Citizens Recognition Night, City Hall, Newark, N.J., October 15, 2001.

7 Mary Beasley Burch: Beloved Philanthropist

Interviews

Dryden, Irma (Pete). Telephone interview: Asbury Park, N.J., November 14, 2001.

Edwards, Elizabeth. East Orange, N.J., December 1, 2001.

Felder, Jewel Smith. Telephone interview: Mobile, Ala., November 13, 2001.

Graves, Carole A. Telephone interview: Newark, N.J., November 6, 2001.

Johnson, Helen. Telephone interview: Verona, N.J., November 18, 2001.

Lowen, Yvonne Counts. Telephone interview: Newark, N.J., November 4, 2001.

Mobley, Robert. Telephone interview: East Orange, N.J., December 12, 2001.

Oliver, Sheila. Telephone interview: Newark, N.J., November 24, 2001.

Payne, Donald M. Telephone interview: Newark, N.J., January 15, 2002.

———. Mary Burch Memorial Tribute. "In Celebration of the Life, Legend and Legacy of Mary Beasley Burch." Burch Theater, Essex County College, Newark, N.J., September 22, 2001.

Payne, William. Telephone interview: Newark, N.J., January 3, 2002.

Peoples, Sesser. Telephone interview: Piscataway, N.J., December 27, 2001.

Ray, Veronica. Mary Burch Memorial Tribute. "In Celebration of the Life, Legend and Legacy of Mary Beasley Burch." Burch Theater, Essex County College, Newark, N.J., September 22, 2001.

Reed, Carolyn Ryan. Newark, N.J., August 3, 2000.

Salley, Arthur. Telephone interview: Newark, N.J., August 3, 2000.

Spellman, Dr. Robert. Telephone interview: Scotch Plains, N.J., December 4, 2001.

Thompson, Connie. Telephone interview: Silver Spring, Md., November 18, 2001.

News Accounts

Bailey, Edna M. "The Leaguers Bring Hope, Guidance to Newark Youth." *Star-Ledger,* March 12, 1985.

Byrd, Frederick W. "Leaguers Chief Assails Newark Funding Stance." *Star-Ledger,* March 21, 1984.

"College Will Honor Founder of Leaguers." *Star-Ledger,* February 24, 1977.

Holly, Dan. "Leaguers History Reflects Four Decades of Service." *Star-Ledger,* August 30, 1985.

Hutchinson, Edith M. "Leaguers Modify Program to Meet Modern Youth Needs." *Newark Sunday News,* November 8, 1970.

Kukla, Barbara. "In a League of Her Own: Friends and Beneficiaries Honor Dr. Mary B. Burch." *Star-Ledger,* December 15, 1993.

———. "Mary Burch, 95: Newark 'Visionary.' " *Star-Ledger,* August 16, 2001.

———. "Organization Is in a League of Its Own." *Star-Ledger,* August 1, 1999.

———. "Tribute to Mary Burch: Payne Committee Honoring Philanthropist at Luncheon." *Star-Ledger,* October 16, 1998.

"Post as College Trustee New Honor for Mrs. Burch." *Sunday Star-Ledger,* July 7, 1968.

"United Women's League Active in Community Work." *New Jersey Herald News,* December 26, 1953.

Wellborn, Zana. "Leaguers Alumni Dinner to Honor Group's Founder." *Star-Ledger,* October 20, 1974.

Woodruff, Connie. "As I See It." *City News,* July 1, 1992.

Other Sources

Burch, Mary B. Letter to Barbara Kukla, March 17, 1993.

———. Letter to Barbara Kukla, September 6, 1996.

———. Letter to Connie Woodruff, September 4, 1975.

Mary Burch Memorial Tribute. "In Celebration of the Life, Legend and Legacy of Mary Beasley Burch." Burch Theater, Essex County College, Newark, N.J., September 22, 2001.

Women's Project of New Jersey. "Mary Allison Beasley Burch." In *Past and Promise: Lives of New Jersey Women,* pp. 217–218. Metuchen, N.J.: Scarecrow Press, 1990.

Yamba, A. Zachary. Mary Burch Memorial Tribute. "In Celebration of the Life, Legend and Legacy of Mary Beasley Burch." Burch Theater, Essex County College, Newark, N.J., September 22, 2001.

8 Marion A. Bolden: Champion of Children

Interviews

Bolden, LaMar. Telephone interview: East Orange, N.J., November 9, 2001.

Bolden, Marion A. West Orange, N.J., November 8, 2001, and January 7, 2002.

Bolden, Reagan. Telephone interview: Orange, N.J., November 9, 2001.

Culver, Doris. Telephone interview: Fanwood, N.J., January 8, 2002.

Dennis, Gary J. Newark, N.J., January 8, 2002.

Dotson, Wertley. Telephone interview: South Orange, N.J., November 15, 2001.

Gaymon, Dr. Alfred. Telephone interview: Newark, N.J., December 20, 2001.

Hawthorne, Darrin. Telephone interview: Newark, N.J., February 27, 2002.

Lindgren, Dr. Raymond M. Telephone interview: East Rutherford, N.J., January 6, 2002.

Manigault, Sam. Telephone interview: Newark, N.J., November 5, 2001.

Manigault, Shannon. Telephone interview: Boston, Mass., January 28, 2002.

Manigault, Sheila. Telephone interview: Scotch Plains, N.J., November 10, 2001.

McFarland, Catherine M. Telephone interview: Montclair, N.J., February 20, 2002.

Munford, Merissa. Telephone interview: Newark, N.J., February 3, 2002.

Otero, Hilton. Telephone interview: East Hanover, N.J., December 5, 2001.

Paschall, Lannie. Telephone interview: Newark, N.J., December 19, 2001.

Potts, Nathaniel. Telephone interview: Newark, N.J., January 3, 2002.

Ryan, Arthur F. Response to written questions: Newark, N.J., January 15, 2002.

Royster, Gloria. Telephone interview: Piscataway, N.J., November 12, 2001.

Vizcarrondo-DeSoto, Maria. Telephone interview: Newark, N.J., January 9, 2002.

Ward, Shirley M. Telephone interview: Newark, N.J., December 13, 2001.

Watson, Cathy (Bubbles). Telephone interview: East Orange, N.J., November 10, 2001.

Washington, Franotie A. Telephone interview: Newark, N.J., November 15, 2001.

News Accounts

Alaya, Ana M. "A Year in the Hornet's Nest." *Star-Ledger,* July 7, 2000.

———. "Ex-Teacher Leads Newark Schools." *Star-Ledger,* September 10, 1999.

———. "Insider Selected as New Head of Newark Schools." *Star-Ledger,* July 20, 1999.

———. "Newark School Chief Tackles Tough First Year." *Star-Ledger,* July 9, 2000.

———. "Saturdays at Library Don't Get Shelved." *Star-Ledger,* April 26, 1999.

"Apprenticeships Offered in Construction Trades." *Star-Ledger,* June 5, 2001.

Braun, Robert J. "Law, Politics Barred Newark Takeover for Years." *Star-Ledger,* July 31, 1994.

"Bulldogs to Christen New Sports Center." *Star-Ledger,* October 4, 2001.

DeJesus, Ivelisse. "Again, the Halls Are Alive with the Sound of Music." *Star-Ledger,* June 21, 2001.

———. "Bolden Rallies Teachers in Newark for New Year." *Star-Ledger,* September 9, 2000.

———. "Corporate World Aids Newark Schools." *Star-Ledger,* March 3, 2001.

———. "Progress Measured in Newark Schools." *Star-Ledger,* January 4, 2001.

———. "School Chief Decision Spurs Protests in Trenton." *Star-Ledger,* February 6, 2003.

———. "Twilight Students See Light." *Star-Ledger,* January 18, 2001.

Kukla, Barbara. "Bolden Backers Vow to Turn Out Tuesday Night." *Star-Ledger,* February 20, 2003.

———. "School Board under Attack." *Star-Ledger,* February 6, 2003.

———. "School-to-Career Program Kicks into High Gear." *Star-Ledger,* June 28, 2001.

———. "Science Center Opens New Horizons for Youngsters. October 4, 2001." *Star-Ledger,* March 3, 2002.

———. Students Reach for the Future at Math Fair and Olympics." *Star-Ledger,* May 5, 2000.

———. "You Can't Say 'Revival' Without 'Rah!' " *Star-Ledger,* January 27, 2000.

Lucas, Caryl R. "Calculus Olympics and Math Fair Spur Newark Students to Achieve." *Star-Ledger,* March 17, 1996.

Mooney, John. "Contentious Chapter in Newark Schools Ends." *Star-Ledger,* May 8, 2003.

"Newark Needs Bolden." Editorial. *Star-Ledger,* February 6, 2003.

"Schools Thank Pru for Gift." *Star-Ledger,* November 29, 2001.

Smothers, Ronald. "After Time of Turmoil, a Familiar Face Runs Newark's City Schools." *New York Times,* August 29, 1999.

INDEX